The Victorians and Race

The Victorians and Race

Edited by

SHEARER WEST

Ashgate

Aldershot • Brookfield USA • Singapore • Sydney

Ch. One   © Douglas A. Lorimer   Ch. Eight   © Donald M. MacRaild
   Two   © Tim Barringer   Nine   © Inga Bryden
   Three © Mary Hamer   Ten   © Deborah Cherry
   Four   © Simeran Man Singh Gell   Eleven © Anita Levy
   Five   © Tim Dolin   Twelve © Reina Lewis
   Six   © H. L. Malchow   Thirteen © Helen M. Cooper
   Seven © Joseph A. Kestner

Published by
Ashgate Publishing Ltd
Gower House
Croft Road
Aldershot
Hants GU11 3HR
England

Ashgate Publishing Company
Old Post Road
Brookfield
Vermont 05036
USA

British Library Cataloguing in Publication Data

The Victorians and Race
(Nineteenth Century series)
1. Great Britain—Race relations.   2. Great Britain—Social
conditions—19th century.
I. West, Shearer.
305.8'00941

ISBN 1–85928–268–7

Library of Congress Cataloging-in-Publication Data

The Victorians and race/edited by Shearer West.
     p.   cm.
   Includes index.
   ISBN 1–85928–268–7 (cloth)
    1. Great Britain—Race relations—History—19th century.
  2. English literature—19th century—History and criticism.
  3. Great Britain—History—Victoria, 1837–1901.   4. Great Britain—
Civilization—19th century.   5. Race in literature.   I. West, Shearer.
DA125.A1V53   1997
305.8'00941'09034—dc20   96–33140
                                 CIP
Reprinted 1998

ISBN 1 85928 268 7

Typeset in Sabon by Manton Typesetters, 5–7 Eastfield Road, Louth, Lincolnshire, LN11 7AJ
Printed in Great Britain by The Book Co, Suffolk

Contents

The Nineteenth Century
General Editors' Preface

The aim of this series is to reflect, develop and extend the great burgeoning of interest in the nineteenth century that has been an inevitable feature of recent decades, as that former epoch has come more sharply into focus as a locus for our understanding not only of the past but of the contours of our modernity. Though it is dedicated principally to the publication of original monographs and symposia in literature, history, cultural analysis, and associated fields, there will be a salient role for reprints of significant texts from, or about, the period. Our overarching policy is to address the spectrum of nineteenth-century studies without exception, achieving the widest scope in chronology, approach and range of concern. This, we believe, distinguishes our project from comparable ones, and means, for example, that in the relevant areas of scholarship we both recognize and cut innovatively across such parameters as those suggested by the designations 'Romance' and 'Victorian'. We welcome new ideas, while valuing tradition. It is hoped that the world which predates yet so forcibly predicts and engaged our own will emerge in parts, as a whole, and in the lively currents of debate and change that are so manifest an aspect of its intellectual, artistic and social landscape.

Vincent Newey
Joanne Shattock

University of Leicester

List of figures

Notes on contributors

Tim Barringer is Lecturer in the History of Art at Birmingham University and formerly Lecturer in History of Art at Birkbeck College, University of London. He was educated at the Universities of Cambridge, New York and Sussex and from 1993 to 1995 was Research Fellow in Victorian Studies at the Victoria and Albert Museum. His book *Representing Labour in Mid Victorian Britain* will be published by Manchester University Press in 1997. He is currently editing books on Frederic Leighton and on *Colonialism and the Object*.

Inga Bryden is Lecturer in English Studies at King Alfred's College of Higher Education, Winchester. Her doctoral thesis, 'Victorian Arthurianism: remodelling the past' was completed at the University of Exeter where she was Tutor in Nineteenth-Century Literature. She has published articles of Victorian historicism and culture, and is a contributor to *The Year's Work in English Studies*. She is currently editing a collection of Pre-Raphaelite writing.

Deborah Cherry teaches at the University of Manchester. She is the author of *Painting Women: Victorian Women Artists* (Routledge, 1993) and co-editor with Jane Beckett of *The Edwardian Era* (Phaidon, 1987) and *Treatise on the Sublime: Maud Sulter and Lubaina Himid* (1990). Her study on feminism and visual culture in Britain, 1850–1900 will be published by Routledge in 1997.

Helen M. Cooper is an Associate Professor of English and a faculty member of the Latin American and Caribbean Studies Centre at the State University of New York at Stony Brook. She is author of *Elizabeth Barrett Browning, Woman and Artist* and co-editor of *Arms and the Woman: War, Gender and Literary Representation*. She is working on a book *'Tracing the Route to England': Nineteenth-Century Caribbean Interventions into English Debates on Race, Slavery and Empire*.

Tim Dolin teaches in the Department of English at the University of Newcastle, Australia. He has published articles on Elizabeth Gaskell, Charlotte Brontë and Thomas Hardy. A study of property, domestic ideology and national identity in the Victorian novel, *Mistress of the House*, will be published by Scolar Press. He is at present working on *Accidental Companions: Six Novels of Dickens and Six Victorian Paintings*, of which the essay in this collection will be a part.

Simeran Man Singh Gell is a research associate at the Department of Social Anthropology at Cambridge University. She is currently engaged in research into the Asian community in Britain and has written papers on second-generation Asian ethnicity, the relationship of the Asian community with the British state and the reinvention of the historical relationship of these communities with Britain. She is the author of a book on a tribal community of central India on the basis of anthropological fieldwork conducted among them over a period of two years as part of her doctoral thesis.

Mary Hamer is a Fellow of the W. E. B. Du Bois Institute for Afro-American Research at Harvard and has taught in Cambridge (England) for many years. Her books include *Writing by Numbers: Trollope's Serial Fiction* (Cambridge, 1987) and *Signs of Cleopatra: History, Politics, Representation* (Routledge, 1993). She has written a memoir about the way a Catholic childhood moulded her own perceptions.

Joseph A. Kestner is McFarlin Professor of English at the University of Tulsa, Oklahoma. He studied at Columbia University under Gilbert Highet and Carl Woodring. He is the author of *The Spatiality of the Novel, Protest and Reform, Mythology and Misogyny* and *Masculinities in Victorian Painting*. He has lectured widely in Great Britain and the United States. In 1992 he was an Honorary Senior Fellow at the Victorian Studies Centre of the University of Leicester. He has chaired the Christian Gauss Award Committee of Phi Beta Kappa. In 1993 he received a Fellowship from the Anne S. K. Brown Military Collection at Brown University.

Anita Levy is Assistant Professor of English at the University of Rochester. She is the author of *Other Women: The Writing of Class, Race and Gender, 1832–1898*, and essays on the Brontës; modernism, gender and professionalism; and the formation of the middle-class subject. She is currently working on a book-length study tracing the relationship between representations of biological and cultural reproduction in eighteenth- and nineteenth-century British writing, provisionally entitled *Reproductive Urges: Popular Novel-Reading, Sexuality and the English Nation*.

Reina Lewis is Senior Lecturer in Cultural Studies at the University of East London. She is the author of *Gendering Orientalism: Race, Femininity, Representation* (Routledge, 1996).

Douglas A. Lorimer teaches history at Wilfrid Laurier University in Waterloo, Ontario. He is the author of *Colour, Class and the Victorians* (Leicester University Press, 1978), and has published articles on black slavery in eighteenth-century England and on racism and Victorian science. He is presently completing a study, provisionally entitled *Race,*

Race Relations and Resistance: A Study of Late Victorian and Edwardian Racism 1870–1914 for the Manchester University Press series on Imperialism and Popular Culture.

Donald M. MacRaild is Lecturer in History at the University of Sunderland. He was awarded a PhD by the University of Sheffield in 1993 for research into Irish migration and culture in nineteenth-century Cumbria. He has written a number of articles on aspects of Irish migration and is currently revising his doctoral work with a view to publication.

H. L. Malchow is Professor of History at Tufts University. His books include *Population Pressures: Emigration and Government in Late Nineteenth-Century Britain* (Society for the Promotion of Science and Scholarship, 1979), *Gentlemen Capitalists: The Social and Political World of the Victorian Businessman* (Macmillan, 1991) and the forthcoming *Gothic Images of Race in Nineteenth Century Britain*. He is the author of a number of important articles on church, class and society in the Victorian period.

Shearer West is Senior Lecturer and Head of Art History at Birmingham University. She is the author of *The Image of the Actor: Verbal and Visual Representation in the Age of Garrick and Kemble* (Pinter, 1991); *Fin de Siècle: Art and Society in an Age of Uncertainty* (Bloomsbury, 1993) and co-editor (with Marsha Meskimmon) of *Visions of the 'Neue Frau': Women and the Visual Arts in Weimar Germany* (Scolar Press, 1995). She is the general editor of the *Bloomsbury Guide to Art* (Bloomsbury, 1996) and is currently completing a history of modern German art. She has also written many articles on aspects of eighteenth-, nineteenth- and twentieth-century art and theatre.

Preface and acknowledgements

This volume originated in a conference on 'The Victorians and Race' held at Leicester University in July 1995. I organized the conference with the hope that I could draw together scholars from many different disciplines in order to concentrate our attentions and energies on a subject which was of critical importance to us all. I was not disappointed in the results, but what I also found was that a subject which has received much academic attention in recent years has only just begun to be explored. The process of selecting papers from the conference to be rewritten for a volume was one of the most difficult tasks I have ever confronted, as the papers were of a uniformly high standard and remarkably relevant to each other in their themes and concerns.

In preparing the conference and the volume, I have accrued debts to many individuals who deserve my most sincere thanks. First, I must thank each of the contributors to this volume, who were faultlessly professional and courteous in their dealings with me and in editing their own essays. They were a pleasure to work with. I would also like to thank, in alphabetical order, the other individuals who participated in the conference as speakers and chairpersons: Andrew Blake, Sighle Breathnach-Lynch, Bill Brock, Julia Courtney, Joan Crossley, Fintan Cullen, Audrey Fisch, Rowena Fowler, Pamela Gerrish Nunn, Simon Katzenellenbogen, Oliver Lovesay, Gail Low, Virginia McKendry, Jan Marsh, David Mayer, Helen Mayer, Vince Newey, Panikos Panayi, Christine Poulson, Joanne Shattock, Stephen Small, Keith Snell, Michael Weiner and Alison Yarrington.

Many others helped with the administration of the conference and made it a success. These include the staff of Beaumont and Stamford Halls at Leicester University; the student assistants: Terry Cavanagh, Lucy Faire, Giovanna di Giovanni, Catriona Miller and Tara Smith; clerical staff in the History of Art department: Krys Wysocki, Joy Fox and Esther Holm; and the members of Leicester University Theatre (LUT) who put together a creative and exciting production *The Jew in Drama* with only a very brief period of rehearsal.

I am also grateful to Colin Holmes for his support of the conference, and to the Humanities Research Board of the British Academy for a conference grant to aid travel for overseas speakers.

Finally, I would like to thank Alec McAulay and Caroline Cornish at Scolar Press for seeing through to publication what began as only an idea.

Introduction

Shearer West

During the past 20 years, there has been an explosion of academic interest in the subject of race. These historical explorations exist uneasily with the tensions between pluralist cultures and violent racism that characterize the world of the late twentieth century. When we tease out the implications of the subject of race within modern academic disciplines, we can only artificially distance ourselves from the cultural concerns of our own time. Race is a ubiquitous yet conflicted issue which arouses passions that cannot be suppressed even by the detached modulations of academic debate. This book seeks to explore the broad subject of race within the context of one nation and one historical period. The contributors to this volume uniformly acknowledge both the necessity of studying contextual and period-specific factors, as well as the impossibility of doing so without acknowledging their own modern consciousness, concerns and preoccupations.

The two questions which need to be addressed at the outset are: why the Victorians, and why 'race'? The latter is perhaps the most difficult question, as the very term 'race' has unstable and often ambiguous implications. In its strictest dictionary sense, 'race' refers to common descent or a group or 'class' of persons with common features; however, it has taken on connotations that suggest a biological categorization of physiological difference, based largely on skin colour. Historically, it has been frequently paired with such loaded terms as 'stock' or 'breed', and it has been used not only as a biological classification of individuals but as a synonym for culture, religion, class, nation and many other factors. Race is, as the Victorian anatomist, Robert Knox, suggested, 'everything', at least by virtue of the imprecise way the term is often used. This is why it has become almost mandatory for academics to refer to 'race' with inverted commas – to show their comprehension of the dangerous ambiguities of the term and to distance themselves from those very implications. As this volume concerns the subject of race as it was understood within a given historical situation, I would like to think that we can consider the inverted commas as implied. The authors here do not consider race to be unproblematic, and many of them address directly the connotations of the term within Victorian culture.

The subject of race has been opened up by twentieth-century scholars, and the ground-breaking historical studies of Lorimer (1978) and Stepan (1982) have been augmented by the theoretical considerations of

Bhabha (1984, 1994), Said (1978), Spivak (1986) and others who have shown the ways in which ideas of race are created and negotiated by western cultures, as well as the psychological and sociological workings of racism. The assumption that race is posited as a simple opposition between 'self' and 'other' has been abrogated by the knowledge that the perpetuation of race theories has led to numerous – and sometimes mutually contradictory – responses. Race therefore continues to be a subject that deserves and demands scholarly attention and exposition.

The reasons for isolating Victorian Britain as the focus of this study are equally manifold. It was a period in which race was 'reified', to use the term of H. L. Malchow in Chapter 6 in this volume. The eighteenth-century debates surrounding the abolition of slavery, which continued to hold force at the beginning of the Victorian period, combined with an era of aggressive imperialism, in which western Europeans had increasing contact with the appearances, manners and customs of non-European peoples. These new relationships engendered changing and ambivalent attitudes which were fed by the advent of modern science, the growth of print capitalism and the spread of literacy. Race, and all its concomitants, was no longer a barely conceived prejudice; it became the subject of both academic discourse and popular journalism.

Finding a way through the morass of evidence – visual and verbal – for the place of race in the Victorian period would be a task that any single individual would undoubtedly find both daunting and frustrating. Furthermore, the monolithic view that such a study would require would perhaps militate against the real need to locate a pluralist and multivalent reading for race during the Victorian period. I have chosen instead to edit a volume which includes the work of contributors in different disciplines and with distinct (and not always compatible) approaches. However, from this diversity has come not a rag-bag of idiosyncrasy, but some important themes which emerge strongly throughout the book. I can characterize the principal arguments of this volume into three general categories: contexts, representations and subjectivities. Each author contributes something to each of these areas, and their essays bear a number of rich and complex relationships to each other. In providing these categories for the reader, I am not attempting to pigeon-hole a diverse and unstable subject, but to suggest some broad areas which contribute to the discourse of race in the Victorian period and which are tackled consistently by the authors who have contributed to this book.

Contexts

To contextualize the subject of the Victorians and race involves an understanding not simply of historical events, such as the expansion of the British Empire, but also a more nuanced reading of what we could call the 'discursive' contexts which fed into ideas of race and were fed by them, such as gender, class and nation. The chapters by Douglas Lorimer and Tim Barringer which begin this volume emphasize the necessity of the former type of contextualized reading; as Barringer puts it 'the concept of race is socially created and thus historically variable'. Race as a semantic category has its own history which, Lorimer points out, we are all too prone to see as static. In reality, the connotations and functions of race vary throughout history and maintained a particularly problematic position in the Victorian period.

It is important, for example, to understand the ways in which theories of race, as perpetuated by 'scientific' texts, permeated popular consciousness through novels, journalism and pictures hung at Royal Academy exhibitions. Strongly held – if often radically divergent – views about the physical, psychological and genealogical properties of certain races invaded these texts in a way that suggested closure even while they opened up endless possibilities of interpretation and (mis)appropriation. The scientific context is where the academic study of race really began, and as Lorimer shows here, nearly 20 years after his seminal study *Colour, Class and the Victorians* (1978), it is possible to explore the scientific dimensions of race in an ever more subtle way. As the Victorian period witnessed the flowering of modern print capitalism, the power of mechanical reproduction in creating and perpetuating ideologies of race cannot be ignored. This subject forms an important focus of the arguments of Barringer (who concentrates on visual aspects of print culture) and Helen Cooper, who uses Benedict Anderson's (1991) idea of an 'imagined community' to help locate a notion of an Englishness fed by popular publications. A cognate, and specifically Victorian, issue was the growth of literacy and the campaign for universal education, which forms a central argument of Tim Dolin's chapter and a powerful subtext of Lorimer's chapter.

A number of authors in this volume deal directly with other contexts and their role in race's history. Helen Cooper, for example, focuses on the twilight of slavery, while Deborah Cherry and Reina Lewis examine particular manifestations of travel in north Africa and the Muslim world, and what has been termed 'Orientalism'. The authors range widely over different outposts of the British Empire from Africa (Anita Levy), to India (Simeran Gell) and the Caribbean (H. L. Malchow). These specific cultural and historical frameworks do not themselves explain the development of theories of race in the Victorian period but they provide a battery of factors which contributed to the formation and inevitable complexity of this cultural category.

However, the contextualized readings of race in this book veer more frequently towards what could be called discursive strategies. These studies involve teasing out the ways in which particular linguistic and cultural formations (such as race itself, class and gender) are constructed and fluctuate within a given place and time. A discourse is formed from numerous fragments of language, belief and desire which cohere fleetingly to comprise the assumed substance of physical and mental life in a particular period. Given the all-embracing presence of race in the Victorian period, it is hardly surprising to see that discourses of race overlap with, help define, and are defined by, other discourses of the Victorian period.

The first, and perhaps most obvious of these, is class. The intersections between race and class in the Victorian period were due in no small part to the fact that both the working classes and 'other' races were making their presences known and felt in Britain throughout the Victorian period. As potential sites of conflict, or as threats to a stable white/middle-class order, both non-Europeans and members of the urban proletariat were seen to be problems to be solved, suppressed or neutralized. This issue is discussed in the chapters by Tim Dolin and Tim Barringer, who show the ways in which stereotypes about 'savages' were employed to demonize the working classes at home. Using Mayhew's (1968) illustrated *London Labour and the London Poor*, Barringer further reveals how imagery undercuts the apparent monolithic nature of the 'poor' savage stereotype, by inadvertently revealing genuine social diversity among the working class. Dolin, on the other hand, discusses how the class/race parallel became an issue about education and civilization in a period in which philanthropy was a middle-class ideal. Class also appears in Chapters 7 and 8 by Donald MacRaild and Joseph Kestner respectively, whose considerations of Celtic stereotypes reveal the ways in which Celticism was often implicitly or explicitly equated with the proletariat.

Apart from class, gender is another discursive formation that is inextricably linked with race in the Victorian period. By gender, I refer to the social constructions of masculinity and femininity, and their physical and psychological manifestations in a given period. *The Victorians and Race* includes a number of chapters which draw particular attention to white women and their problematic role in relation to Victorian imperialism. One of the most difficult issues for feminists to negotiate in a study of Victorian gender is the problem that western white women were potentially as imperialist as their male counterparts, although their imperialism manifested itself in missionary zeal, rather than military conquest. However, this fissure between western and non-western women means that any study of Victorian gender must also bring race into the equation. Deborah Cherry and Anita Levy tackle this problem in different ways. Cherry problematizes the notion of 'feminism's imperialism' by showing how Algeria became a site of focus and exchange for women of the Langham Place circle and contributed positively towards the formation of modern gender identity: 'Discourses on western and Algerian women ... collided, abutted, interrupted, and supplemented each other.' In her analysis of Olive Schreiner's *Story of an African Farm*, Levy also deals with the potential racism of Victorian feminism, but she shows the ways in which this race-consciousness paradoxically fostered the construction of the late Victorian 'new woman'.

The relationships between gender and race are central to, or emerge in, the chapters by Mary Hamer, Reina Lewis, Helen Cooper and Joseph Kestner, the latter of whom focuses on constructions of masculinity as implicit in imperialist views of selfhood and otherness in the Victorian period. Kestner takes the military man as a trope of Victorian masculinity and reveals the ambiguities of contemporary responses to Scottish soldiers who both conformed to and resisted the stereotype of English masculinity their role implied. As Levy indicates in Chapter 11, race and gender are too often seen as parallel but unrelated discourses, whereas it is essential to consider the two together. Given the all-encompassing nature of Victorian ideas of race, the intersections of race with class and gender, as well as religion (explored in the chapters by MacRaild and Hamer) and nation (examined by Cooper and Bryden) cannot be taken for granted.

Representations

The proliferation of race theories in the nineteenth century was in no small part fuelled by both visual and verbal texts which served to plant certain ideas of race into the minds of their audiences. However, as with any text that is mediated by the perspective of the reader/viewer, art and literature of the Victorian period served to reinforce existing stereotypes as well as contributing to the creation of new ones. The issues of *what* is represented, as well as *why* and *how* must be considered, as well as the ways in which representations modulate and feed on existing preoccupations. Changes in language and culture do not simply reflect historical 'reality' but engender further change in that 'reality'.

Visual representation is the theme of a number of the authors in *The Victorians and Race*. Given that race was seen to be encoded in such specificities as skin colour, gesture and costume, the contribution of painting, sculpture and graphic art to the formation of race theories should not be underestimated. This truth is taken for granted by authors in this volume, who concentrate instead on the question of how such visual signals were read and understood or misunderstood. Mary Hamer, for example, concentrates on William Wetmore Story's white marble statue of Cleopatra, the medium of which evokes the classical canon while its appearance was read by Nathaniel Hawthorne in terms of contemporary notions of race. As Hamer puts it, 'Here white means black', and she tackles the problem of a work of art's potential open-endedness which is really only a putative legibility. Simeran Gell and Tim Barringer also consider ways in which representations of a racial body can be misread or deliberately appropriated for other ends. The apparent legibility of painting and engraving was undermined by the Victorian idea that works of art were open to interpretation. The space left by this openness allowed room for the intrusion of private and public mythologies, desires and expectations.

What could be called the mythological aspects of representation – especially literary representation – are of particular concern to a number of authors. Both the visual arts and fictional literature served to evoke imaginary worlds which fed the fantasies of their contemporary audiences. However, these fantasy spaces opened up new possibilities, allowing the reader to impose his or her vision on them; they thus pulled the reader 'back and forth between the imagined world of literature and the "real" world of historical experience', as Malchow puts it in Chapter 6. Malchow is concerned with the way language was used in the Victorian period to demonize mulattos by employing associations between them and the monsters of Gothic fiction. Inga Bryden also explores the openness of mythologies in her analysis of Bulwer-Lytton's *King Arthur*, whose fictional evocations of the Anglo-Saxon and Celtic racial heritage serve only to create 'vertiginous perspectives' and a plurality of possible contemporary associations. Literature, as well as art, manufactured imaginary spaces from fragments which could be read as 'real' to Victorian audiences; the hints and associations of these shards of fictional experience enhanced the complexity of Victorian racial self-consciousness.

Representations of race vary further and provide different messages and meanings when the genre of the work and its status in the contemporary canon are explored. *The Victorians and Race* contains analyses of a wide selection (although by no means an exhaustive one) of types of Victorian art and literature. In terms of art, both 'high' and 'low' genres, as well as the media of painting, sculpture and engraving receive attention. Different types of popular painting are shown to convey conflicting Victorian perspectives of race: Kestner shows the ways in which battle painting conflates race with masculinity, or negates that very association; while Gell tackles imaging of the body in portraiture, and Lewis teases out the different meanings that can be discerned in Orientalist subjects by women artists.

Many more authors explore the manifold possibilities of literary productions for creating and perpetuating ideas of race. Novels – one of the most popular literary forms in the period – are analysed by Dolin, Hamer, Levy and Lewis, whose discussions of Dickens, Hawthorne, Schreiner and Charlotte Brontë respectively show how many diverse discourses of race can be subsumed within the apparent simplicity of a Victorian narrative plot. Inga Bryden similarly plumbs the racial mythologies of an epic poem. Other authors deal with non-fictional literary forms, which in some ways become alternative fictions of the Victorian period, susceptible as they are to the same misreadings and misappropriations as fiction. This is most apparently the case in Lorimer's discussion of both academic and popular scientific writing, in which apparent 'objectivity' about non-British races becomes soured by a remarkably blunt introduction of superstition and prejudice. Other characteristically Victorian forms of non-fiction – the exposé of the lives of the poor and literature of exploration – are dismantled by Barringer to reveal the racial, even racist, core beneath.

The place and purpose of non-fictional literary genres within the wider problematic of Victorian race theory is the subject of the chapters by Helen Cooper and Deborah Cherry. Cooper tackles the problem of a recorded oral history – in this case the memoirs of the former slaves Mary Prince and Mary Seacole. The imposition of an editor into the outpourings of Prince's oppositional voice is shown to have created difficulties for her self-expression and the public perception of her. Cherry's chapter on the women of the Langham Place group discusses the letters which passed between members of the group from Algeria to England and back again, but she moves away from an examination of the content of the letters to consider the importance of the letters' physical presence and role as tokens of exchange.

Aside from visual and literary representations – and the issues which accompany them – the authors also consider more ephemeral modes of representation and their impact on prevailing constructions of race. This is especially true of Donald MacRaild's chapter on the rituals of the Victorian Orange Order – specifically their celebration of the 'Glorious Twelfth' and how race was configured or understood through ritual. Race was not simply encoded in the more lasting forms of art and literature, but it structured social ritual, public behaviour and even language. Lorimer takes up the issue of language in his arguments about the ways in which neologisms of race relations appeared and became accepted into common linguistic currency before the First World War. How people spoke, as well as the ways they understood such representational forms as paintings or novels structured their thinking about race, as well as embodied or realized their prejudices, misapprehensions or concerns. What could appear to the public as a scientific truism about racial difference between peoples, cultures or nations was overwritten by the sentiments, fantasies and desires of visual culture, literature, public ceremony and the language of social life itself. The theoretical separations between science and sentiment, fact and fabulation, were undermined by a subconscious blending of oppositions that double-coded race as both a biological reality and a Victorian mythology.

Subjectivities

The contexts of Victorian discourses of race, as well as the representational strategies which both reinforced and augmented Victorian ideas about race, are incomplete without considering the real individuals who received these signals, digested them and converted them into lived experience. However, what could be called the subjective qualities of Victorian race theory are perhaps the most complex and elusive for a historian to identify and discuss. Like any aspect of history, subjectivities are historically situated, in flux and subject to the circumstances of a particular period. When speaking of subjectivities, I am not referring simply to the mental processes of single individuals, but to how those mental processes are formed at least in part by culture and which aspects of the 'inner life' appear to have been shared by different sectors of the population. The study of subjectivities is both vast and elusive; therefore, the authors in *The Victorians and Race* tackle this problem in a variety of ways.

Underlying many of the essays in this book is an acknowledgement that Victorian middle-class English men either saw themselves (or thought they should see themselves) as exemplars of a civilized society – perhaps the *only* civilized society. As Simeran Gell points out, 'the notion of "self-image" is to a certain extent a contradiction in terms', given that any image is created in part from the observations and prejudices of others. But certainly in the English case, a unitary notion of selfhood was remarkably persistent throughout the Victorian period. It is when we examine this idea of self – as many authors here do – that the fissures and inconsistencies become apparent. The English middle class did not simply see themselves as more civilized, more physically perfect, more morally correct than non-European peoples, but they defined themselves equally in opposition to other Europeans, non-Protestant religions, the Irish, the Scots, and even the working class (whether or not they were, by strict Victorian racial definition, of 'Anglo-Saxon' stock). As Cherry points out, simple oppositions between 'self' and 'other' are not enough to explain the workings of race theory in the Victorian period. The closer we examine the 'self', the more its illusory unity and predictability begin to crumble.

This object underlies Gell's chapter on representations of the Sikh, Dalip Singh, a favourite of Queen Victoria who wholeheartedly embraced English ways and attitudes even while maintaining the manners and dress of a Sikh. Gell shows how Dalip Singh's external 'otherness' was counterpoised against an internal conformity to English customs. This was recognized by the English and allowed them to assimilate him as both an exotic other and a familiar self. Dalip Singh's own subjective negotiations of his dual role in Victorian life further reveal how complex an identity could be when configured in terms of race.

Unitary notions of self were further eroded by the inescapable presence of the Celts within all aspects of Victorian English culture. From the chapters in this volume by Bryden, MacRaild and Kestner, it becomes clear that many English people had a deeply ambivalent attitude towards their fellow citizens of Celtic descent. On the one hand, as MacRaild shows, the real variety of Irish culture was eschewed or ignored by the English, who tended to stereotype all Irish – regardless of religion or class – as inherently similar. On the other hand, Bryden reveals how racial myths of King Arthur acknowledged his Cymrian associations and used this as a way of creating a mythical racial unity between the Anglo-Saxon and Celtic strands of British culture. The problem of incorporating Celticism yet keeping it at arm's length is handled most directly by Kestner, whose phrase 'the colonized in the colonies' reveals the strategies that allowed the English to accept the Scots as honorary Anglo-Saxons, as long as they were fighting non-western races in the outposts of the empire. The presumed stability of British notions of selfhood is in all the chapters of this volume shown to be not only illusory but very fragile.

Concepts of identity and selfhood were fed in the Victorian period by a greater cultural exchange between nations – fed by emigration, immigration, exploration and colonization. Such travelling back and forth proved to be a threat to unitary notions of identity, as it further ruptured the stability of a nation with a strong self-image. In following up this problem, many of the contributors to *The Victorians and Race* examine the effects of travel on identity and self-image. They investigate why people leave; what they see when they go; what they bring back with them; how this changes the way they perceive their own home; and (perhaps most tellingly) how this changes the way they are perceived. The latter point is tackled by Dolin, who – in his discussion of Dickens' *Edwin Drood* – reveals the reception of Helena and Neville Landless, returning to their provincial village from Ceylon, and seen as little more than savages in their own community. Cherry shows how the factor of women travelling, sometimes alone, to the French colony of Algeria could add a new dimension to their activities and attitudes. New places were seen to taint or enhance their visitors by adding something to their character or to the way they were understood at home.

'Home' here is the key word, as these transports and shifting identities were configured around a stability that was rooted in English domesticity. Not just England as home, but the domestic space of the hearth itself was seen as something inherently English – hence rejecting it and travelling away was transgressive. However, Levy considers the ways in which the habits of English domesticity could be rendered both alien and ridiculous when transplanted into the African Boer community in *The Story of an African Farm*. The character of Lyndall, the 'new woman' of the novel, can be read perhaps more sympathetically because the independence she exerts in Africa can be seen as excusable within an alien environment, despite the fact that these very actions were construed as destructive of all domestic values at home in England.

The contribution of travel to Victorian subjectivities can also be read through the experiences of non-English peoples who travelled to England. These subjectivities are harder to gauge, given the dearth of evidence from outside the canonic strands of white Anglo-Saxon male writing. However, Helen Cooper presents a convincing argument for the ways in which 'the colonized who sailed to England imagined themselves as participating in England as a nation'. In Cooper's analysis, the former slaves Mary Prince and Mary Seacole wrote themselves into a unitary notion of Englishness in their autobiographical narratives. Notions of 'selfhood' and 'otherness' become utterly confused here, as Seacole, for example, with her nickname 'Mother' makes herself a symbol for the 'Mother Country' itself.

All of these subjectivities discussed so far are implicated with a Victorian sense of racial identity. *The Victorians and Race* deals thoroughly with this subject, but its authors also plumb the possibilities of subjectivity further in their assessment of the workings of desire within Victorian culture. Both Edward Said (1978) and Robert Young (1995) have analysed what Young called 'colonial desire', or the longing and fascination which Britons felt for their colonial others – their physical selves, as well as their nations and cultures. The authors in *The Victorians and*

Race test these and other notions of desire to show the ways in which desire feeds into particular racial concerns. Malchow and Cooper both reveal how the racial and sexual overlap in Victorian understandings of 'half-breeds', whose very existence implies what was then felt to be a sexual impropriety as well as a contribution to the dissipation of English national vitality. Both Cherry and Lewis analyse the role of desire in the formation of gender self-consciousness. Lewis considers Orientalist paintings which are traditionally understood to be the domain of male artists produced for the salacious tastes of male audiences. But in her analysis of women who painted such works, she considers both the issue of how women artists chose to view the harem and how female and male audiences chose to interpret women's views. Overturning Laura Mulvey's (1975, 1981) insistence that women spectators are compelled to assume an artificial male viewpoint, Lewis posits the possibility that Orientalist paintings can represent women's views and desires – not sexual desire for a physical body, but spiritual desire for liberation or philanthropy. The place of racial desire – however ambivalent or conflicted – in the formation of modern subjectivities is thus a crucial area for exploration when considering the role of race in the Victorian period.

The essays in *The Victorians and Race* are not arranged chronologically. In fact, the first and last chapters, to an extent, offer a reverse chronology. Douglas Lorimer takes us up to the First World War in his bleak view of the ways in which the reality of anti-racism in Victorian society was undermined by the all-powerful scientific community and its perpetuation of racial divisiveness. The more optimistic Chapter 13 by Helen Cooper, which ends the volume, is set primarily in the early days of Victoria's reign, when the English could assume an abolitionist stance while looking towards their slave-owning American cousins, and when former slaves could become English and impose themselves into the racial bastion of Anglo-Saxonism. Lorimer presents to us the smug voices of the academic establishment, while Cooper unveils the oppositional voices of a Victorian 'other'. These two poles of the book in many ways stand for all the oppositions and ambiguities that are considered by the authors whose chapters rest between them. Race is never a straightforward issue; it is always conflicted, diverse, problematic and terrifyingly complex. *The Victorians and Race* seeks to show that divergent modes of thinking can coexist and relate to each other subtly and richly even though it is only ever possible to scratch the surface of the argument and grope towards an elusive truth.

CHAPTER ONE

Race, science and culture: historical continuities and discontinuities, 1850–1914

Douglas A. Lorimer

As a historian of Victorian racism and race relations, I have one persistent fear. My fear is simply that in studying the racism of the past, we unavoidably reconstruct the racism of the present. This realization flows from two considerations: first, our vision of the past, in this case of the Victorians, is intimately connected with our perception of the present; and secondly, the subject of race is at root a question of power and is, therefore, whether we like it or not, profoundly political. The responsibility of those engaged in the academic study of race and racism is to make their scholarship a source for liberation, and not an instrument of oppression. As a class, of course, those of us who are professional academics, or prospective professional academics, are peculiarly unsuited to fulfil that role.

/Between the mid-nineteenth century and the Second World War, there is a troubling historical correspondence between the emergence in modern western societies of a professional intelligentsia cloistered within the universities and the origin and dissemination of the ideology of race. In so far as science became the paradigm of authoritative knowledge, those academics considered to be scientists had a leading hand in this process, but racism was not so exclusive in its associations. In addition to the scientists, historians, novelists, travel writers, journalists, artists, and their assembled professional critics both shared in, and gave fuller articulation to the pervasive racism of the Victorian age.

A cursory read of recent scholarship on the Victorians and race readily reveals a presumption that a fundamental discontinuity exists between our present and the Victorian past. Professional academics who produce this scholarship stand largely as critics of the Victorian legacy of racism, yet, to my mind it is not clear whether we claim to be liberated from this past or whether our racism in the present is just differently constituted from that of the nineteenth century.

Both histories of scientific racism, and the recent burgeoning field of literary studies of colonial discourse run the risk of colonizing the

Binary opp'
Victorians + other | vics considered a
                     otheress eg- women, homosexuality
                                w/c working women
                                        Irish
RACE, SCIENCE AND CULTURE   13

Victorians. This act of colonization, to use the language of colonial discourse, involves the making of the Victorians into our 'others' – that is, by our selective reading of the sources, both scientific and literary, we create a binary opposition in which the Victorians are made into advocates of a stereotypical racism in implicit contrast to our presumed anti-racism. A more comprehensive reading of the sources, attuned especially to areas of disagreement among the Victorians, will suggest that a variety of racial attitudes existed, and that there may well be a greater continuity between the racism of the late nineteenth and of the late twentieth centuries.

In an effort to explore the continuities and discontinuities in the history of racism, this essay will look at race and science, and its relationship to Victorian culture, particularly in the period between 1850 and 1914. Much of the scholarship on science and race focuses on the initial efforts to classify races hierarchically in the late eighteenth century, and on the more formal origins of scientific doctrines of racial inequality in the mid-nineteenth century (Banton, 1977; Bolt, 1971; Curtin, 1964; Stepan, 1982). In the quest for origins, scholars have found that racial stereotypes show a remarkable stability over time. Struck by the persistence of stereotypes of racial groups, and desirous of offering a critique of racism, scholars, especially analysts of colonial discourse applying the psychology of projection, have looked to ahistorical forms of explanation which give little scope for the dimension of change over time (Brantlinger, 1988; Young, 1990).

There are a number of perhaps unintended dangerous consequences which follow from this focus. To replace the outmoded biological determinism which characterized scientific racism, we may well be constructing an equally oppressive historical, cultural, psychological or linguistic determinism. If our studies of the racism of the past do not address the question of change over time, and the role of human agency in effecting change, then we are left with long-term continuities deeply rooted in our psychology and culture, and impervious to change in the past, and by implication in the present and in the future.

The Victorians and race

'Race' is obviously the defining concept in the ideology of racism, and our problem as scholars is whether we can use the concept of race at all, without being prisoners of racism. This difficulty is compounded by the fact that our scholarship gives us a licence to replicate the racism of the Victorians. Even if we accept that 'race' is a mental construct and not a biological entity, the relationship between ideas of 'race', and the identities of 'nation' and 'culture', which are clearly human creations out of particular histories, leaves ample scope for ambiguities and conflict. In the clarification of these cultural and historical relationships, the Victorians may be more of a hindrance than a guide. The Victorians themselves were often uncertain about what meaning they assigned to 'race'. Furthermore, they differed among themselves, and their meanings changed during the course of the long nineteenth century.

In 1841, when Thomas Arnold attempted to define the features of the modern period of history, he identified its origins with the coming into existence of four features of those nationalities currently active on the world's stage. Those four features were: race, language, institutions and religion. He identified race with 'blood' which suggests a biological inheritance or descent, but he took pains to treat his four features as co-equal and independent. He identified the Germanic races, and particularly the Anglo-Saxon branch, as at the vanguard of progress. Other races existed under conditions of modernity created by the energies of the dominant Anglo-Saxons, and they confronted two options. Some, especially aboriginal peoples under the impact of colonization, faced decline and even extinction. For others, including peoples of European and non-European ancestry, Arnold held out the promise of assimilation to the language, institutions and religion of the dominant race. In using 'race' as one of the defining elements of modern history, Arnold, in common with many of his contemporaries, gave it at best an ambiguous meaning confusing the historical relationship between race and culture (Arnold, 1842, pp. 27–41, 200–2; Barksdale, 1958; Curtin, 1964, pp. 375–6).

In assessing Arnold's use of 'race', and similar uses by his contemporaries, we need to be wary of a temptation to tease out a more precise meaning, when its ambiguous, and even contradictory, character was the source of its utility. To take another famous example from the 1840s, Benjamin Disraeli in his 1847 novel, *Tancred*, had his characters engage in a discussion of the basis of civilization and progress. Sidonia declared: 'All is race; there is no other truth.' In this instance, the qualities of the Saxon race explained why England led the world, while formerly greater European powers were in a state of decline. Even England faced the prospect of decline, for, according to Disraeli: 'The decay of a race is an inevitable necessity, unless it lives in deserts and never mixes its blood' (Disraeli, 1970, pp. 148–50). In his biography of Lord George Bentinck, Disraeli (1852, p. 331) reaffirmed that 'All is race'. In contrast to *Tancred*, though, he pined for the decline of the Norman aristocratic element, and associated the ascendancy of Saxon attributes with middle-class, industrial and reforming enthusiasms he particularly disliked (Brantlinger, 1988, pp. 146–57).

In a fuller statement in the same biography, Disraeli addressed the relationship between race and the idea of human equality. He identified Jews with the 'Semitic principle', which was spiritual, aristocratic and conservative, and opposed to pernicious egalitarian ideas. On the basis of adding a conservative weight to the body politic, he favoured the emancipation of Jews from civic disabilities. He then turned to the Continent, and there within the destructive insurrectionary movements of 1848, Jewish radicals, contrary to the principles of their race, associated with atheists, communists, and 'the scum and low castes of Europe'. Here was proof of the destructive impact of a Christian persecution which led these natural conservatives to align themselves with alien political forces (Disraeli, 1852, pp. 496–8). In the case of Disraeli, and of other Victorians, the ambiguities and contradictions in their conception of race can only be understood in the light of the author's specific historical and political context.

Contemporaneous with Disraeli's observations on race were the lectures and publications of Dr Robert Knox, the discredited Edinburgh anatomist, often identified as the British equivalent to Gobineau as a founding father of modern racism. In a frequently quoted statement, Knox claimed that 'Race is everything: literature, science, art, – in a word, civilization depends on it' (Knox, 1862, p. v; see also, Biddiss, 1976; Richards; 1989b). Knox complained that his contemporaries frequently and imprecisely used the word 'race', and incorrectly linked it to religious, philosophical, political, social and environmental influences. He associated these 'Utopian visions' with James Cowles Prichard, the pre-eminent ethnologist of the 1830s and 1840s. In contrast, Knox thought that humans had both a 'zoological' and an 'intellectual' history, and that race, the 'zoological' or biological element, determined the 'intellectual' (Knox, 1969, pp. 9–17).

Knox also complained that perceptions of race were too closely linked to colonial encounters with peoples visibly distinct in their physical appearance, especially skin colour. He observed that 'When the word race, as applied to man, is spoken of, the English mind wanders immediately to distant countries; to Negroes and Hottentots, Red Indians and savages' (Knox, 1969, p. 39). Knox's intention was to convince his readers that racial differences among European peoples, especially Saxons and Celts, were as real, and as deeply rooted in anatomy. Furthermore, races were inevitably in conflict. The sources of that conflict were also rooted in human nature, and not in the environment, nor in social and political circumstances (Knox, 1969, pp. 24–35, 1862, pp. 119–20, 231–2, 598–9).

Knox saw himself as an outsider, advancing an unpopular but none the less truthful case. During the last half of the nineteenth century, elements, but certainly not all, of Knox's opinions came into wider currency. Nevertheless, we need to be wary of the tired game of intellectual history in which we try to trace commonplace ideas to specific authors. In the case of the discourse on race, we are not finding the proverbial needle, but rather straws, in a haystack. The Victorian use of race was so pervasive that to attribute the origins of racist ideas to a single writer or group of writers invariably ignores or distorts the context of racial inequality and ethnic conflict which gave rise to this discourse.

Despite Knox's efforts at clarification, the Victorians continued to confuse race and culture, and at times they used notions of race in a fashion which has misled their late twentieth-century interpreters. There was no clearer example than Charles Dilke, whose influential account of his world-wide travels, *Greater Britain* (1869), gave greater currency to the idea that the English-speaking peoples of the British Isles and the United States belonged to a common, pre-eminent Saxon race. This picture of the young Dilke, as a disseminator of a transatlantic Anglo-Saxon racism, overlooks other aspects of his ideas and political career, and consequently oversimplifies both his racism and the racism of the larger community of like-minded liberal thinkers. For example, in *Greater Britain*, Dilke not only gave new weight to Anglo-American racial origins, but new currency to the term 'imperialism'. He was critical of British rule in India which managed to 'reduce the government to a mere imperialism, where one man rules and the rest are slaves' (Dilke, 1869, p. 520; Koebner and Schmidt, 1964, pp. 87–91).

When Dilke set out on his travels, in 1866, he was a young radical. He opposed slavery, and travelled to Virginia to see the results of emancipation. The liberated slaves, in his opinion, could only protect their new freedom with the possession of both land and the vote. At the same time, he worried about the decline in British abolitionist enthusiasms, noting that

> if it is still impossible openly to advocate slavery in England, it has, at least, become a habit persistently to write down freedom. We are no longer told that God made the blacks to be slaves, but we are bade to remember that they can not prosper under emancipation. (Dilke, 1869, p. 31)

Despite this trend in opinion, Dilke continued to defend Afro-Caribbean and African American peoples, as well as other non-Europeans subject to colonial rule. In his conclusion to *Greater Britain*, Dilke affirmed:

> There is much exaggeration in the cry that self-government, personal independence, and true manliness can exist only where the

> snow will lie upon the ground, that cringing slavishness and imbe-
> cile submission follow the palm-belt around the world. If freedom
> be good in one country it is good in all, for there is nothing in its
> essence which should limit it in time or place. (Dilke, 1869, p. 530)

Dilke's message was not simply liberal rhetoric, for in his political career following the disaster of his divorce scandal, he became a leading parliamentary advocate of the political and legal rights of persons of colour. From his return to Parliament as a Liberal backbencher in 1892 until his death in 1911, he spoke and lobbied on behalf of the Aborigines Protection Society, and performed a similar role for E. D. Morel and the Congo Reform Association. In the debates on the new South Africa, he led a rump of MPs who defended African rights to land, the vote, and to equal standing before the law, and was a leading critic of abuses of African labour in other British colonies (Gwynn and Tuckwell, 1917, vol. 2, pp. 368–86). To understand the power of Victorian racism, our histories need to comprehend that Dilke's Anglo-Saxon racism and his liberal advocacy of the rights of persons of colour were not necessarily contradictory.

Dilke recognized that in the course of his political career since the 1860s, the discourse on race had undergone a transformation. At the anniversary meeting of the Aborigines Protection Society in 1901, he reminded his audience that, unlike their founders at the beginning of Victoria's reign in 1837, they could rely neither on influence within Parliament nor a sympathetic public (Dilke, 1901, pp. 3–5).

The late Victorian and Edwardian survivors from this earlier humani-tarian tradition were isolated both intellectually and politically. Recent scholarship runs the risk of replicating this isolation by ignoring these forgotten Victorians who belong to the history not of racism but of anti-racism. For example, Catherine Impey, a Quaker spinster from Street, Somerset, and founder of the Society for the Recognition of the Brotherhood of Man, declared in the first number of her magazine, *The Anti-Caste*, in 1888:

> It is our belief that all arbitrary distinctions (or disabilities) based
> on differences of social rank, are 'contrary to the mind of Christ',
> and that of all such distinctions the meanest and most cruelly
> irritating to the victims are those which are based purely on *physi-*
> *cal* characteristics – sex, race, complexion, nationality – in fact
> form or deformity of any kind. (Impey, 1888, Introduction, p. 1;
> Ware, 1992, pp. 173–221)

Our conception of the Victorians and race needs to include Catherine Impey and her friends and supporters. Among her circle were members of racial minorities within British society who were both victims of, and active in resistance to, the prevalent racism of the age.

Our scholarship also needs to take into account differences in opinions, to pay particular attention to conflicts in view and to be aware of the profound changes in both the metropolitan culture and colonial world of the periphery during the course of Victoria's reign. In 1908, in a confidential memorandum on restrictive immigration policies of the self-governing dominions, C. P. Lucas, of the Colonial Office, noted the unexpectedly regressive character of the change in opinion in the last half of the nineteenth century. He observed that 'contrary to what might have been hoped and expected, and undoubtedly was hoped and expected half a century ago, the growth of democracy and science and education has not diminished but increased antipathies of race and colour' (Lucas, 1908, p. 53). Lucas was an informed observer whose administrative responsibilities included the task of addressing what he termed 'the colour question'. He called it 'The greatest difficulty in the British Empire', and he feared that the twentieth century promised to be less tolerant than the nineteenth (Lucas, 1912, p. 97).

One important, though not by any means exclusive, agency in affecting a change in the climate of opinion came from the new intellectual authority of science. Scientists frequently expressed frustration at the imprecise uses of 'race', and attempted to provide a more exclusively biological definition of the term. In this task, they were never entirely successful. Before the British Association in 1881, W. H. Flower (1831–99), Hunterian Professor at the Royal College of Surgeons, President of the Zoological Society, 1879–99, President of the Anthropological Institute, 1883–85, and from 1884 Director of the Natural History Museum, poured scorn on the contradictions in his contemporaries' views of race. He ridiculed 'the great inconsistency between a favourite English theory and a too common English practice – the former being that all men are morally and intellectually alike, the latter being that all are equally inferior to himself in all respects: both propositions egregiously fallacious' (Flower, 1881, p. 436). Despite the efforts of Flower and other comparative anatomists to establish their authority over the definition of race, they were never successful, and nineteenth-century usages remained diverse, contradictory and imprecise (Lorimer, 1988).

In an article, subsequently cited in the *Oxford English Dictionary*, the *Spectator*, commenting on the squabbles in the Bohemian Parliament in 1890, expressed both the ill-defined and the essential character of race. Describing the conflict between the Czechs and the Germans as an instance of 'race-hatred', the *Spectator* ascribed its ultimate source to 'the indefinable aggregate of inherent differences which we call "race"'. Extending its vision from Bohemia to the whole of Europe, the article identified competing nations as 'races', and drew the conclusion that 'A difference, often a secret difference, as to the ends of life is usually the most marked of the separating qualities of two civilised races, and as it is incurable, it tends, as both advance in consciousness, to separate them still further' (*Spectator*, 1890, pp. 109–10). In making the claim that differences of race were 'indefinable', 'inherent', 'secret', related to 'the ends of life', and 'incurable', the *Spectator* accurately reflected the newer sensibilities of the 1890s.

In a sense, Disraeli and Knox may be correct after all. In Victorian discourse, 'race is everything', though in being everything it also becomes nothing. We need to keep in mind the fluid and contradictory character of Victorian claims about race. These features account for the power of racism, and force us to consider the role of the specific historical context in giving meaning to the all-inclusive terminology of race. As Homi Bhabha has observed about the character and potency of stereotypes:

> It is the force of ambivalence that gives the colonial stereotype its currency: ensures its repeatability in changing historical and discursive conjunctures; informs its strategies of individuation and marginalization; produces that effect of probabilistic truth and predictability, which, for the stereotype, must always be in *excess* of what can be empirically proved or logically construed. (Bhabha, 1986, pp. 148–9)

To illustrate, let me reiterate a point from my book *Colour, Class and the Victorians*, about the contradictory attributes of common racial stereotypes, as exemplified by that of the 'Negro'. In the perception of the Victorians, the physical characteristics of peoples of African descent remained constant, but the psychological and social attributes assigned to the stereotype of the 'Negro' altered according to changes in the context of the observer. The 'Negro' was depicted as both 'the obedient, humble servant, and the lazy, profligate, worthless worker; the natural Christian and the unredeemable sinner; the patient, suffering slave, and the cruel, vengeful savage'. These contradictions were not simply an expression of polarized views of those identified as 'Negrophiles' or 'Negrophobes', for 'Evangelicals thought Africans were natural Christians and unredeemable savages; the advocates of the planting interest thought Negroes were lazy and profligate, yet particularly suited to vigorous physical labour in tropical climates' (Lorimer, 1978, p. 203). The mental construct which we identify as a racial stereotype cannot be abstracted from its context, for it is the context which gives meaning to the attitude to the observer.

contradictions

Victorian science, race and context

Within the history of science itself, the role of context as a source of change involves more substantive issues between those usually characterized as 'internalists' or 'externalists'. The 'internalists' see change as a product of the logic of scientific discovery itself, whereas the 'externalists' put greater emphasis on changes in the social and historical context. Even though the science of race, unlike higher mathematics or theoretical physics, invariably had immediate social implications, these differences are present in the history of scientific racism. Those who emphasize the continuity of racial stereotypes over time within the changing form of biological determinism from comparative anatomy, Darwinian evolution, and eugenics tend to be in the internalist camp. The externalists put greater emphasis on the links between science and the defence of race slavery and of nineteenth-century colonialism, on changes in the institutional basis of science and the social background of scientists, and on the association of professional science and the State in articulating the hegemonic racism of the late Victorian and Edwardian periods. To some degree, the crude polarities of 'internalist' and 'externalist' have now been surpassed, as historians of science attempt to place the development of scientific ideas within the broader context of Victorian culture. This contextualist approach leaves scope for the creative response of scientists seeking to understand natural phenomena, while recognizing that the scientists' perception and conceptualization of nature owed much to their social and cultural milieu (Appleby et al., 1994, pp.160–97; Lightman, 1996; MacLeod, 1977; Young, 1985b). This perspective applies particularly to the biological sciences, for in Robert Young's notable phrase, 'Darwinism *Is* Social'. In fact, Young uses remarks about race by T. H. Huxley and other scientists to demonstrate the social character of Darwinian biology and its applications (Young, 1985a, pp. 609–38).

The role of context in informing the scientists' perceptions of racial differences becomes more evident if one bears in mind the form of racial typologies. The scientists assumed that a correlation existed between anatomical features and mental and psychological traits. In fact, descriptions of racial groups often gave a simple list of both physical, and social and mental characteristics without elaborating on the relationship of biology to social behaviour. In his entry on 'China' for *Cassells' Storehouse of General Information*, A. H. Keane, one of the more prolific popularizers of racial typologies, began with a brief general description of the physical features of the Chinese, but quickly slid into generalizations about psychological attributes:

> Physically the Chinese are below the middle height, averaging about 5 feet 4 or 5 inches, with somewhat coarse thick-set frames, prominent cheek-bones, oblique eyes, small nose, broad flat features, yellowish complexion, long lank black hair, sparse or no beard, inanimate expression, with great staying power and capacity for enduring fatigue and hardships on poor fare.

The entry then extended the description of Chinese social and psychological traits, as Keane observed, 'they are naturally frugal, thrifty, and parsimonious, though given to reckless gambling, excessively courteous among themselves, but rude and aggressive towards strangers'. He also claimed the Chinese suffered from 'excessive gregariousness', resulting in 'a low state of morals', and thus justified exclusionary immigration regulations (Keane, 1894, pp. 97–8).

The scientists adopted the description of the mental and social traits of races, often drawn from travel literature or other sources, as established 'knowledge', and they showed little interest in testing these claims. The focus of scientific enquiry was upon the 'new' knowledge of human biology, especially comparative anatomy and evolution. The scientists no doubt promoted a form of biological determinism, but their typologies were not simply a creation of their science. The attributes assigned to races, especially significant social and mental traits, were incorporated, often uncritically, from the common cultural context. As the historical context was subject to dramatic changes in the course of the nineteenth century, so too was the ideology of race.

A brief comparative note on the familiar triumvirate of class, gender and race may illustrate this point. Social histories of class and gender readily recognize that differences in social rank and differences in the roles of males and females existed in the past and exist in the present, yet the inequalities of class and gender were subject to significant changes over time. Consequently, historians and others are faced with the complex task of reconstructing past languages of class and gender (Corfield, 1991; Higginbotham, 1992; Jones, 1983; Joyce, 1991; Scott, 1988). Studies of race, on the other hand, offer by implication a rather crude measure of historical development. Racism either exists or does not exist. Since significant social and political distinctions on the basis of 'race' have been made in western culture during the whole of the modern period of history, let us say since Columbus if not before, then racism has a continuous existence.

This perspective begs the historical question. For example, was the racism of the late eighteenth century the same as that of the late nineteenth or of the late twentieth centuries? Dramatic changes in the historical context, including the creation of a new form of social order and culture with the Industrial Revolution, and the making of a new world order by modern imperialism, transformed the character of race and racism. Both were subject to historical changes as significant as those we are now accustomed to address in studies of class and gender.

In an essay on the abolition of the slave trade and its relationship to European racism, Seymour Drescher, quite correctly in my opinion, argues that the period of the ascendancy of the anti-slavery movement, from the late eighteenth century to the 1840s, marks a fundamental discontinuity in the history of racism (Drescher, 1992). The African slave trade and race slavery in the New World had long been defended by intellectual and moral authorities within western culture. When these time-honoured practices came under attack, some supporters of the slave traders and planters, for example Edward Long, attempted to use science to defend these forms of racial oppression. As abolitionist opinion gained ascendancy in the early nineteenth century, within both élite and more significantly in popular culture, the advocates of racism retreated into the isolation of the unorthodox and the eccentric.

Drescher runs into difficulty when he turns to address the re-emergence of racism into the position of orthodoxy after 1850. Partly, on a misreading of *Colour, Class and the Victorians* (Lorimer, 1978), Drescher argues that this revival of racism reflects a historical continuity with the earlier racism of the late eighteenth century. A more accurate reading of this history, in my opinion, would argue that racism in the second half of the nineteenth century was reconstituted as the orthodox position in western science and culture, but on a new institutional basis and within an altogether different historical context (Lorimer, 1978, 1988). Therefore, racism no doubt existed in the late eighteenth and the late nineteenth centuries, but these defences of racial inequality and oppression were as distinct as the comparable defences of inequalities of class and gender in the late eighteenth century and the late Victorian periods. It is only through paying attention to this historical dimension that we can come to understand both how oppression changed form over time and, more importantly, how movements of resistance and liberation emerged, developed, and under certain historical circumstances achieved some, if not all, of their goals.

The disturbing question, for which our historiography supplies only partial answers, is why, in the late nineteenth and early twentieth centuries, did science, which we associate with reason, enlightenment and progress, sanction the forces of oppression rather than of liberation? In the case of Victorian England, modern racist ideology, and the role of science in its creation, grew out of the intersection of the metropolitan and colonial spheres, and served to reconcile, with only partial success, the contradictions between democracy at home and imperialism abroad. Those Victorians in the liberal and radical tradition, for example, John

Stuart Mill, Charles Dilke, Catherine Impey, L. T. Hobhouse, Graham Wallas, H. M. Hyndman, Annie Besant, Ramsay Macdonald, and Sydney Olivier, feared that the exercise of empire abroad would serve to weaken and corrupt a fragile democratic culture within the British Isles (Porter, 1968; Taylor, 1991).

As scholars of the Victorians and race, we all to a greater or lesser degree suffer from tunnel vision in limiting the Victorians to our own inevitably restricted selection of the sources. In the history of science and race, the danger is that our research never goes beyond the scientists, so the Victorian discourse on race is equated with social biology. A broader sampling of sources readily establishes that there were competing ideologies of race in the nineteenth as in the twentieth century.[1]

Victorian discourses on race encompassed a struggle between two rival visions. The advocates of humanitarian causes and the civilizing mission espoused a goal of assimilation, and believed in the common origin and psychic unity of human beings. Their opponents, at least the extreme racialists among them, argued that the races had separate origins, and distinct, unequal characteristics. Depending on the historical context, they advocated a strategy either of exclusion or of separate and unequal development. Both positions, the assimilating cultural imperialism and the exclusionary doctrine of global apartheid, were variants of racism. Both presumed that the agents of western civilization had the power and the right to transform other peoples' lives, and both assumed that in the resultant new order a hierarchy of races, like a hierarchy of social classes, would exist.

In the mid-nineteenth century, under the liberal certainties of *laissez-faire* capitalism, it was still possible to believe that the abolition of an imposed system of racial oppression, such as slavery, was in itself sufficient to provide for conditions of individual freedom and economic prosperity. By the late nineteenth century, colonial advocates aiming to establish viable capitalist economies relying on indigenous or migrant wage-labour recognized that such an order, including the subordination of non-Europeans within white *herrenvolk* democracies, had to be artificially constructed in the law, in political institutions, and in social practice (Davis, 1984; Foner, 1983; Smith, 1982; Trapido, 1980; van den Berghe, 1967). Within this changing context, the older cultural imperialism of assimilation lost credibility, while the strategy of segregated, and unequal, development seemed more in harmony with reality and common sense. Ironically, the man-made edifice of separate development, according to some scientists, was constructed in accordance with the dictates of nature.

By the late nineteenth century, the community of scientists was in a more powerful position to influence the direction of racial discourse for institutional as well as intellectual reasons. The professionalization of science, even a late bloomer such as anthropology, created a community of experts socially selected from the expanding professional middle class, and confident in the authority of its specialized, scientific knowledge. Among anthropologists, the comparative anatomists, both from their specialized training and from their affiliation with the medical profession, claimed pre-eminent status as scientists (Stocking, 1987, pp. 238–73; see also Lorimer, 1988).

This bias within professional science was reflected in the form of the popularization of scientific images of race in the late nineteenth century. Unfortunately, the existing historiography places too great an emphasis on the mid-Victorian period, and too little attention has been given to later in the century. Technological innovations in printing and the extension of literacy through state education, began to have a noticeable effect from the 1880s onwards. By that time, it was possible to produce affordable texts for school and university students, and encyclopedias, serialized reference works, or what were termed 'self-educators', for a mass market. At the same time, visual, non-literary representations of race experienced a comparable development. These innovations occurred both at the institutional level of ethnographic displays at museums, and as part of popular commercial exhibitions such as Buffalo Bill's Wild West Show and the Earl's Court exhibit of Savage South Africa (Coombes, 1994; Dunae, 1989). In numerous encyclopedia entries and popular texts, Professor A. H. Keane, a Professor of Hindustani at University College, London, was a leading publicist of the racial typologies of the professional scientists. Trained as a linguist rather than as a biologist, he evaded the technicalities of biological inheritance and specialized in providing succinct descriptions of mental as well as physical characteristics of what he termed 'ideal' racial types. He also pioneered the use of photographs to illustrate his typologies. Ethnographic photographs provided a means to avoid the dull technicalities of anatomical description. They also objectified their subjects, making the presentation appear more authentic, while freezing people in time as unchanging specimens of nature (Edwards, 1992; Fabian, 1983; Green, 1984; Keane, 1899, 1908; Keane et al., 1905; Lorimer, 1990, 1996).

Science and the politics of race

The racial typologies were commonplace, and eventually reached a more popular readership with the innovations in publishing, photography and marketing in the two or three decades prior to 1914. They became the target of the critiques of population geneticists and others from the 1930s onwards, but to define Victorian scientific racism too narrowly in these terms omits forms of racist thought which have had a longer duration (Barkan, 1992; Kuklick, 1991; Livingstone, 1992).

It may be more useful to see scientific racism not simply in terms of racial typologies, but more broadly in terms of late Victorian scientists' belief in what has been termed 'scientific naturalism' (Lorimer, 1996; Richards, 1989b; Turner, 1974). This doctrine, which looked for a symmetry between processes in nature, and in the human dimensions of history and culture, was more evident in schemes of human biological and social evolution than in the typologies of comparative anatomy. In this vision, forces of change, as for instance in geology, were seen to be uniform, universal and incremental. In making human beings into natural objects, questions of human consciousness, will and agency were seen to be outside the realm of science. Consequently the decline and, even, genocide of aboriginal peoples was depicted as a natural process working according to a scientific or Darwinian law. This perspective denied the colonizers' role as morally responsible historical agents, and similarly denied the role of historical agency to indigenous peoples whose resistance was seen simply as an outburst of savage instinct.

This detachment from troubling moral, not to say explosive political issues was part of the scientists' creed of objectivity. The claim to a scientific detachment from ethical issues involving racial conflict and oppression developed over time, and was more securely fixed by the end of the nineteenth century than in the early or mid-Victorian periods. In the late eighteenth century, contemporaries identified scientific claims of racial inequality with the defence of the slaveholding interest then under attack from the abolitionists. When the abolitionist movement had gained the moral, intellectual and political ascendancy, leading ethnologists such as Prichard openly expressed their confidence in the compatibility between science and humanitarianism.

Finding the political activities of the Aborigines Protection Society consumed all its time and attention, Dr Thomas Hodgkin led some fellow members, anxious to pursue academic studies of human racial and cultural varieties, to found the Ethnological Society of London in 1844 (Rose, 1981). The lingering connections of the Ethnological Society with humanitarian causes through its founding core of Quaker physicians and their belief in monogenesis, or the common origin of the world's peoples, came under attack in the 1860s. In the midst of the intellectual ferment associated with Darwinian evolution, the issue of race became an intellectual and political testing ground for many of the new directions in science. The racial determinism of Dr Robert Knox in his *Races of Man* (1850, revised 1862) received a wider publicity through Dr James Hunt, a young speech therapist, who broke with the Ethnological Society and its humanitarian links in 1863, and founded the Anthropological Society of London (Burrow, 1970, pp. 118–36; Hunt, 1863; Lorimer, 1978, pp. 134–61; Rainger, 1978; Stocking, 1971).

In the 1860s, the claim that the races represented distinct and unequal species with separate origins was still contentious, and Hunt deliberately provoked controversy. Through the Anthropological Society's publications, Hunt and his supporters defended slavery and the Confederacy in the American Civil War, justified Governor Eyre's brutal use of martial law to suppress the Jamaican Insurrection of 1865, and criticized the missionary societies for pursuing impractical schemes in defiance of the biological facts of race. Hunt's politics and his management of the Anthropological Society became a scandal to the scientific community. T. H. Huxley with the support of Darwinian friends in the X-Club, worked to reunite the ethnologicals and the anthropologists, and to restore respectability to the scientific study of race. The eventual reunion in the newly founded Anthropological Institute in 1871 represented, according to George Stocking, a political compromise (Stocking, 1987, pp. 254–7; see also ASL, 1869; Huxley, 1901).

The new institute rejected both the older humanitarian affiliations of the ethnologists and the newer politics of Hunt's racial determinism. This compromise was not free of its own political implications. In their annual addresses, Presidents of the institute promoted the anthropological study of race as a science necessary for the administration of a multiracial empire. Their most ambitious scheme, the creation of a state-financed Imperial Bureau of Ethnology, was rejected for budgetary reasons by Asquith's Liberals. None the less, the anthropologists did win imperial recognition, when in 1907 their learned society became the 'Royal' Anthropological Institute (RAI, 1907, 1909, 1911, 1912).

The politics of professional anthropology becomes clearer when contrasted with the racial discourse of its originating body, the Aborigines Protection Society (APS). The APS served as a political lobby, often acting as the agent of colonized peoples in general, and of West and South Africans in particular. Up until 1914, the APS, despite its old-fashioned advocacy of aboriginal entitlement to land and equality before the law, still had more influence at the Colonial Office than did the anthropologists. Although the humanitarians were viewed as a nuisance by colonial secretaries such as Joseph Chamberlain, the efforts of H. R. Fox Bourne, the APS Secretary, to seek redress in specific cases still required Colonial Office attention and response (Bourne, 1899).

A comparison of APS pamphlets and of the *Colonial Intelligencer and Aborigines' Friend* with scientific publications such as the *Journal of the Anthropological Institute*, the magazine *Nature*, and of popular illustrated serials of geography and travel, shows that a variety of racial discourses still existed in the late nineteenth century. By that time, according to the test of contemporary science, the Aborigines Protection Society was an anachronism. If its members no longer believed in noble savages, they still believed in natural rights, and defended aboriginal entitlement to land and to legal standing within that tradition (APS, 1837, 1900a; Bourne, 1899). In contrast, prior to 1914, the anthropologists contributed little to the discussion of the political, legal and social conditions which might enable indigenous peoples to preserve and nurture their customs and traditions. The anthropologists with their more informed ethnography and their scientific understanding of evolutionary change thought that questions of natural entitlement or rights rested more upon 'sentiment' than upon knowledge.

This division between sentiment and knowledge was to some degree reflected in the membership of the two organizations. Despite the founding links of the scientific study of race with the APS in the 1840s, after 1870 none of the leading members of the APS belonged to the Anthropological Institute. Similarly, no prominent late Victorian anthropologist belonged to the APS, or participated in its various public campaigns against racial injustice. This detachment of the scientists from the principal political lobby for the rights of colonized peoples was most striking in the controversies about the formation of the new Union of South Africa. The anthropologists offered advice to the government about the management of 'native races', whereas the APS, criticized the use of Chinese indentured labour in the Rand, defended African entitlement to land and to the vote, and opposed discriminatory legislation against Indians in Natal and the Transvaal (APS, 1900b, 1908; Bourne, 1900; RAI, 1900).

By the 1890s, the Anthropological Institute had about 350 members, whereas the APS had declined to around 200 subscribers. The APS was still dominated by Quaker families, many connected with private business enterprises, whereas the anthropologists were drawn mainly from the professional middle class. Over time amateurs such as army officers and clergy declined in numbers, whereas the number of institute members who were colonial administrators or university lecturers increased. The most striking difference between the two societies, though, was in the gender of their subscribers. The admission of women had long been a contentious issue for the learned societies, and under its founding terms the Anthropological Institute specifically excluded women. In contrast, approximately 40 per cent of the subscribers to the Aborigines Protection Society were women, and prominent among them were wives, mothers, daughters, and sisters from leading Quaker families (APS, 1908, pp. 14–15; Lorimer, 1988, p. 407; Richards, 1989a).

This gender division reflected Victorian sensibilities on the question of race. The world of science was a masculine world, in which the scientist prided himself on his mastery of his subject, and his realistic, detached and objective view of the world, free of sentimental attachments including the humanitarian enthusiasms of the past. On the other hand, the philanthropic agencies were, after the 1860s, viewed as old-fashioned, unrealistic and sentimental. Catherine Hall has argued that in this late Victorian world, in which knowledge and sentiment were identified as incompatible, racial dominance became an expression of masculine virtue, and humanitarianism belonged to the sphere of women's work and feminine weakness (Hall, 1992). In 1911 press headlines on the Universal Races Congress captured these polarities. The *Daily News*, a Liberal daily, posed the question directly, asking if the Congress dealt with 'SCIENCE OR SENTIMENT?' (*Daily News*, 29 July 1911, p. 4d). On the other hand, the *Daily Express'* headline, 'RACES IN CONGRESS – WOMEN PLEAD FOR CHINESE AND INDIANS' was itself a not-so-subtle rejection to this effort to address issues of racial oppression and race relations (*Daily Express*, 28 July 1911, p. 3h).

Social science and race relations

To assess the longer-term legacy of the Victorians, that is the legacy for the 1990s rather than for the 1930s, we should shift our focus from the scientists' racial typologies to the social science of race relations. Here, too, important innovations occurred during the course of the nineteenth century, and particularly between the 1890s and 1914. The phrase 'race relations' came into use *circa* 1910 (Archer, 1910, p. x; Olivier, 1970, pp. 172–3). In addition, the following terms, among others, entered this vocabulary during the two decades prior to the First World War: segregation, discrimination, colour bar and racialism. Out of the discussion of what was termed the 'native' or 'colour' question, the words 'non-European' and more rarely 'non-white' were coined as authors attempted to describe an emerging global pattern of political and social relations (Wallas, 1948, pp. 6–8).

This language of race relations grew out of the older humanitarian tradition of the abolitionist movement. As late nineteenth-century colonialism focused less on questions of the acquisition of new territories, and more on economic development requiring the recruitment of local or migrant labour, the language of race relations was overtaken by colonial promoters, administrators, and other informed experts, some claiming the authority of science. Much of this discussion was informed by American innovations and experience, including the institution of legalized segregation in the South, and widespread incidents of lynching. The American example had particular relevance for the making of a system of social and legal segregation in the new Union of South Africa (Cell, 1982; Frederickson, 1981). This shift in focus, from the older humanitarian language of racial injustice to the newer academic and scientific study of race relations, involved a change from a concern with the liberation of oppressed peoples to the justification and management of racial subordination.

In this fashion, the Victorian concept of 'colour prejudice' underwent a remarkable change in the late nineteenth century. The expression, 'prejudice against colour', or more simply, 'colour prejudice', originated in abolitionist discourse in the 1820s and 1830s. From the 1840s through the 1860s, African-American fugitive slaves played a particularly prominent part in bringing this theme before their audiences as they contrasted their reception in Britain with their experience of prejudice in the United States (Blackett, 1983; Lorimer, 1978; Spiers, 1992). After the American Civil War, as anti-slavery attentions shifted to Africa, this critique of colour prejudice became less common, except for the activities of more radical abolitionist survivors such as Catherine Impey and the Society for the Recognition of the Brotherhood of Man.

More importantly, increasing racial hostility and exclusiveness in the United States, in the self-governing dominions, in South Africa, and in the jurisprudence and administration of crown colonies and India led to efforts to uncover the roots of such prejudice. By the end of the century, the older terminology of 'colour prejudice' was superseded by the new language of 'race instinct'. This use of race instinct developed at the same time that the newly established discipline of psychology focused its interest on instinctive or irrational behaviour. Such behaviours, often associated with hyper-sexuality, male observers attributed to groups identified as the 'other' by gender and race (Jones, 1980, pp. 121–39; Levy, 1991b). 'Instinct', of course, naturalized 'prejudice' making it no less irrational, but making it legitimate as an expression of human nature.

The racial animosity evident among white populations became proof that this instinct was not subject to control, but rather part of the new political reality. In 1900, in his essay on 'The Exploitation of Inferior Races', for *Liberalism and Empire*, Gilbert Murray, a classics professor at the University of Glasgow, rejected the liberal standards of the past: 'Let us frankly abandon for the present the ideal of one universal British law – we have never really acted upon it' (Murray, 1900, p. 156). In its place he called for protective legislation for coloured labourers restricted to admittedly inferior conditions and status. In some measure, this realism was well founded. The mid-Victorian vision of a colour-blind empire was an illusion. At best its advocates assumed that without the institutional framework of discrimination in law, the legitimate inequalities of social class would exist, and these by and large would conform to distinctions of race. The late nineteenth-century experience of the United States, Canada, Australia, New Zealand and South Africa suggested that white voters insisted upon protection of a privileged status by the exclusion of non-white migrants, and by entrenching existing forms of racial subordination (Huttenback, 1976). Within colonial territories outside the areas of white settlement, the new language of race relations also served to counteract the demands of African and Asian nationalists for greater representation within legislative councils, and for self-government.

This late Victorian and Edwardian discourse on race relations has had a longer-term legacy in the twentieth century than the racial typologies of Victorian anthropologists. This discourse of race relations also became institutionalized within new academic disciplines. Authors such as Sydney Olivier, James Bryce, L. T. Hobhouse, Gilbert Murray and Graham Wallas moved readily between politics, government service, journalism, and the university lecture hall. Even at this founding stage of the social sciences, the divisions which still characterize the academic study of race relations were evident.

In the Romanes Lectures for 1902, James Bryce, a Liberal, a pro-Boer, and a distinguished jurist and diplomat, attempted to describe the newly emergent pattern of race relations out of his experience in the United States, India and South Africa. Comparing the innovations in global race relations at the beginning of the twentieth century with the historical initiatives that followed upon Columbus's landing in the Americas, Bryce's lectures on *The Relations of the Advanced and the Backward Races of Mankind* became one of the more frequently cited works on this theme.

As his title suggests, Bryce contrasted racial groups by their level of development, but to his mind racial conflict derived less from innate inequality than from the psychology of interracial contact. Using the phrase 'physical repulsion' rather than colour or race prejudice, Bryce thought that there was a fundamental 'dissimilarity of character' between races. Consequently, while he was ready to admit that the so-called backward races had the capacity to advance in 'intelligence and knowledge', such progress only served to intensify racial animosity (Bryce, 1979, pp. 5–10, 18–20, 27–36; Stone, 1972). This antagonism was rooted in human nature. Pointing to the hostility toward Chinese labourers in Australia and California, he observed that 'Nature may be supposed to know better than we do; and the efforts of man to check her have been often foolish and most ineffective' (Bryce, 1979, pp. 33–4).

Bryce offered a psychological rather than a biological view of race relations, yet this form of social science shared much in common with the scientific naturalism of his forerunners in Victorian biology and physical anthropology. Once again, racial divisions and conflict were not the work of responsible human agents, but part of the dictates not so much of nature as of human nature.

Bryce's view of race relations became the new orthodoxy of his Edwardian contemporaries. While there may be traces of similar ideas as far back as Edward Long, or in the mid-Victorian science of Robert Knox, in its vocabulary and in its uses of recent historical experience, largely of former slave societies after emancipation and the new colonial creations of late nineteenth century, Bryce and his contemporaries created a new form of discourse about race and race relations. They did not, though, establish exclusive control of the field.

In contrast, Sydney Olivier, Colonial Office civil servant, former Governor of Jamaica, and Fabian Socialist, offered a rival picture of race relations. In many ways, Olivier still thought in terms of familiar racial stereotypes, especially about Africans and their New World descendants. None the less, his experience as a colonial administrator and his socialism gave him an unusual perspective. Concerned with questions of colonial development, and especially the problem of recruitment of wage labour, Olivier recognized that patterns of labour in non-industrial societies conformed to traditional practices, whereas the unusual and historically unprecedented patterns of regular, disciplined, intensive labour were a recent product of industrialization within western societies. The problem of labour was not one of the 'lazy native', but how to replicate the unusual regularity and intensity of industrial labour in a non-industrial colonial context (Olivier, 1970; see also Lee, 1988).

In addition, Olivier's experience gave him a sense of comparative differences in race relations. He contrasted patterns of institutionalized segregation and virulent racism in the United States with his knowledge of the West Indies. There he claimed neither formalized segregation, nor such violent racial prejudice existed. Furthermore, he feared that South Africa was imitating the United States, and from there the whole of colonial Africa would be infected.

Olivier rejected claims of racial superiority which he saw were at the root of what he termed the 'race-barrier' theory or the 'race-differentiation theory'. In *White Capital and Coloured Labour* (first published 1906), he offered the contrasting and admittedly unconventional view that:

> If we carefully compare the essentials of the situation as between a modern industrial community and a tropical dependency, where white enterprise is exploiting native resources, we shall, I believe,

be forced to recognise that inhuman social conditions arise in them
much more out of the opposition in the categories of Capital and
Labour than out of the opposition in the category of race or colour.
(Olivier, 1970, p. 122)

Dissident voices, such as Olivier, and before him more obscure figures
such as Catherine Impey or H. R. Fox Bourne, cannot be ignored if our
picture of the Victorians and race is to be complete. The issue at stake is
not whether Bryce or Olivier offered a more persuasive view of race
relations, but rather to recognize the fact of their differences. This
recognition will force us to acknowledge the profoundly political character of race, and will afford us the possibility of confronting the reality
of change over time.

Conclusion

It is only in this fashion that we will be able to avoid the crude
determinist trap set by racism in its various forms. To this end, I have
tried to argue that we need to pay more attention to the discontinuities
in the history of racism. The sources of change derived in the first place
from tensions and contradictions within racist discourse itself. The
Victorian language of race may well be ubiquitous within the culture,
but its power flowed from its flexibility rather than from its rigidity. In
fact, one of the limitations of the typologies of the scientists was that
they tried to fix racial traits as a natural inheritance just at the time
colonialism was transforming the economic, political and social conditions of people's lives. The divergent patterns of development between
these worlds, best summed up in the Victorian radical concern for the
contradictions between democracy at home and imperialism abroad,
were themselves sources of tension and change. Consequently, the Victorians, as observers and participants within this changing world, differed among themselves and altered their opinions over time.

By pursuing the differences within Victorian racial discourse, as between the humanitarian activists and the professional scientists, one can .
gain a clearer sense of the direction and dynamics of historical change.
Regrettably, in the second half of the nineteenth century, we need to
confront the reality that racism grew in power, in sophistication and in
intensity. Within the metropolitan culture, part of the explanation for
this regressive pattern lies in the emergence of a professional intelligentsia supportive of the exercise of imperial expansion and racial domination.

In assessing the racist legacy from the nineteenth century, we need to
be wary lest we focus too exclusively on the racial typologies of the

biological sciences. This form of racism came under attack during the 1930s, but in a longer-term historical perspective it was a kind of scaffold, a buttress and perhaps a necessary support, for the construction of new institutional inequalities of race. When the scaffold was partly dismantled from the 1930s through to the 1960s, the structure of racial inequality remained largely intact. The surviving Victorian legacy is primarily that structure of inequality, but nineteenth-century developments also contributed to its surviving ideological defence. The defences of systemic racism had already emerged in the new social sciences, and in the new language of race relations which came into being from the 1890s to 1914.

In this sense, the Victorian legacy for our racism may be more immediate than the existing historiography recognizes. Within the limits of their time and place, the Victorians were none the less active historical agents making choices from the options open to them. The disturbing question for scholars in 1990s is that our academic predecessors, including some of the best minds of the Victorian age, exercised their historical options for oppression rather than for liberation.

Notes

1. These reflections grow out of my research for a forthcoming monograph on Victorian racism and race relations. Much of the Victorian discussion of race relations engaged writers with either a background in colonial administration or with some connection with philanthropic lobbies such as the APS. The themes in this non-fiction prose, including the advocacy of assimilation, do not appear to have engaged the sympathies of prominent writers of fiction, at least in so far as that genre is represented by Brantlinger (1988). It is striking that one of the most popular novels in Victorian England, Harriet Beecher Stowe's *Uncle Tom's Cabin*, was both American in origin and, despite its racial ambiguities, a narrative of liberation. As Raymond Williams has taught us, we cannot write the social history of the Victorian working class from the novel; nor can we reconstruct Victorian race relations from contemporary fiction.

CHAPTER TWO

Images of otherness and the visual production of difference: race and labour in illustrated texts, 1850–1865

Tim Barringer

Respectable society in Victorian Britain defined itself through a series of structured oppositions by which any group thought to adhere to different concepts of social and sexual behaviour, of work and time discipline, of value and of religion, was accorded the status of an inferior and potentially hostile other. Ludmilla Jordanova has recently offered a useful definition of otherness as 'the distancing of what is peripheral, marginal and incidental from a cultural norm, of illicit danger from safe legitimacy'. Jordanova outlines characteristic themes in the response to otherness:

> the other [is treated as] an object, something to be managed and possessed, and as dangerous and threatening. At the same time, the other becomes an entity whose very separateness inspires curiosity, invites enquiring knowledge. The other is to be veiled and unveiled … the process of unveiling is called science and it depends on new modes of vision. (Jordanova, 1989, pp. 109–10)

The most powerful concept which could be deployed in asserting the otherness of social groups was that of race. A fundamental assumption here is that the concept of race is socially created and thus historically variable: essentializing definitions of race, which assert that discrete groups of people are fundamentally different from others, are treated as discursive constructions (Gates, 1986, Introduction; Lévi-Strauss, 1985, p. 15; Stepan, 1982, pp. ix–xix).

During the mid-nineteenth century, as often before and since, the idea of racial difference was mobilized in various ways to distance an empowered group – in this case white, middle class and respectable – from others both at home and abroad. The field of visual representation offered a site for the production and dramatization of powerful distinctions between self and other, in which normative categories of body-type and behaviour could be presented in contrast to those of others, constructed as deviant. The problematic of race is fundamentally linked to the process of looking at the body; physical appearance has commonly been considered to be the primary visible signifier of racial affiliation. The role of images in fixing essentialized definitions of race in the consciousness of dominant groups is, accordingly, of primary importance. Not only were visual representations of physiognomies and body-types read for signs of race: these representations also played an active role in establishing the tropes through which the idea of racial difference was articulated. An abiding and often unspoken assumption in the analysis of images is that visual representations constitute a passive and reflective record of appearances; the central assertion of this chapter is, by contrast, that visual representations play an active and formative role in cultural discourses, notably that of race.

In examining the visual production of racial difference, I shall not examine images usually incorporated in the privileged category of 'art', but rather mass-circulation, wood-engraved illustrations for popular works of non-fiction. This type of image, which appeared in illustrated newspapers, travel books, scientific and religious literature, was, and often still is, commonly understood as reportage, a direct transcription of things seen. There is an apparent absence of those processes of considered artistic mediation which make Victorian academic paintings, for all their efforts at verisimilitude, look so obviously rhetorical. For the same reasons, art history has ignored this corpus of imagery, except in so far as it might have provided source material for works of high art. Yet these unspectacular illustrations were central to mid-Victorian visual culture: the steam press had made the automated production of large print-runs of illustrated books and newspapers inexpensive and speedy; wood engravings were cheaper and quicker to produce than engravings on steel and copper and could reach a mass market (Wakeman, 1973, p. 73). With the founding of the *Illustrated London News* in 1842, visual reportage came to play an increasingly influential role for the middle-class reading public (Anderson, 1991; Fox, 1988). These images circulated more widely than all but the most famous fine art engravings, and yet their ideological content and role in Victorian visual culture has barely been examined. It is important, then, to disrupt the rhetoric of authenticity which surrounded the production of these images and which has allowed them to continue to circulate, almost unnoticed, treated as unmediated factual data. Popular illustration deserves, I suggest, analysis as rigorous as that routinely applied to works of high art.

This chapter examines illustrated books from the 1850s and early 1860s which take as their subjects population groups unfamiliar to the majority of the mid-Victorian reading public. From the extensive exploration literature relating to sub-Saharan Africa derive two works by the missionary and explorer David Livingstone, *Missionary Travels* (1857) and *Narrative of an Expedition to the Zambesi* (1865), and a further volume of travel writing, John Hanning Speke's *Journal of the Discovery of the Source of the Nile* (1863). Each is concerned with the indigenous populations of areas of Africa being staked out as potential sites for colonial expansion during this period. By contrast, Henry Mayhew's vast study *London Labour and the London Poor*, based on extensive social investigation carried out between 1849 and 1851, represents in text and images a domestic other consisting of those in London who were perceived as deviating from behavioural norms: casual labourers, street-traders and the urban poor, criminals, vagabonds, vagrants and prostitutes.[1] Through the juxtaposition of these works I shall draw attention to the similarities between representations of otherness at the fringes and at the heart of empire, indicating the visual cross-references and slippages which, through a visual language of race, bind Mayhew's darkest London to Livingstone's dark continent.

Parallel strategies are employed in these texts to identify their subject-matter as other, as distant and different: typically, the other group is reached by a journey into an ethnographic territory which Mary Louise Pratt has called the 'contact zone ... where disparate cultures meet, clash, and grapple with each other, often in highly asymmetrical relations of domination and subordination' (Pratt, 1992, p. 4). Mayhew described himself as 'a traveller in the undiscovered country of the poor'[2] whose role was that of 'adducing facts so extraordinary, that ... until his stories are corroborated by after investigators, [he must] be content to lie under the imputation of telling such tales, as travellers are generally supposed to delight in' (Mayhew, 1968, vol. I, p. xv). The explorers' accounts characteristically opened with a description of a long and dangerous journey into the African 'interior' undertaken in order to investigate the 'dark continent' (Brantlinger, 1986). Speke solemnly claimed: 'I profess accurately to describe naked Africa – Africa in those places where it has not received the slightest impulse whether for good or for evil from European civilization' (Speke, 1863, p. xiii). The picture, Speke continues, is a 'dark one'. This process, whereby the territory of the other is mystified and presented as exotic, might be seen in Jordanova's terms as the veiling of the other. Yet Speke's claim to offer 'accurate description' and Mayhew's insistence upon 'adducing facts' promise a counterbalancing process of unveiling.

This mapping out and making visible of unknown territories, physical and social, had direct political consequences, both abroad and at home. Mayhew noted that *London Labour and the London Poor* was 'curious' in 'supplying information concerning a large body of persons, of whom the public had less knowledge than of the most distant tribes of the earth – the Government population returns not even numbering them among the inhabitants of the kingdom' (Mayhew, 1968, vol. I, p. xv). As Mayhew's comparison of his work with the official collection of statistics implies, mapping the alien social and physical geography of London's East End was significant in relation to debates about public health and political unrest in the aftermath of Chartism. In terms of the African landscape, surveying, mapping and naming were more important still, signifying the imposition of western structures of knowledge on a zone which was previously a blank on the map. Various incursions by explorers from the eighteenth century onwards had opened up Africa as a discursive field, a site of possible colonization by British beliefs and ideologies as well as a site for the extension of industry, commerce and, ultimately, political control (Cairns, 1965; Coetzee, 1988; Pratt, 1992). The frontispieces to both of Livingstone's books record from a raised vantage point the view of the falls on the Zambesi which, in a frankly imperialist gesture prompted by Roderick Murchison of the Royal Geographical Society, he renamed the Victoria Falls (Jeal, 1973; Livingstone, 1857). Surveillance of landscape with a view to potential agricultural and commercial uses was a significant part of the explorers' brief, and considerable attention is paid to this in their published accounts. In the image of the Victoria Falls engraved in 1857 by Josiah Wood Whymper for *Missionary Travels*, some fanciful African figures appear in the foreground. Although overshadowed by the sublime grandeur of the scene in this frontispiece, it was the human body, and not physical geography, which was subjected to the most intense scrutiny, visual and verbal, throughout the book. For Livingstone and Speke, as for Mayhew, physical and cultural geography provided a mere setting; the body's text was susceptible to more detailed and nuanced readings.

Jordanova describes the veiling and unveiling of the other. These two modes of understanding were held in constant tension during this period. Taxonomic analysis provided the basic method and scientific theories of race contributed to the epistemology of each author, yet the deployment of these methods was premised on the assertion of a radical discontinuity between author and readers of the books on the one hand and the subject of their enquiries on the other. The most powerful trope of otherness through which this distinction could be articulated was that of civilized versus savage. The discursive formation of the savage is a familiar and recurring one in metropolitan culture. By the mid-nineteenth century the reading of the savage as a natural man had given way to the idea that savagery resulted from a process of degeneration from a state of primal grace (Stocking, 1987). Furthermore, the distinction between civilized and savage was taken to be racial, ensuring that the categories were held in a permanent and inalienable state of difference. In Victorian popular and metropolitan culture, this idea of the savage was constantly reinforced through texts, exhibitions, illustrations and stage shows. Richard Altick has described the stage show of 'Ojibbeways' mounted in 1844 by the American artist and explorer George Catlin, which, it turned out, consisted of a group of poor men and boys from the East End of London dressed up in feathers (Altick, 1978, pp. 280–1). A satirical sketch of them in *Punch*, punning on the supposed similarities between the grotesque physiognomies of the poor and those of the savage, explored a possible slippage between social and racial difference, a theme to which I shall return later. A wood engraving from the *Illustrated London News* represents a group of !Kung Africans, known in colonial parlance as Bosjemans or 'Bushmen', exhibited at the Egyptian Hall in 1847. Difference is vividly inscribed in the illustration, *The Bosjemans at the Egyptian Hall, Piccadilly*, through the placing of the proprietor at the apex of a pyramid formed by his charges, the standing African figure's face darkened by a shadow to emphasize the contrast in skin colour. The text in the *Illustrated London News* notes that:

> It was strange ... in looking through the windows of the rooms into the busy street, to reflect that by a single turn of the head might be witnessed the two extremes of humanity – the lowest and highest of the race – the wandering savage and the silken baron of civilisation. (*Illustrated London News*, 12 June 1847)

The next year, 1848, was to see the publication of Henry Mayhew's letters on 'Labour and the Poor' in the *Morning Chronicle*, the precursor of *London Labour and the London Poor*, which entered the space of the London streets and discerned this same contrast of wandering savage and civilized man within the population of Britain.

A similarly dramatic juxtaposition of savage and civilized underpins the illustration *Grant Dancing with Ukulima* (See Figure 2.1) from John Hanning Speke's *Journal of the Discovery of the Nile*. The figure of Speke's travelling partner, James Augustus Grant, dressed in a heavy checked shirt, linen or woollen knickerbockers and a cloth helmet, is inserted into a stereotypical, exoticized scene of savage revelry. Homi Bhabha has suggested that, in analysing colonial texts, 'what does need to be questioned ... is the *mode of representation of otherness*, which depends crucially on how the "west" is deployed' (Bhabha, 1986, p. 151). The figure of Grant here is significant not because it documents the sartorial habits of ex-army officers of the 1860s, but because it signifies the maximum distance from the clothes – or absence of clothing – of the savages surrounding him. The implication is that the values for which Grant stands – broadly those of the British establishment –

Grant dancing with Ukulima.

2.1 *Grant Dancing with Ukulima*

are universal, applicable across the world irrespective of local context, be it climate or custom. The unified western subject – the Imperial I – is characterized as being essentially different from the savage who is the object of the collective gaze of the explorer and the readers of his book. By personifying civilization in the figure of Grant, divisions within western society along lines of class and gender are suppressed; through this strategy, the whole of western society is discursively subordinated to white, male paternal authority. Grant stands for civilization in the same way that the paterfamilias was held to stand for the interests and identity of the bourgeois nuclear family. The figure of Ukulima, surrounded by his armed supporters, is in this image represented as being subject to the authority of a lone, white male figure. Seen dancing with Grant in the place of a female partner, Ukulima is presented as other to Grant's masculinity and authority, and in the image appears feminized and disempowered.[3]

At work in this illustration is the most powerful of all tropes of difference, that of skin colour. Bhabha puts it well:

> skin is the key signifier of cultural and racial difference in the stereotype; it is the most visible of fetishes, recognised as common knowledge in a range of cultural, political and historical discourses, and plays a public part in the racial drama that is enacted every day in colonial societies. (Bhabha, 1986, pp. 165–6)

Wood engraving of this type does not allow for subtleties of shading or tinting; the movement of the engraver's hand determines whether an area is white or black. Here, Grant is as white as the paper on which his image is printed; Ukulima and his fellow savages mainly appear an inky black. I am not, however, ascribing the production of racial difference specifically to the engraver, and certainly not to Grant's sketch in which the figure of the explorer does not even appear. It is not a question of individual intentionality but of a discourse of racial difference operating across a wide range of representational practices. The perceived absolute differences between black and white, clothed and naked, were conceived in terms of a Manichean dualism (JanMohamed, 1986) between civilized and savage, a dualism which was understood in explicitly racial terms.

The visualization of difference is achieved somewhat differently in *Lake Ngami, Discovered by Oswell, Murray, and Livingstone* (see Figure 2.2), a plate from the best-selling *Missionary Travels* of 1857, where an image of David Livingstone and his family is superimposed on a landscape which the explorer claimed to have discovered. The family portrait provided a sign of an ideal, respectable bourgeois family, like Grant, unchanged in appearance and behaviour by their location in malarial East Africa. A pyramidal family structure is graphically dem-

From a Drawing made on the spot (1850) by the late Alfred Ryder, Esq.

LAKE NGAMI, DISCOVERED BY OSWELL, MURRAY, AND LIVINGSTONE.

2.2 *Lake Ngami, Discovered by Oswell, Murray, and Livingstone*

onstrated, in which female labour and black labour are directed by, and subordinated to, Livingstone. It is worth noting the formal similarities of this group to contemporary paintings such as George Elgar Hicks's *Woman's Mission: Companion of Manhood* (1863, Tate Gallery) and Thomas Jones Barker's *That is the Secret of England's Greatness* (1861, National Portrait Gallery) where similar pyramidal structures are headed by males. The image of the Livingstone family presented by the illustration contrasts vividly with the private correspondence of Mary Livingstone, itself a problematic source, which bitterly records the miserable physical conditions which led to the death of the child she is seen nursing here following Livingstone's insistence that she travel with him (Schapera, 1960, pp. 70–1). Mary Livingstone's face is obscured in the image; she functions here as a subordinate element within the Livingstone family unit, which, as with the image of Grant, stands for the dominant values of respectable British society. Livingstone's well-known formulation that commerce and Christianity could alone save Africa (Stanley, 1983) implied the imposition of British, middle-class norms on the African landscape and population. A hint of this future can be seen in the figures of the African workers employed by Livingstone, who, far from enjoying the rewards of a respectable lifestyle, are cast as a new proletariat. There is an implicit contrast between the black prepared to labour for white masters and conform to western behaviour – the reformed, converted savage – and the untamed savage, beyond the frame of this image (but seen in *Grant Dancing with Ukulima*), even though the fundamental distinction between white and black is not effaced.

Elements of British society not conforming to this ideal picture of the respectable nuclear family and paternal authority were likewise constructed as deviant. Banished from society's self-image, wandering street-traders, gypsies, prostitutes and the homeless, paupers, criminals and vagrants were assimilated to the other. It was this urban other that formed the basis of Mayhew's study of *London Labour and the London Poor*.

The opening of Mayhew's text implies that his study will be more explicitly scientific in organization than the travel books of Livingstone and Speke. Mayhew's central authorial acts are the collection of detailed information about the economic, social and sexual behaviour of the urban poor, and the organization of that group into taxonomies on the basis of the information collected. These procedures, borrowed from the natural sciences, were far from impartial in operation; they centred on the ordering of selectively acquired material into pre-or-dained categories which were highly judgmental and evaluative. Mayhew divided the poor into the categories 'those that *will* work, those that *cannot* work, and those that *will not* work' (Mayhew, 1968, vol. I, title page).[4] This set of criteria, as much moral as economic or social, echoes the language and classifications of the 1834 Poor Law Amendment Act, and also resonates with the moral discourses of labour central to the writings of Thomas Carlyle and others (Barringer, 1994). More radical was Mayhew's application of the contemporary science of the human race, ethnology, to the discussion of people resident in Britain, albeit outside the body politic (Bolt, 1971; Stepan, 1982; Stocking, 1987). Ethnology, extensively referred to in the texts of Livingstone and Speke, was, as Stocking notes, 'the most general scientific framework for the study of the linguistic, physical and cultural characteristics of dark-skinned, non-European, "uncivilised" peoples' (Stocking, 1987, p. 47). *London Labour and the London Poor* opens with an astonishing assertion drawn from ethnological theory:

> Of the thousand million human beings that are said to constitute the population of the entire globe, there are – socially, and perhaps even physically considered – but two distinct and broadly marked races, viz., the wanderers and the settlers – the vagabond and the citizen – the nomadic and the civilised tribes ... Each of these classes has its peculiar and distinctive physical as well as moral characteristics. (Mayhew, 1968, vol. I, p. 1)

Mayhew invokes the authority of Sir Andrew Smith, a leading ethnologist, zoologist, explorer and colonial administrator who provided drawings of African subjects for reproduction in Livingstone's *Missionary Travels*. Mayhew, however, found it 'curious' that:

> no-one has as yet applied the above facts to the explanation of certain anomalies in the present state of society among ourselves. That we, like the Kaffirs, Fellahs, and Finns are surrounded by wandering hordes – the 'Sonquas' and 'Fingoes' of this country – paupers, beggars and outcasts possessing nothing but what they acquire by the depredation of the industrious, provident and civilised portion of the community; – that the heads of these nomades [*sic*] are remarkable for the greater development of the jaws and cheekbones rather than those of the head; – and that they have a secret language of their own. (Mayhew, 1968, vol. I, p. 2)

Mayhew presents the spectacle of a world riven in two between a dominant group whose 'industrious' virtues singularly resemble those of the bourgeoisie in Victorian England and an 'other' group which consists of a mass of 'nomades', united not only by common morals but also by distinguishable physical characteristics. A social distinction between a dominant group and its others is naturalized into racial difference. Pursuing this theme, Mayhew drew on a key work of ethnology during this period, James Cowles Prichard's *Natural History of Man*, which had been republished in a single, lavishly illustrated volume in

1848. Mayhew quoted at length Prichard's suggestion that a 'prognathous jaw' or 'lozenge shaped head' might mark out the lower races, simplifying and distorting Prichard's scheme, and disregarding the provisos and injunctions to caution which characterize Prichard's text.

The concentration on physical characteristics as bearing legible information about racial type indicated in Mayhew's introduction inevitably focuses attention on the illustrations to his volumes; indeed among the data of ethnology, the visual image played a crucial role. The anthropologist Johannes Fabian has identified the importance of visual surveillance in western modes of knowing the other, and indicates the linkages between visual representation and political domination:

> Early ethnological practices ... established seldom articulated but firm convictions that presentations of knowledge through visual and spatial images ... are particularly suited to the description of primitive cultures ... The hegemony of the visual as a mode of knowing may thus directly be linked to the political hegemony of an age group, a class, or of one society over another. The ruler's subject and the scientist's object have, in the case of anthropology ... an intertwined history. (Fabian, 1983, p. 121)

In Prichard's book, illustrations were offered as value-free data adduced to 'prove' a hypothesis. Specific points were made with wood engravings positioned on the text pages, but most significant are the hand-coloured full-page engravings on steel, usually focusing on a single figure implicitly typical of a racial type, such as the *Inhabitant of Tikopia*. Like the plates in Prichard's ethnology, Mayhew's illustrations generally show a single typical example, labelled not with the name of an individual, but a type. In Prichard as in Mayhew, the illustrations form an important part of the text, authenticating the descriptions given. However, in one way at least, the development of new technology enabled Mayhew to go one step further than Prichard. Central to the rhetoric of authenticity which surrounded Mayhew's illustrations was the claim that the new technology of photography had been used in their preparation; most of the illustrations are captioned 'from a Daguerreotype' or 'from a photograph'. As with Prichard, the illustrations are positioned as an authenticating archive, adduced to 'prove' the arguments of the text.

Yet if the hundred or so Mayhew illustrations are examined as a group, discontinuities and contradictions become apparent. The divergence of the visual evidence from the textual thesis contributes to the anarchic and disordered effect of Mayhew's study overall. The physiognomic argument lifted from Prichard, asserting the racial unity of the wandering 'nomades', immediately collapses; the *Groundsel Man* and the *Comb Seller* have little in common but their submissive posture, poor clothing and the desperate need to sell low-value goods.

But if an audience alert to reading representations of the body for nuances of racial type would find little evidence of the 'prognathous jaw' as characterizing the poor as a unified race apart, other more traditional signifiers of racial difference are much in evidence. The Jewish street-trader was a familiar and much maligned figure in popular culture from the Middle Ages to the Victorian period (West, 1993), and makes regular appearances in sets of Cries of London (Beall, 1975). The type was brilliantly harnessed by Dickens in his creation of Fagin. In spite of the claim printed underneath of a source in a daguerreotype by Richard Beard, the image of the *Jew Old-Clothes Man* (see Figure 2.3) closely resembles Cruikshank's famous illustrations to *Oliver Twist*.[5] The sardonic expression is replicated, as are the beard and the stereotypically hooked nose. The production of racial difference, in other words, follows the traditional methods of the caricaturist. Mayhew's illustration, which is signed, was drawn onto wood by Archibald Samuel Henning and engraved by William Frederick Measom. Henning was a comic draughtsman who designed the first cover of *Punch*; Measom was an engraver on the *Illustrated London News*. While it is not adequate simply to assert that the racial inflection of this image was produced by draughtsman and engraver, there is no question that genre and traditions of caricature and comic illustration are in play here. The proximity of so-called reportage and the world of comic exaggeration and caricature is even clearer in Mayhew's street market scenes of Petticoat Lane and Rosemary Lane. The assertion that there existed identifiable and separable ethnic groups among the urban poor undercuts Mayhew's idea of a unified nomadic other; his text and plates serve to emphasize the ethnic diversity of the London poor, Doctor Bokanky the Street Herbalist, vendor of the Kalibonka Root, being one of many non-white street-sellers whom Mayhew interviewed and depicted.

Livingstone, too, included wood engravings of single figures as exemplars of race, and claimed that he intended to produce a major work of ethnology. Thomas Baines, the artist who accompanied Livingstone's Zambesi expedition of 1858–63, was instructed by the doctor 'to furnish me ... with a series of portraits of natives for the purposes of Ethnology, giving them if necessary in groups so as to show the shapes of the heads and bodies as accurately as you can' (Livingstone to Baines, 11 July 1859, quoted in Wallis, 1941, pp. 170–1). Baines made a range of carefully observed watercolours and oil paintings which were, however, not used in Livingstone's published account because of a dispute ending quite unfairly in Baines's dismissal. They display a sophistication of technique and a willingness to blend anthropological annotation with a sensitivity to individual character. Unlike the pub-

THE JEW OLD-CLOTHES MAN.

Clo', Clo', Clo'.

[*From a Daguerreotype by* BEARD.]

2.3   William Measom after a drawing by Archibald Samuel Henning from a daguerreotype by Richard Beard, *The Jew Old-Clothes Man*

lished illustrations in Livingstone or Mayhew, they are inscribed with the name of the depicted individual, indicating a respect for the sitter deriving perhaps from the western portrait tradition, a mode concerned with the representation of the self rather than its others.

I have outlined two interlinked modes of imaging otherness: one premised on the notion of savage and on caricatural and essentialized tropes of racial difference, the other based on the traditions of ethnological representation, themselves ideologically inflected. But in the most vivid, and undoubtedly the most popular, of Mayhew's studies the representation of previously unrepresented figures in Victorian London was achieved through the blending of so-called scientific investigation with literary and visual convention. Mayhew drew successfully on the pre-existing tropes of the urban Gothic, familiar from the works of Eugène Sue, Victor Hugo and the early work of Dickens. In describing the lives, and publishing engravings, of the *Mudlark* and *The London Scavenger* (See Figure 2.4) for whom dead bodies at five shillings were the most prized discovery, Mayhew produced images of London life at its furthest from respectable domesticity; a world of Gothic awfulness, a stone's throw from home. Dirt and darkness were the primary characteristics of the illustrations, especially of those who worked underground like the *Sewer Hunter*, sieving sewage for lost pennies.

If there are hints here of a slippage between the visual rhetoric of the darkened skin of the lowest of manual labourers and the dark skin which was considered the primary determinant of racial otherness, these became explicit in the case of the chimney sweep. Mayhew's extensive investigation into the life and habits of the sweep revealed that 'the need of reformation in the habits of the working sweeps is extreme, and especially in respect of drinking, gambling and dirt' (Mayhew, 1968, vol. II, p. 364). Mayhew entered a sweep's home with the artist Archibald Samuel Henning whose sketch was 'made on the spot' (See Figure 2.5). The whites of the young sweeps' eyes stand out brilliantly as in the contemporary stereotype of the Negro, exemplified by George Cruikshank's illustrations to the 1852 edition of the best-selling emancipation novel *Uncle Tom's Cabin* by Harriet Beecher Stowe.[6] Mayhew goes on to describe the mature sweep in the following terms: 'The savage was intoxicated, for his red eyes flashed through his sooty mask with drunken excitement, and his matted hair, which looked as though it had never known a comb, stood out from his head like the whalebone ribs of his own machine' (Mayhew, 1968, vol. II, p. 368).

Mayhew draws together his portrayal of the poor as an ethnic group in a passage enumerating the ways in which costermongers 'resemble many savage nations'. His ten-point checklist can be matched detail by detail in the African travel literature:

THE LONDON SCAVENGER

[From a Daguerreotype by BEARD.]

2.4 William Measom after a drawing by Archibald Samuel Henning from a daguerreotype by Richard Beard, *The London Scavenger*

THE SWEEPS' HOME.

(From a sketch taken on the spot.)

2.5 William Measom after a drawing by Archibald Samuel Henning, *The Sweep's Home*

The nomad then is distinguished from the civilized man by his repugnance to regular and continuous labour – by his want of providence in laying up a store for the future – by his inability to perceive consequences ever so slightly removed from immediate apprehension – by his passion for stupefying herbs and roots, and, when possible, for intoxicating fermented liquors – by his extraordinary powers of enduring privation – by his comparative insensibility to pain ... – by his love of libidinous dances ... – by the looseness of his notions as to property – by the absence of chastity among his women, and his disregard of female honour – and lastly, by his vague sense of religion – his rude idea of a Creator and utter absence of all appreciation of the mercy of the Divine Spirit. (Mayhew, 1968, vol. I, p. 2)

Yet this absolute formulation of difference collapses under the close interrogation made possible by the revelations of Mayhew's texts and those of the explorers. Ultimately the double act of veiling and unveiling cannot be sustained. The unity of the urban other and the colonial other discussed in the texts I have considered proves to be mythical; the racial characteristics which were presented as uniting them disappear amid the disparate nature of the evidence. A fatal challenge to the unitary categories of self and other is posed by the internal incoherence of each, an incoherence particularly evident within Mayhew's category of the urban poor. A vast social distance separates the scowling *Vagrant from the Refuge in Playhouse Yard, Cripplegate* (illustrated in Mayhew, 1968, vol. II, opposite p. 406) from the suavely dressed *Street Dogseller* (illustrated in Mayhew, 1968, vol. II, opposite p. 54), who is barely distinguishable from his shadowy bourgeois clientele. Mayhew's project of mapping an otherness of race onto that of class collapses because his attempt to read the poor as a single body is overwhelmed by the diversity of social life in the modern city. The separation of the nomadic race from respectable life, too, emerges as a fiction, since Mayhew's text and images clearly indicate the constantly renegotiated relations of mutual social and economic dependence which linked Mayhew's poor with the inhabitants of London's West End, just as theorists of colonial discourse have insisted that the colonial power is bound to the colonized (Bhabha, 1994; Young, 1990). As the voices of London street-traders are heard and their faces are seen in Mayhew's text, albeit mediated by forms of representation which they did not control, the signs of inequality remain, but grand notions of difference collapse. Likewise, the explorers relied on African knowledge and African labour-power to support their expeditions and missionary outposts. The dying Livingstone was supported by Susi and Chuma, his two servants, who embalmed his body and carried it on a five-month route march across Africa; the leaping savages were recast as civilized and tidily clad protectors of a British saint and martyr. It must be added that the apparently secure category of bourgeois selfhood was as much of a fiction as the unified and racially distinct other against which it was defined. Livingstone, Speke and Mayhew were all individuals whose personal lives can now be seen to have transgressed in one way or another the norms so insistently promoted in their published works.

The juxtaposition of these two sets of images indicates the complex and inconsistent visual rhetorics through which Victorian notions of otherness were imaged. The notion of racial difference, though a powerful one, especially in visual form, relied on essentialized and polarized distinctions which bore little relation to the complexities of the situation either in the Victorian city or in proto-colonial Africa. While the visual image allows the chiaroscuro of race a vividly physical form, the closing-off of possible readings of the represented body demanded by the idea of a dualism between self and other, a racial split between black and white, is virtually impossible to achieve visually. The very complexity of the process of visual representation determines the multivalent nature of the image, even images like those I have discussed, which are habitually thought of as straightforward and unproblematic. The multiple iconographic and genre traditions at play, the technical characteristics and limitations of the medium, and the caprice of their individual and collective makers, always leave the image open to a variety of readings. A close examination of these images disrupts an interpretation of popular book illustrations as simple reflections of the ideas included in the text, and problematizes the role of visual representations as evidence. The purportedly separate traditions of scientific illustration, graphic journalism and caricature are revealed as being intimately and inextricably linked, and it becomes clear that the visual production of difference occurred right across the diverse field of visual culture in the Victorian period.

Notes

1. The complex publication history of Mayhew's *London Labour and the London Poor* is summarized by Humpherys (1977). All references here are to Mayhew (1968), the Dover edition, with an introduction by John D. Rosenberg, which reprints unabridged the Griffin, Bohn and Co. four-volume edition of 1861.
2. The phrase seems to derive from William Thackeray, reviewing Mayhew's column 'Labour and the Poor' which appeared in the *Morning Chronicle* between 1848 and 1850. (*Punch*, 9 March 1850).
3. It is significant in this context that in a recent article, Grant is described as dancing with one or two 'topless females' (Bridges, 1994, p. 21). This article discusses the transition from Grant's original drawing (National

Library of Scotland) to the wood engraving which appeared in Speke's book. Much of the scene, including the figures of Grant and Ukulima, is entirely imaginary and does not appear in the drawing.

4. These distinctions were first suggested in the initial letter published in the *Morning Chronicle* on 19 October 1849. Mayhew argued there 'I shall consider the whole of the metropolitan poor under three separated phases, according as they *will* work, they *can't* work and they *won't* work' (Mayhew, 1980, p. 40).

5. George Cruikshank, *Fagin in the Condemned Cell*, from Charles Dickens, *Oliver Twist*, London: Charles Bentley, published serially 1837–39.

6. See, for example, George Cruikshank (1852) *George Shelby Giving Liberty to his Slaves*, Stowe 1852. Wood engraving by W. F. Measom.

CHAPTER THREE

Black *and* white?
Viewing Cleopatra in 1862[1]

Mary Hamer

William Wetmore Story of Boston threw up his career as a lawyer when his father died and went to Rome in 1856, to join the community of sculptors there. Only a few years later he was on the point of admitting defeat and going home again when his name was made by the success of two of his pieces at the London Exposition, a *Libyan Sibyl* and a *Cleopatra* in white marble (see Figure 3.1). The *Cleopatra* in particular was hailed as the most outstanding work of sculpture on display. The names of these two famous women from antiquity that he invoked were resonant, but this explains only some of the warmth with which his statues were received. It seems likely that pleasure was also taken in the image of subjected femininity that these statues offered, a subjection which stood to be read in terms of race.

The story I have to tell concerns the second of Story's statues, the *Cleopatra*, and the part it played in training viewers to look out for and interpret the signs of race. That white marble statue had an almost magical power to create and maintain difference in the minds of viewers: difference between blacks and whites, between men and women, between black women and white women and between good women and bad ones. Viewers simply had to be taught how to look.

The person of Cleopatra had a history in the city of Rome, where Story set up his studio and worked on his image of her. Contemporary sculptors were drawn to Rome by the collections of antique sculpture for which the city was famous; since the beginning of the sixteenth century these statues had been the most prestigious objects in western art. Touchstones of 'beauty' and of 'taste', the cultural capital of the west was most densely concentrated in these stone bodies and body fragments, most of them white. The premier among these collections was housed in the Vatican and one of its most celebrated statues was a reclining marble figure called 'the Cleopatra' (Haskell and Penny, 1981, pp. 184–7). It had been bought for the Vatican in 1512 by Pope Julius II when he was first setting up its collection of antique sculpture.

Owning this image had a strategic importance for Julius, in his campaign to represent himself as heir of the Caesars and the papacy itself as

3.1 William Wetmore Story, *Cleopatra*

inheritor of the imperial authority of Rome (Garrard, 1993, pp. 262–3). Pope Julius had imperial ambitions of his own; under him the papal territories were extended by conquest until they reached the widest extent ever recorded. It was the heritage of classical authority to which Julius laid claim by installing a Cleopatra in the Vatican; his namesake, Julius Caesar, the lover of Cleopatra, had honoured her by setting up a gold statue of her as Venus Genetrix in the temple of his ancestral deity (Cassio Dio, LI, 22, 3; Harvey, 1937, p. 445). An alternative approach had been demonstrated by Augustus, the ruler who established the new world order of law, literature and architecture on which so much of what the West calls civilization is based. He had an image of Cleopatra

made only because the woman herself had eluded him by her act of pre-
emptive suicide. Augustus had meant to lead an enslaved Cleopatra in
triumph after him through the streets of Rome; rather than be balked of
his desire, he had an image of the dead woman carried in his procession
(Hamer, 1993, pp. 20–1). It is this aspect of imperial tradition which
appears to have been dominant in the Rome that was ruled by the pope
of Story's day.

In the early years of the sixteenth century, when Pope Julius was
buying a Cleopatra for the Vatican, the ostensible justification for be-
stowing that name on the reclining figure of his choice was slight, as
Winckelmann pointed out nearly three centuries later when he demoted
it to an anonymous nymph. What had once been seen as a living snake
wound about the arm was now admitted to be more like a bracelet.
Support for the eroticized tone of male viewing now came from the
suggestion that the piece might be a Venus.[2] Story's sculpture, by contrast, was intended to be unmistakable, with every detail designed to
secure a positive identification, starting with the name, 'Cleopatra',
standing out in relief across the base. The image was meant to encour-
age a reading that had other concerns beside individual identity, however. It invited a viewer to speculate on the race of the body in question
and it offered the tools for making a reading of that race.

In the nineteenth century, the people who went to look at exhibits of
ideal sculpture, like this *Cleopatra*, placed a premium on accuracy and
the specific. They valued recognizable and realistic details, because they
gave the viewer a starting-point for framing a response. Meanwhile the
marble itself was supposed to offer a guarantee of moral value. Discourses of purity, chastity, aloofness and white silence which circulated
about white marble statues claimed for them an unspoken language of
disinterest and truth (Kasson, 1990, pp. 46–72). But the case of this
Cleopatra gives that assumption the lie. In this sculpture detail is used
in order to engage a highly politicized rhetoric of race, purity and
colour. Here white means black. It is still possible to trace the process
by which spectators were invited to 'see' and interpret a blackness that
existed only inside their heads.

When Story's *Cleopatra* was put on show in the London Exposition
of 1862, the *Athenaeum* review indicated that the sculptor had been
successful in achieving legibility. Both the pose and the garments could
be read. We know that Story had taken pains over the disposition of
Cleopatra's hand and his communicative effort was evidently not thrown
away; the reviewer read it like a book 'the … [hand] is outstretched
upon her knee, nipping its forefinger upon the thumb thoughtfully as
though some firm wilful purpose filled her brain, seeming to set those
luxurious features to a smile as if the whole woman "would"' (Phillips,

1897, p. 132). The question of exactly what 'the whole woman' wanted or intended is left to the imagination or simply assumed; isn't it clear that all Cleopatra wants is her own way?

Dress, headgear and jewellery were also designed to prompt the viewer to active interpretation. The same review saw Egypt written all over the piece. It claimed that the 'gown was the characteristically Egyptian one that gathers about the torso and falls freely around the limbs' and that the coif was also recognizably Egyptian, with its uraeus and wide side lappets. Recent scholarship has endorsed this emphasis on legibility rather than interrogating it. Jan Seidler Ramirez has shown that Story probably did use details from a collection of Egyptian jewellery discovered in Rome to model the necklace (Ramirez, 1985, p. 470). Making objects recognizably Egyptian was not just an antiquarian exercise, however. It constituted a move towards focusing on racial and cultural difference. Disputes over the authenticity of those features intended to signify racial or cultural origin in the image surely miss the point. Whether or not the detail would now be authenticated as Egyptian, at the time of its first exhibition viewers received the sculpture as boldly marked with the signs of Egypt. The image was designed to engage notions of racial and cultural difference by means of its detail, and designed to do so as an important end in itself.

This was not an eccentric gesture on Story's part. Since the late 1840s the claims of race to be the supreme determinant of human potential had become ever more widely disseminated both in Europe and North America. Previously ethnologists had studied languages, cultures and physical type, working within a framework that was broadly Lamarckian. This had permitted the current position of different cultures and races to be charted on an evolutionary scale without implying that any one of them had reached the limit of their achievement. From the 1840s it began to be argued that physical type – a set of categories that in this argument were determined by the subject's racial origin – could and did impose limits on cultural achievement. Some races, to put it plainly, were not capable of the fullest human development. The debate, which had centred on the comparison of skulls and head shapes, polarized around skin colour during the 1850s as the conflicts around slavery were building towards civil war in the United States.

Defining the limitations of blacks was by no means an exclusively American concern, however. One of the most influential exponents of the supreme importance of race was Dr Robert Knox, an English anatomist. Knox's book, *The Races of Man*, was published in 1850 and came out in a second edition by 1862 – the year this *Cleopatra* was put on show and the same year that Lincoln promised the end of slavery. Knox argued that racial difference was the motor of human development and claimed that the struggle between races was the only source of human creativity and progress (Curtin, 1964, p. 379). As an educated man, like Pope Julius, Knox looked back to Augustan precedent; for Knox, though, the Pax Romana established by Augustus was something to be deplored since it put an untimely, if temporary, stop to international conflict.

In his own time Knox won the assent even of the sophisticated. In the 1850s his theories concerning racial inequality and the need for conflict can be seen to underpin the arguments of writers in journals like the *Edinburgh Review* and the *Westminster*, journals which had a previously liberal attitude towards questions of race. Darwin was to quote Knox approvingly (Curtin, 1964, p. 378). The primacy of the category of race and the part it had to play in determining cultural achievement were not considered speculative but were widely accepted as premises.

Knox described the drive towards human development unambiguously, in terms of a struggle between light and dark races, and like some other ethnologists he worked to create the difference he wanted to see installed:

> Look at the Negro, so well known to you, and say, need I describe him? Is he shaped like any white person? Is the anatomy of his frame, of his muscles or organs like ours? Does he walk like us, think like us, act like us? Not in the least. (Knox, 1862, pp. 243–4)

This appeal, to identify absolute difference between the bodies, cultures and behaviours of blacks and whites – no walking, thinking or acting like us – was one that could only be achieved by the manipulation of evidence or indoctrination of the viewer. It required educated looking.

Geography as well as anatomy came into play here, as the work of the ethnographer J. C. Prichard demonstrates. Using apparently natural boundaries, Prichard drew an imaginary line across Africa, one that separated the northern, 'more civilized' parts from the southern interior. Above the chain known as the Mountains of the Moon lay what Prichard described as the 'comparatively civilized region containing the Mohammedan states': below it lay a region inhabited by African races 'whose aspect displays the characteristics of the Negro fully developed and in the highest degree' (Prichard, 1855, p. 320). First the fantasy of a pure Negro type was created, then it was given a location apparently removed from the history of European development by a natural boundary of extremely tall mountains.

South of this demarcation, Prichard explains, lay a wilderness, inhabited by various nations who painted their bodies in strange colours and had no acquaintance with any form of social or political structure. The people of Mandara were such a group. The reports of their looks and habits that he quotes accord only too well with what the enquirer already expects to find; the Mandara wear their hair down to their eyes and they decorate themselves with bits of bone and teeth apparently taken from the bodies of the enemies they have killed. Not interested in communication with the outside world, all they want from travellers is the gift of a horse that they can carry off to kill and feast on (Prichard, 1855, p. 321). When Prichard or his later editor Edwin Norris offers an engraved illustration of a native of Mandara, they set it side by side with a member of the Bornawi, who have been described as close to the

3.2   Native of Mandara and native of Bornu

3.3   Native of Haussa and Abbas Gregorius

ideal Negro, that is to the racially, culturally, and geographically extreme type (see Figure 3.2).

How hard the ethnographic text has to work at this fabrication of
racial types, this making of invidious distinctions, can be seen by comparing Figure 3.2 with Figure 3.3. The man in the red hat in Figure 3.3
is a native of Haussa and he comes from north of the critical boundary
drawn at the mountains. Like the native of Mandara in Figure 3.2 he
wears a red hat, but in every other way, physically, morally, geographically, according to Prichard, the man from Haussa is a finer, more
developed being. The Haussa, as Prichard reports, 'are described as
handsome people, with woolly hair and a jet black complexion' (Prichard,
1855, p. 324). The 'specimen of the race' given in Plate xiii (Figure 3.3),
the text goes on, was taken from 'a native' who happened to be found
in London. Geography, even its temporary accidents, seems to guarantee racial type here too. The features under this red hat Prichard encour-
ages us to see as 'remarkably good, [they] appear to have little resemblance to those of the natives of Guinea'. That is, they are quite different from the features of the people who were born in a place from
which slaves were taken, a crucial distinction. Word has it, Prichard
adds, that the Haussa are 'acute, intelligent and industrious'. The authority he quotes for this belief is his fellow Englishman, 'Mr Jackson',
who sees in the Haussa, as perhaps might have been expected, given the
fact that Haussa can be found on the streets of London, 'a peculiarly
open and noble countenance, having prominent noses and expressive
black eyes' (Prichard, 1855, p. 324). Though Prichard does not spell
this out, it is clearly implied that the intelligent viewer could tell just by
looking at the man from Haussa that under his black skin lay a bone
structure and a moral development that was much closer to the European than a man would have if he had been born further to the south.

This is the kind of instructed reading that the detail of Story's *Cleopatra* invites. Sculpture had first been pressed into the service of ethnography by Johann Friedrich Blumenbach, who invented the term Caucasian, but it was not until the middle of the nineteenth century that the
genre of ethnographic portraiture really took off in Europe (Honour,
1989, pp. 100–6; Le Normand-Romain, 1994, pp. 33–50). In the Great
Exhibition of 1851 in London, Charles Cordier, a French sculptor who
had trained in the studio of François Rude, showed two busts, a *Nègre
de Tombouctou* and a *Vénus africaine*. These were so well received that
at least eight copies of the pair in bronze were sold; members of the
British royal family were among the buyers. Five years later, in 1856,
Cordier obtained funding from the French government to visit Algiers
and record the 'types' that he found there. Acknowledging individual
human identity by name was not the object in making these busts of

Africans; they were often built up as composites from separate models. Ethnographic busts are much closer to the mounted heads produced by big-game hunting, a collection of specimens or trophies. The use of polychrome marbles in the most expensive versions gave an effect of brilliance and luxury while helping to throw bone structure and skin colour into relief. The fact that they were often produced in couples even supported the impression that they might be offered as an example of a breeding pair. Purporting to embody truth, whether contemplated as art or as science, Cordier's busts were greeted as equally suitable for display in the ethnographic gallery or the salon. Bronze versions of some of his work were on show in the London Exposition in 1862. Though Story's work was destined exclusively for the salon, it was created and viewed in an international context where sculpture was already expected to support a 'scientific' interest in race.

Story's salon viewers accepted that it was their task to construct a narrative around the image that they came to see. When ideal sculptures were exhibited they were often accompanied by pamphlets intended to teach viewers how to pick up the visual cues that pointed the way to the 'correct' story. It was recommended that male visitors would read aloud to the women who came with them (Kasson, 1990, pp. 32–45). Something similar happened in the case of this piece but on a grander scale. Before the *Cleopatra* had left the sculptor's studio in Rome, where it was created, it had become famous on account of an extended description of it given in a novel by the American writer, Nathaniel Hawthorne. This novel, *The Marble Faun*, was published in London in 1860. After that visitors to Story's studio would arrive with copies of the novel in hand, meaning to have the text read aloud as they viewed the statue. It is by turning to Hawthorne's account that a reading conducted on the premises of a contemporary theory of race can be reconstructed.

In Hawthorne's novel, the image of Cleopatra is the work of a sculptor called Kenyon, who is shown displaying it to a woman visitor. He starts by unveiling it. This preliminary gesture seems to make a special address to the women among the viewers who stand outside the fiction; it teaches both women and men that they are to go about reading the Cleopatra before them by removing its outer layers too. Hawthorne was merely following the lead set by Story in offering an evidently layered image. The dress leaves one shoulder bare, encouraging the viewer to set aside the covering in order to view the body separately. On the surface the image is presented as Egyptian. The reader is told that the costume has been derived from 'the strange sculpture of [ancient Egypt], its coins, drawings, painted mummy cases, and whatever other tokens have been dug out of its pyramids, graves and catacombs' (Hawthorne, 1968, pp. 125–6). In its sophistication, Egyptian culture can almost be assimilated to Europe and perhaps more importantly here, the woman associated with this culture can be reconciled with European notions of the feminine. On the surface the sculpture looks almost sedate.

It is something of a surprise, two paragraphs later, then to find that the race assigned to Cleopatra is to be understood as Nubian. As the novelist moves from categorizing the garments that are worn to naming the race of the body beneath them, his assessment of racial origin is modified. 'The face was a miraculous success. The sculptor had not shunned to give the full Nubian lips, and other characteristics of the Egyptian physiognomy' (Hawthorne, 1968, p. 126). The surprise in this statement for a late twentieth-century reader is considerable; the racially specific features that Hawthorne claims to detect are not so unarguably present for us, yet he was not alone in seeing them (see Figure 3.4). The critic James Jackson Jarves in his first review of the piece spoke of them as 'African' in 'type' (Jarves, 1960, p. 224).[3] Again, in spite of the downright claim to specificity, a certain equivocation seems to have come into play. 'Nubian' and 'Egyptian' do not map onto each other with the ease that Hawthorne at one moment seems to imply. The term 'Egyptian' has been used in the passage to appeal directly to an ancient culture and a civilization, while the word 'Nubian', even up to the time of the recent opening of the Nubian Gallery at the Boston Museum of Fine Arts, tended to suggest not a culture but an African body, the most beautiful of African bodies according to some versions of western aesthetics (Lewis, 1995, p. 96). Intelligent viewers took the hint and read this white marble face as black.

If the connotations of the terms Hawthorne has used tug in opposing directions it is not a matter of accident. The meaning of Cleopatra's ethnicity is being extended by stages that move inwards; the reader is being led to see the figure as progressively darker and by implication more 'primitive'. At the centre of this primitive body, enclosed by the skin now mentally revisioned as black, is the locus of black female sexuality, or as Hawthorne puts it, of 'a great smouldering furnace, deep down in the woman's heart' (Hawthorne, 1968, p. 126). The language identifies this sexuality firmly with the tropical heat of Africa and an ungovernable animal ferocity: 'she might spring upon you like a tigress and stop the very breath that you were now drawing midway to your throat'. (The tigress, of course, only confuses the ethnicity issue further since tigers are found only in Asia.)

This journey into the body takes the sexuality of black women as its destination. The fantasy of black women's sexuality had many attractions for contemporary white viewers. The figure suggested first the white authority which called it up and put it on show, locked under a

3.4 William Wetmore Story, *Cleopatra* (detail)

marble constraint, as in this image. Soothing the anxieties of white women it flattered the continence of white men, by posing them as the indifferent witness of black seductiveness. Hawthorne actively promotes this form of spectatorship by suggesting that in the sculpture Cleopatra is depicted in despair over the self-restraint of Octavius, the man who would later take the name of Augustus when he founded his authority on her defeat (Hamer, 1993, p. 22). 'It was the repose of despair, indeed, for Octavius had seen her and remained insensible to her enchantments' (Hawthorne, 1968, p. 126).

When reviewers praised Story's courage in making this representation it was perhaps its bold statement of frustrated, black female sexuality that they had in mind. It has a very specific contemporary reference and manages to finesse one of the most touchy issues of its day. White male slave-owners were accused by abolitionists of using their black women slaves to breed. The increase in the number of mixed race or mulatto slaves, many of whom looked more white than black, seemed to bear out this charge.[4] Hawthorne's marble image acknowledged contemporary anxieties raised by the question of sexual connection between blacks and whites but in a minimally disturbing form, by putting black female sexuality on show and implying that it was of a radically different order from that of white women and one that was geographically ordained. This permitted spectators to believe that mulattos were the product of a black mother's lust, though of course it did rather compromise the absolute self-command attributed to white men. There was also a subtler point structured into the image; reading reinforced the imaginary dialectic of white against black, a dialectic with particular force in a print culture. There was no intermediate term. The sculpture denied the very problem from which the image took its charge; the person of mixed and essentially unfixed colour, whose racial origin could not be determined at a glance. So, far from being a specially abolitionist image, Story's *Cleopatra* perpetuates one of the fictions of its day, that slaves were always blacks and whites were always free.

It would be a pity to leave this white marble Cleopatra without asking why the current pope, Pius IX, took such an interest in it. One answer might be that the image addressed the question of women, the question of all women, black and white. In teaching viewers to penetrate below the cold white surface of a woman's body, the sculptor had invited them to envisage a darkness at its centre, a deeper stain that indicated the place of desire which was also the place of generation; in this all women might be sisters under the skin.

Perhaps it is time to explore how the generous action of Pius IX, in making Story's reputation, served the Pope's own rhetorical and political turn. When the statue was sent to London and put on exhibition it was in the name of the papacy, not of America, and it was housed in the Roman pavilion. The American selectors had turned Story's work down and the Pope paid for both pieces, the *Cleopatra* and the *Libyan Sibyl*, to be shipped to England. According to some accounts, he paid for every completed work in the studios of Rome to be shipped; a floating collection of Vatican sculptures, to rival the creation of his predecessor, Julius II (Phillips, 1897, p. 135).

There was a still more ancient precedent for his act. The figure of Cleopatra had been put to political use before, when Augustus made her image the sign of his own success. He dated his own rule in Rome from the time of Cleopatra's defeat and death. Augustus was supported by poets and historians who were his propagandists. They defined Cleopatra in terms of her alien origin and values (Hamer, 1993, pp. 28–

9). The absolute difference that Robert Knox, the anatomist, would later locate in the person of a black was attributed under Augustus to the person of a woman.

This was the tradition that the popes had elected to join. Pius showed no inclination to distance himself from it personally. Like eight pontiffs before him, on his accession Pius IX took the name that aligned him with 'pius Aeneas', the hero of Virgil's account of the founding of Rome. In the story presented by Virgil the crucial test of piety in Aeneas is his readiness to steel himself to disregard what his lover, Dido, feels for him and to abandon her. From the time when Virgil was giving readings from his still unpublished poem, listeners have recognized in Dido, queen of Carthage the African city, a reference to Cleopatra, queen of Egypt. In Virgil's *Aeneid*, the rule of Augustus boasts that it is grounded in the sacrifice of a woman and her desire, a woman so firmly held at arms' length that she is said to come from Africa. Skin colour was almost certainly not the issue, for in Augustan Rome black skin appears to have had no shameful connotations (Snowden, 1970, pp. 169–95). The force of Virgil's myth within the culture of Rome seems to have lain in encouraging men to cut themselves off from sympathy with women and to deaden their own instinctive identification with them.

It is impossible now to reconstruct the conscious motivations and choices of Pius IX, but his political predicament is quite clear. Sending Cleopatra to London was the manoeuvre of a man who had been forced to relinquish secular power, a man who then made a compensatory bid for unprecedented moral authority. In the years when Story was still working on this sculpture in his Rome studio, Pius IX had been presiding in that same city over the dismantling of the secular power of the papacy. Before him popes had ruled for 700 years as monarchs. Now there was a drive throughout Europe to separate church and state that took its impetus from the French Revolution. With the rise of Italian nationalism secular voices were growing in authority, and they questioned the way that the papacy discharged its temporal responsibilities. First Pius IX was asked to reform his rule of the Papal States, then to surrender them. In April 1861 he had finally been obliged to see its remaining territories incorporated in the new kingdom of Italy. From then on all that was left to him was the city of Rome itself. A principal opponent of the Pope's attempts to halt this humiliating decline had been Great Britain. Between 1858 and 1861 both Whig and Tory governments had steadily encouraged the establishment of a secular kingdom in Italy (McIntire, 1983, pp. 2–4). It was to the courts of his foes that Pius sent the white marble armada.

It was a gesture of defiance and perhaps also one of reiteration. Although he was unable to stop the papacy being stripped of its secular power, Pius IX made a later bid to claim absolute moral authority by having papal infallibility declared an article of faith. He is notorious for that bid today, though at the time of the exhibition of these statues in 1862 only the first shots in the battle to reassert his own supremacy had been fired. Pius began the public campaign to restore his own dignity in 1854 when he declared the doctrine of the Immaculate Conception an article of faith. It was a matter of personal pride to him that he did it quite unilaterally. In later years, before he revealed the full extent of his ambitions by claiming infallibility, he would remind listeners that he had not invited the assembled bishops to vote when the doctrine was formalized. On his own independent authority he had declared the Immaculate Conception, previously only a traditional belief of the faithful, to be an official doctrine of the Church. Paying to send white marble statues across the sea offered one more opportunity for Pius to remind the world about himself and 'his' Immaculate Conception.

Even the doctrine Pius used to advance his own claims seems to dwell on the triumphant isolation of a single figure. According to its official interpretation, the Immaculate Conception states that Mary, the mother of Jesus, was preserved from original sin from the moment of conception: she 'alone among women' was 'free from sin even in her mother's womb'. Although all humans, not just women, are said to be born in a state of original sin, the force of the doctrine is to emphasize the purity of a single exceptional woman, at the cost of implying that all others bear a stain. The form of words 'free from sin even in her mother's womb' further implies that the uterus is normally a tainted place. The effect of publishing the doctrine of the Immaculate Conception, outside the debate of theologians, is to broadcast an authoritative reminder that women are carriers of an inward contamination.

The Immaculate Conception invites the attention to focus on the interior of a woman's body just as Story's marble image of Cleopatra does. It is not immediately evident in the case of the doctrine, any more than it was in the case of the white marble figure, that women's desire is the issue at stake. Yet both statue and doctrine could be read as warnings to men who want to retain their masculine supremacy, warnings of the contamination that they risk, the erosion of their masculinity, if they let women close the distance that should be kept between them. Story's image goes even further and specifies: what men risk by intimacy with women is humiliation. They might lose the sense of their own superiority and difference. The sculpture has a measure for this threat; it compares the loss to the humiliation of blacks, those who have been robbed of all their human rights and enslaved.

Let me close with a question. A fantasized maternal body lurks at the core of both doctrine and statue. This is no minor observation, for Luce

3.5   House of Simon Vostre, *Anne with the Virgin and Christ in her Womb*

Irigaray has claimed that western culture is founded on the murder of the mother. She argues that representation of the maternal body is the suppressed foundation of all other imaging; do these examples give her assertion the lie (Whitford, 1991, pp. 75–97)? Or would it make more sense to counter that the maternal body as it is indicated in these two mid-nineteenth-century constructs does not receive representation but is merely elided and implied?

Early visualizations of the Immaculate Conception do not hedge. They centre on an image of the maternal body, in a tradition that was lost after the Renaissance, the moment when the classical body began to command respect. In illustrated manuscripts of the fourteenth and fifteenth centuries the woman depicted in images of the Immaculate Conception is not Mary herself but Anne, who was Mary's mother. In these images the impregnated body of Anne is shown marked with the radiance that is the sign of 'grace'. Anne is shown with the child in her womb, her daughter Mary, visible and glorified (D'Ancona, 1957, pp. 39–41; O'Connor, 1958, pp. 464–8). At the core of the mother's body there is not darkness but splendour.

Before this tradition was finally lost it was modified. The icon of the generative female body was adapted to accommodate the male. As Irigaray observes, the maternal body is exemplary in its tolerance of difference (Irigaray, 1993, p. 45). In the image from the end of the fifteenth or early sixteenth century that is shown as Figure 3.5 the glorified double of mother and daughter is expanded to include a male figure: at its centre stands a tiny image of Jesus in Mary's womb.

Notes

1. I should like to express my thanks to Karen Dalton, Marilyn Richardson and Michael Hanchard for their helpful comments on earlier drafts of this essay.
2. Nowadays it is given the name of a woman undergoing punishment for betraying her father and is known as the *Sleeping Ariadne* (Haskell and Penny, 1981, p. 186).
3. Twenty years later when he came back to the *Cleopatra* during the period of Reconstruction, at the time when America was making its first attempt to change the meaning of blackness, Jarves no longer expressed admiration for the features: 'her face has no ethnological decisive type and the mouth is vulgar' (Gerdts, 1966, p. 498).
4. It is claimed that mulatto slavery in the US went up by 66 per cent between the census of 1850 and the one of 1860. Over the same period black slavery went up only by 19 per cent (Williamson, 1983, p. 63).

CHAPTER FOUR

The inner and the outer: Dalip Singh as an Eastern stereotype in Victorian England

Simeran Man Singh Gell

The Sikh kingdom established by the great Maharaja Ranjit Singh was finally extinguished with the removal of his youngest son Dalip Singh, aged 15, to England in 1851. There he was to remain for the rest of his life. He had already converted to Christianity and eagerly anticipated his complete assimilation into the imperial culture of his British minders, Sir John and Lady Login, even as his own mother languished as a prisoner in Lahore fort. Recently, I inadvertently attempted to reverse history and effect a homecoming for this tragic Sikh. While preparing for a visit to meet family and friends in India I carefully packed four large posters bearing his portrait (see Figure 4.1), happy in the belief that I had discovered a gift that would arouse excitement among my wider family who would gratefully acknowledge its superiority over the standard gifts of toiletries, ties, etc. After all, I thought, the poster depicting Winterhalter's stunning portrait of the tall, fair, youthful Maharaja Dalip Singh swathed in magnificent silken robes and abundantly bejewelled is the original apotheosis of the aristocratic Sikh form – as firm a declaration as any of British esteem for the Sikhs, and as such could not fail to be appreciated by my family, all of whom are staunch, image-conscious Sikhs. So I was somewhat taken aback by the distinct lack of enthusiasm displayed by those to whom these posters were intended, who, while not wishing to hurt my feelings, nevertheless communicated their acute discomfort with possessing this particular image. The posters remained in my suitcase, and travelled back to England with me.

Why should this image be repugnant to the sensibilities of Sikhs? British Sikhs are more likely to find something positive here in that this picture evokes the aristocratic Sikh heritage and tends to bolster the Sikh image vis-à-vis other south Asian diasporic communities. But they, too, circulate this image in crucially modified forms (Gell, forthcoming). And what makes it so attractive to the British? This image is perhaps the most acceptable face of 'the Raj', as seductive now as when

4.1   Franz Xaver Winterhalter, *The Maharajah Dalip Singh*

it was originally painted – witness the fact that Dalip Singh's portrait was the principal image used to publicize 'The Raj' exhibition held at the National Portrait Gallery in 1992. Winterhalter's portrait of Dalip Singh was commissioned by Queen Victoria in 1854 very shortly after his arrival in England. It shows a youth with a light beard and magnificent jewelled turban, his head and body tilted towards the viewer with his hand resting grandly upon a sword sheathed in its opulent scabbard. The portrait is luminously redolent of the sensuality and beauty of the East – as idealistic a representation of the Oriental body as it is possible to find. Queen Victoria visiting Winterhalter during the Maharaja's sitting reported that 'Winterhalter was in ecstasies at the beauty and nobility of the young Maharajah' (Alexander and Anand, 1980, p. 45), and this feeling certainly shines through.

I believe the reason for both its repulsiveness to Sikhs and attraction for Britons, goes beyond the political – the subjugation of the Sikh body vividly proclaimed by the miniature of Queen Victoria the Maharaja wears at his throat – and lies in the difficult domain of the representation of selfhood and alterity. In this chapter I take the view that Dalip Singh was a signifier par excellence of Britain's Indian empire to the Victorians because his 'objective' arbitrariness enabled the unrestrained inscription of alterity, but an impotent alterity that could be neutralized and transcended at the same time, enabling a confirmation of Victorian selfhood as simultaneously incorruptible and all-embracing, stolidly unchanging as well as dynamic and progressive, protectors of the other and protected by the other. But for the Sikhs it is a different matter in that the phenomena of Dalip Singh conveys the estrangement, appropriation and fetishization of the self by the other, the overglorification of form and trivialization of content. For the Sikhs, Dalip Singh is an alienation of the self wherein the self is diminished, depleted of substance, and defencelessly laid open; for the British the self is enhanced, amplified by its incorporation of otherness. The Dalip Singh image is focused on externalities; the viewer's gaze is gripped by his accoutrements of gaudy silk and jewels, incessantly drawn away from the person of Dalip who appears to shrink behind them, haplessly attempting to measure up to the grandiloquence of his costume. But this overemphasis upon form serves only to throw into relief the image's subliminality; indeed it is only by acknowledging the picture's multilayered composition that it is possible to understand its sentimental impact. On the one hand the strong element of display within the picture appears to affirm Victorian optimism that the gaze of the observer was sufficient to establish knowledge and control, and yet the ethereal aura enveloping Dalip Singh seems to question the efficacy of this technique when directed towards alien people who had undeniably 'natures', 'souls' etc. as well as (surface) bodies.

The Victorians placed faith in the ability to read the inner from the outer. This belief was based upon a conviction that 'differences of external form are the result and measure of pre-existing differences of internal character – in other words, configuration corresponds with organisation and function' (S. R. Wells, *New System of Physiognomy*, 1866, quoted in Cowling, 1989, p. 12). Yet the East confounded the efforts of its colonial rulers to apply this simple inductive method, since Easterners appeared to split their inner and their outer selves with the greatest of ease. It was this observation that lay behind the Victorian stereotype of the deceptive, lying and inscrutable Easterner. Dalip Singh remained very much the deceptive Easterner in that he was not inwardly what he appeared to be outwardly. But it was the inscrutability of the East, turned back upon itself; this time it was the British who knew the true 'internal character', and the Orientals themselves who were fooled.

I treat the colonial discourse on the 'similarity' of the Sikhs as significant in the decision to select Dalip Singh, of all available Indian princes, as representative of 'otherness'. Ultimately I believe the Winterhalter image of Dalip Singh, like the man himself, draws its appeal from the equivocality of its composition; the vanquished Prince posing as commandingly regal, an Eastern prince in a pose evocative of the tragic Charles I in the famous Van Dyck portrait, a fellow Aryan – 'almost but not quite white' – bedecked in unmistakable Oriental garb, the epitome of handsome masculinity but with a disturbingly feminine appeal in his eyes, the pendant with Queen Victoria's face reassuringly foregrounded against a murky landscape suggestive of the East – the turret of a fort is dimly visible. It is the flagrant representation of 'otherness', but at the same time, its ambivalence gives this picture its dramatic appeal. Its success as a representation of selfhood is owing to its ability to communicate ambiguity and ambivalence, both a mutual desire for the other and fear of the other, so that the self is silhouetted in the liminal 'in-between-spaces' of 'disavowal and designation', in Homi Bhabha's terms, which is the only space for the articulation of identities in a cross-cultural colonial milieu (Bhabha, 1994, p. 50).

The image of the Sikh typified in Dalip Singh, that the British were so determined to uphold, must therefore not be regarded in terms of simple negativities – colonial repression and falsehood opposing native authenticity. One must not forget the colonial desire that shaped British sentiments towards the Sikhs who were always regarded as among the foremost of the empire's valiant defenders. Indeed to what motive other than desire, can one ascribe the fact that it was the very people who were regarded as 'approaching much nearer to the European character than any of the other classes of Hindustan' (Thompson, 1943, p. 159) who were singled out to represent the 'otherness' of Hindustan, for this is what Dalip Singh's presence at the Victorian court embodied. It would seem that the Sikhs and the British were imbricated in a relationship of 'mimesis and alterity' (Taussig, 1993) in which the self is transformed and alienated in its replications or mimetic images; it is almost as if Dalip holds up a mirror wherein the British can see a reflection of their own altered, orientalized selves, their bodies abandoned to rich Oriental finery and ennobled with jewels. And this is so even as Dalip is precariously confined to the very margins of Victorian society – which Englishman would ever dare to appear in the strikingly gaudy colours of Dalip's attire in the black sobriety governing Victorian convention? Dalip is clearly a transgressive symbol to Victorians – a dangerous portent of the temptations of the East, as well as a significant trophy with which to boost Victorian and Christian pride.

The same ambivalence is discernible at the Sikh end. Indeed it would be disingenuous to claim an integral selfhood for the Sikhs uncompromised by desire for the other. The Sikhs could hardly fail to be flattered by the image accorded them by the British, nor by the fact that it was a Sikh prince the colonial rulers deemed fit to dine at Queen Victoria's table and hob-nob with her family. 'The term Sikh is a name to conjure with in the minds of the ordinary British citizen' wrote Sir George MacMunn (1933, p. 251), and such sentiments were recorded for posterity in Queen Victoria's journal, wherein she wrote: 'Dr. Login says that the Sikhs are a far superior race to the other Indians' (Alexander and Anand, 1980, p. 46). The Sikhs accepted the British insistence upon image, and to this day a Sikh is identifiably different by the bearded, turbaned image he presents. This is not to say that the British were the inventors of the image – the Sikhs had their own theological and political reasons for conforming to this image, referring to pronouncements believed to have been made by their last spiritual leader, Guru Gobind Singh shortly before his death in 1708. But it is fair to say that the British inflated the importance of image and assigned it rigid meanings that were certainly not part of the Sikh corpus. The British insisted that Sikh recruits to the British Indian army conform to the Sikh image, and Richard Fox in his book on Sikh ethnogenesis has speculated that it is probable that Sikhism would have relinquished the look with which it is identified, had it not been for British strictures forbidding Sikh recruits from doing so. The Sikhs were forced to accept this image which has now acquired the moral force and indubitability of traditional practice.

What is apparent is that the relationship between the Sikhs and the British is entangled and reflexive. It will therefore be necessary to present a background to this relationship, and then present a counter-example of a Sikh hero's visual representation in India, when the British were no longer in control. If the face of Dalip Singh is so satisfyingly and unmistakably Sikh to British eyes, it is hardly surprising that the face of a stalwart Sikh martyr in the cause of Indian independence should be affixed as one of a moustachioed Edwardian dandy complete with trilby and suit. I will conclude with a description of this man, whom one may regard as the antithesis and antidote to Dalip Singh in Sikh historical consciousness – a case of the empire writing back.

The British and the Sikhs

The British encounter with the Sikhs took place during the final phase of the establishment of the Raj, when most of the sub-continent had already yielded to the colonial presence. The progression of the British was from east to west, and south to north, and the Sikhs in the north and west of the country remained immune for a long time from the British advance. (Indeed the last integral native kingdom to fall to the British was that of the Sikhs, almost a hundred years after the British arrived in India.) By the time the British became entangled in Sikh affairs, they had acquired a conviction of their destiny as rulers along with a reasonable familiarity with the people of India. They had grappled with the arcane mysteries of Hindu religion and society, commissioning teams of Brahmans to codify it, and they had assimilated the symbolism of Mughal court rituals. The forbidding complexity of social arrangements in other parts of India was the accretion of centuries of relative freedom from foreign invasion, which Punjab, located at the northern corridor into the sub-continent, had not been spared. Punjab's past was singularly turbulent, marked by the regular depredations of awesome invaders of the ilk of Tamurlane, Mahmud of Ghazni and Nadir Shah in search of the fabled riches of the Hindu kingdoms further south, and its population was both constantly denuded by the massacres of marauding armies and augmented by drifting foreign soldiers who chose to stay. The British believed that this background imprinted the people of Punjab with certain racial traits:

> Essentially the Punjab breeds peasants and fighters; tall, sturdy men with the blend of many martial races in their veins, descendants of Aryan invaders, of Scythians, Greeks, Afghans. Every invader of India has passed through the Punjab, leaving his trail blazed by fire and sword, leaving also a legacy of racial qualities finely blended in the Punjabis of to-day. (Diver, 1942, p. 224)

The difference in social climate – the more chaotic, decentralized, democratic and, indeed, individualistic character of the Punjab, its freedom from the fussy hierarchy that inhibited social intercourse in other parts of India – undoubtedly impressed the British, from the start. A Captain Mathews who travelled in the Punjab in 1808 wrote 'enthusiastically' that he found it

> impossible to fancy myself in a foreign country, the inhabitants are so very attentive, and seem to look upon me as their deliverer. I do think the Siques and Singhs are the very best people in Hindustan, approaching much nearer to the European character than any of the other classes. I am constantly applied to for Wine, and had I brought a hundred Dozens I could have got rid of it by according to their wishes ... The Singhs bear a great similarity of character to British sailors, spending their money as fast as they get it in the pleasures of Women and Wine. The concourse of fine Women who go to bathe at the Temple in a morning is prodigious, they are far superior in Symmetry of Person ,and beauty of Countenance to those of any part of India I have seen. (Thompson, 1943, p. 159)

The resemblance with the British was further stimulated by the resemblance of Sikhism to Christianity, and by the openness of the Sikh faith that did not place barriers of commensality or entertain notions of pollution in relation to the social exchanges between Sikhs and the British. Sikhism was an Oriental religion but purged of Oriental irrationality and mercifully free from idolatry and hierarchy. In the words of Sir George MacMunn (1933, p. 121) the Sikh 'Bible' containing the writings of the founder Guru Nanak had, 'Christian affinities. In fact it has been said, from an examination of the Granth from certain aspects, that Nanak taught nothing but the story of Christ from Birth to Ascension'.

The Sikhs were then equivocal others – too much like the British to be beyond the pale as the rest of the Indians, but tainted with the Eastern character – being 'stupid' and impulsive. The cultural equivocality of the Sikhs extended to their very bodies which appeared both highly gendered – the masculinity of the Sikhs and the beauty of their women was remarked upon – and ungendered. The practice of keeping long hair was seen as womanly: 'The Sikh's hair is wisped up and confined with a comb like a woman's' (MacMunn, 1933, p. 252), and this physical androgyny is conveyed in the Winterhalter. The Sikhs and the Sikh body was seen by the British, as a clean sheet waiting to be written upon.

Dalip Singh (c.1837–92)

Dalip Singh was the youngest of the seven acknowledged sons of the legendary – and original – 'Lion of the Punjab', Maharaja Ranjit Singh, who founded a centralized empire over the entire length and breath of the dangerous and chaotic north-western region inhabited by warring tribes of Afghans, and of armed bands (*misl*) of Sikhs who had established volatile control in the aftermath of the dissolution of the Mughal empire based at Delhi. British–Sikh relations during his lifetime were friendly, tempered by a realization of the mutual benefits of alliance – the British needed Ranjit's goodwill to secure rights of navigation on the Indus river among other things, and Ranjit was genuinely impressed with – and made efforts to emulate – the discipline with which the British controlled their troops and with their advanced military technology. Ranjit mistrusted the erstwhile foes of the British, the Maharajas and rebuffed their overtures to form an alliance to overthrow the foreigners – and this act of his must surely have struck a cord in the British. Ranjit's kingdom, however, did not survive his death. Dalip was only five years old when proclaimed Maharaja, under tense circumstances brought about by the violent deaths of all five of Ranjit Singh's sons and mutinous insurrection by the powerful Sikh army. He was about 11 years old when the British succeeded in annexing the kingdom after a series of particularly bloody encounters with the Sikh army. Its defeat had been engineered by the treacherous connivance of Dalip Singh's royal council with the British. The royal council had more to fear from their own army, than from the British poised in the wings. The army were known to retain feelings of loyalty to the sons of their great leader, Ranjit Singh, and neither Dalip Singh, nor his mother were in any danger from them, but the same could not be said of the royal council which the army were known to hate almost to a man. The Sikh army had always displayed populist, democratic tendencies arising from their adherence to the Sikh creed and its anti-hierarchic ethos.

The British determined upon a policy designed to neutralize the vast army of Ranjit Singh that they had barely defeated. They insisted upon its rapid demobilization and, at the same time, strengthened the moral constraints upon it by bolstering the symbolic role of Dalip Singh, as son and heir of Ranjit Singh. And from the start they displayed a great interest in the promulgation of portraits of Dalip Singh wherein he was shown surrounded with all the trappings of royalty. While the pomp of Indian royalty had always excited the imagination of the British and contemporary British portraits of other Indian royals were hardly uncommon, no other Indian prince seems to have been the object of portraiture commissioned at the highest official levels, to the extent of Dalip Singh. Thus Lord Dalhousie, the Governor-General had a portrait painted of Dalip Singh by George Beechey, and this interest in the iconography of Dalip Singh climaxed in the interest that Queen Victoria was to take.

Dalip Singh's political importance earned him the diligent attention of the British who never let him out of their sight. His mother was banished from the Punjab, and Dalip Singh was made a ward of state with a Scottish medical officer, Dr John Login, to oversee his education. Login and his wife removed him from Punjab, and ensured that his appearance remained scrupulously that of a Sikh monarch – and Dalip was made available for exhibition as such:

> Login encouraged the Maharajah to keep up considerable state. One of the more picturesque sights at Futteghur was the elegant cavalcade attending his daily rides – the prince on his high-stepping horse, hawk on outstretched wrist, accompanied by the Shahzadah and his English friends ... followed by a detachment of the Body Guard in scarlet uniforms and troopers of the famous regiment Skinners Horse ... sometimes he would go out on his elephant with its silver howdah, or ride in his smart carriage with its four grey Arabs, driven by his English coachman, Thornton. (Alexander and Anand, 1980, p. 24)

But even as his appearance was affixed, Dalip Singh was to be internally changed and improved by a constant exposure to English learning and culture. He was confined to Fattehghar, a place some distance from the Punjab where his only companions were, apart from the Logins, two English boys specially selected for the purpose, and a Sikh cousin. It was not surprising that within a year Dalip announced his desire to embrace Christianity causing Dalhousie to exclaim 'This is the first Indian prince of the many who have succumbed to our power or have acknowledged it, that has adopted the faith of the stranger. Who shall say to what it may lead?' (Alexander and Anand, 1980, p. 37). He requested permission to cut his hair,

> this he thought would make him more like his English boy companions; and it was much against his will that he was persuaded by Login to defer the shearing of his locks until he had been, for at least a year, under probation. When at length his hair was allowed to be cut off, and he brought it to Mrs. Login as a memento, it was long and abundant as a woman's. (Malleson, 1889, p. 278)

The relinquishing of a crucial identifying mark – the long hair – of a real Sikh did not ruin the illusion of his being Sikh to those to whom he was exposed, since the turban kept his shorn locks from view.

After consultation between the Court of Directors of the East India Company and Lord Dalhousie, it was decided to accede to Login's and Dalip's desire to visit England. 'He is dying to see Europe and all its wonders. He told me he used to dream every night he was visiting the Duke of Wellington', wrote Dalhousie in a letter to his friend (Alexander and Anand, 1980, p. 39). In England he was immediately summoned to an audience with the Queen, and the strong impression he made was recorded in her diaries:

> The Maharajah ... is extremely pleasing, sensible and refined in his manner. His young face is indeed beautiful and one regrets that his peculiar headdress hides so much of it. He speaks English remarkably well and seems to prefer doing so, more than his own language which he thinks he will forget. (Alexander and Anand, 1980, p. 44)

She wrote to Dalhousie of her impressions and he responded with declaring a proprietorial pride in the young Dalip, stating that personally 'he feels some pride in the acquirements, such as they are, in the manner, feelings and above all, in the character of the Maharajah, contrasting so honourably as they do, with those of other youths in India of his age' (Alexander and Anand, 1980, p. 45). Queen Victoria drew numerous sketches of him, and he was extensively photographed by Prince Albert. His photographs were commercially available in London as well.

He became a familiar figure at court; Queen Victoria's partiality towards him aroused dissenting murmurs, but it was he who led the foreign princes at Prince Edward's wedding. Queen Victoria wrote of 'the amiable disposition of the Boy and his extreme truthfulness – an exception to Orientals in general – that his own good sense and the principles of Christianity had helped to make him overcome the natural indolence of disposition, inherent in all Easterners' (Alexander and Anand, 1980, p. 59).

He returned to Calcutta briefly to rendezvous with his mother who had been granted permission to visit him in England, and wrote from there to Login. 'I must tell you that India is a beastly place ... I hate the natives, they are such liars, flatterers, and extremely deceitful. I would give anything to be back in dear England, among my friends' (Alexander and Anand, 1980, p. 91). Back in England, he entered heartily into the high life of the upper classes – entertaining lavishly at the estate he bought through a mortgage advanced him by the East India Company, and becoming an avid punter at London gaming clubs and an impulsive giver of jewelled trinkets to pretty girls who took his fancy.

Dalip Singh was regularly invited to court functions, and arrived suitably attired as a Sikh Maharaja:

> Around his neck he wore strings of pearls and hanging from them the miniature of the Queen, which had been given to him by Lord Hardinge, in his ears were large gold ear-rings and on his shorn head a brocade turban adorned with dripping emeralds. He swathed a tissue shawl around him and bound it about his waist with an embroidered belt, from which hung an impotent sword in its scabbard. (Aijazuddin, 1979, p. 82)

When his mother visited him, however she thought it appropriate to wear English dress, presenting a sight that amused Lady Login, who described the effect in her *Recollections*:

> she had wished to pay me a special compliment by appearing in European dress; and as she could not entirely abandon her native garments for English under-clothing, she had donned an enormous bonnet with feather, mantle and wide skirt over immense crinoline, on the top of all her Indian costume! No wonder she was utterly unable to move hand or foot, and found it impossible to take a seat, encumbered with the crinoline, till two of her servants lifted her bodily up on to the settee, where she could sit comfortably cross-legged, her crinoline spreading all round her like a Cheese.
> (Alexander and Anand, 1980, p. 92)

Dalip's mother misunderstood her position as a colonized subject and the fact that it was a travesty that *she* could imagine to use *her* outer form to ingratiate the British; the fact that the Rani adopted a dress on the outside that was at complete odds with the one she had on inside, perhaps reveals that she had learnt the lesson of masquerade from her son, and mistakenly assumed it to be the order of the day! The perceived ludicrousness of Dalip's mother's efforts throws into relief the abject dictatorship exercised by Victorian tastes in the matter of Dalip Singh's attire – he could only hope for admiration and approval if he conformed to his 'proper' Oriental attire.

Further description of his life at this point is unnecessary. Suffice to say that although British political interest in him waned after the 1857 Mutiny when Sikh troops displayed their loyalty to them, interest in him as an Oriental show-piece and oddity continued. In this connection one may mention a coat of arms that Prince Albert designed for him which was 'an unintentional, if unfortunate, repetition of the Lion of the Punjab theme, which belonged more appropriately to Ranjit Singh', with a 'lion standing beneath a coronet surmounted by a five-pointed star'. Appositely and poignantly, it had the following motto invented by Prince Albert: 'To do good rather than be conspicuous'. Dalip had by then long since become 'to visitants a gaze, or pitied object' (Aijazuddin, 1979, p. 74), the most conspicuous Victorian Oriental of all.

The British publicly overstated the link between Ranjit Singh, the famous Lion of the Punjab, and Dalip Singh, even though, in accordance with their habitual denial of the legitimacy of Indian princes, they believed that no biological link existed. When one considers father and son, one encounters the same strange antipathy of form and content in both. According to all available accounts Ranjit Singh was a physically unprepossessing man; physiognomically he did not correspond to the sturdy martial type so admired by the British of his fellow tribesmen

Jats, being 'diminutive' rather than stout and burly – very different from the other legendary adversary of the British, Tipu Sultan whose imposing black physique had spawned so many British portraits. The relative impotency and physical incapacity of Ranjit Singh's exterior – remarkable enough in some ways – hid an interior, an inner constitution that was indomitable, martial and fearless; the two aspects – the inner and the outer being at odds with each other, the one giving no hint of the other. It would appear that it was the contradiction of these two aspects of the man that added to his mystique. This mystique was exacerbated by the almost ascetic plainness of his apparel and disdain for personal ornamentation. The only jewel worn by him was the Kohinoor in a clasp on his arm.

Dalip Singh was, of course, very different 'inside' from that which he was on the 'outside' – his real significance inheres in this splitting of inside and outside. But this time it was the British who could determine the form that both inside and outside could take. They chose to construct in Dalip Singh a perfect decoy to delude the Sikhs, by insisting that he conform – only in so far as his exterior was concerned – to the 'form' bequeathed him by his origins, i.e. a brave Sikh aristocratic form, although they 'improved' this form in various ways, and at the same time, ensured that internally he was as passive and non-Sikh as possible. Externally the epitome of Sikh-ness, he was internally to mirror the British. Ultimately the British were themselves confused as to what was 'real' and what 'constructed'; were they to take Dalip Singh's inner similarities as proof of a real compatibility, one that was already there so to speak, or were they to treat his externally different form as a reminder of the pitfalls of assuming identity with their colonial subjects where there was none? Was the outer more 'real' or evidential, than the inner? Would it ever be possible to separate form from content? If not then British attempts to connect themselves to the colonies was doomed, but if so, then there was always the danger of contamination and loss of an original British identity. It was safer to assume that despite all differences of form, there was a real brotherhood of mankind that could be established based on inner similarities acquired through British instruction. But such notions of sameness within difference could only credibly and safely be entertained with a Sikh since it was they who, of all people on the sub-continent, seemed to be the racial and cultural counterparts of the British. Indeed it was not outlandish to entertain the notions expressed by Colonel, later Lord, Sleeman in the following letter written to Lord Login on the eve of Dalip Singh's departure to England on the connections between Dalip Singh by birth a Jat Sikh, and the Jutes of Kent:

My dear Login,
I have been reading up the book I spoke to the Maharajah about
('Pictorial History of England'), since he left. You must get for him,
and let him see for himself that he is of the same race as the men of
Kent. They were from Jutland and came into England with the
Saxons from Friesland and Angles from Holstein, who dispos-
sessed the old Britons in the fifth century. They were the Juts or old
Getae of the Greeks and Romans, who came from the countries
about Kashgar. Some came down and settled on the banks of the
Indus, whence they spread to the Jumna and Chunbal; whilst others went and settled in western Europe (Sweden and Denmark);
from them Jutland received its name. Tell his Highness that their
chiefs, Hengist and Horsa, were Juts, like himself; their family
came from Kashgar and the Caspian and settled in Jutland; while
his part of the family settled on the Indus, spreading to the Punjab.
The Juts took possession of Kent, and some of the first kings were
Juts, like the Maharajah's ancestors, and both might, with equal
justice, boast descent from Odin, the god of war; they also took
possession of the Isle of Wight and the Isle of Thanet. All the old
Kentish families are descendants of Juts, and of the same race as
Duleep Singh. You can show him some of the beauties of Kent, as
you go up the Thames, and he will have an opportunity of seeing it
if he visits Lord Hardinge. Tell him, with our kind regards that we
would be very pleased if he would present the beautiful ring which
he did Mrs. Sleeman the honour of offering her to the first pretty
Kentish girl he sees, and claim brotherhood with her, on the authority of an old Indian officer, his friend Colonel Sleeman. If she is
of pure Kentish descent, he may feel assured that they are members
of the same great family! (Malleson, 1889, p. 326)

By an overemphasis upon the appearance of the Sikh in Dalip Singh, the
British could even convince themselves that they could control both the
form of their Indian subjects, as well as the 'content' of their inner
selves, thus achieving a total subjection. Furthermore it was only they
who were to be cognizant of the deception involved since their simple-
minded subjects, the Sikh soldiery, would succumb to believing the
truth of what was presented to their eyes; only the British knew better.
Sikhism did indeed develop an obsession with its own 'image', yet its
seemingly straightforward adoption of the image of a turban-wearing,
unshorn Sikh betrays a deeper ambivalence towards 'image' generally
(Gell, forthcoming). Ultimately, however, it is debatable as to who had
the last laugh as image-makers – the British or the Sikhs. It is true that
the Sikhs were themselves seduced, and internalized the image presented
by Dalip Singh; they began to present themselves to the world as the
British wished them to. But there is nothing disturbing about this since
the notion of a 'self-image' is to a certain extent a contradiction in
terms. However, by altering the frame they changed the terms of the
meaning of form and, ultimately, subverted its message. As a pendant to

the Dalip Singh phenomena which informs us about Victorian representation of the Sikhs, it is necessary to consider the inverse case of Bhagat
Singh (1907–31). This demonstrates the self-representation of Sikhs
during the struggle for independence from the British, a representation
that radically departs from and undermines Dalip Singh's significance.

Bhagat Singh is universally acclaimed as 'the most famous of all
terrorists in the annals of Indian revolutionary history' (Khushwant
Singh, 1977, p. 226n), whose sudden mass popularity took Nehru and
other contemporary political observers by surprise. He is known for
two acts, namely that of firing at and killing J. P. Saunders, a probation-
ary Assistant Superintendent of Police in Lahore on 19 December 1928
and of throwing a bomb at the Central Assembly, without causing
injury, while he was still at large after the first incident. The killing of J.
P. Saunders was a mistake, a case of misidentification (brought about
possibly by the fact that to Sikh eyes one Englishman looked much the
same as another?). The intended target was the Superintendent of Police, a Mr J. A. Scott, who had given an order for the police to charge at
a civil demonstration led by a nationalist leader named Lala Lajpat Rai,
who subsequently succumbed to the injuries he received during this
police assault. The avenging of Lala Lajpat's death was to be accom-
plished by the death of Scott. Bhagat Singh was eventually tracked
down and hanged, with his two companions, on 23 March 1931.

Figure 4.2 is the image of Bhagat Singh that is broadcast in India
today, based on a studio photograph that he had taken of himself a few
days prior to the bomb incident. It was believed that he and his friend
had evaded the police, and hoodwinked the security guards controlling
entry to the Assembly because 'they were smartly dressed in European
costume' (Sanyal, 1931, p. 49). So this image is equally suggestive of
both the importance of appearance and a daring defiance of the imperatives of 'ethnic' appearance as these were dictated by the British for all
Indians, but foremostly for the Sikhs who were made to 'look' different
from everyone – other Indians and British alike. The reason why Bhagat
Singh became so amazingly popular was, I believe, not merely because
of his brave revolutionary acts and subsequent martyrdom – there were
many other martyrs who remained obscure – but because of the image
of Bhagat Singh drawn from the fortuitous photograph. This image was
correctly perceived by the British as seditious and suppressed. This is
apparent from the collection of Bhagat Singh posters, bearing captions
such as 'Bhagat Singh's wonderful presentation', and 'Bhagat Singh
ascending to Heaven' etc. that are now available for inspection in the
'publications proscribed by the Government of India' section of the
India Office library. The image of Bhagat had such popular appeal
because it conveyed the idea of a fundamental liberation of the Indian

4.2   Bhagat Singh in his conventional calendar art form

body. It presented a handsome Sikh who would *not* submit his body to the reading of racial and ethnic signs, all the while epitomizing the courage of the Sikh to stand out and look different – but this time 'differently' British. If the British were smug in the belief that the Sikhs, of all Indians, could be relied upon to abide by the injunction contained in 'The Indian Gentleman's Guide to Etiquette' published in 1919 to 'have the courage to show that you are not ashamed of being an Indian, and ... identify yourself with the race to which you belong' (Allen, 1975, p. 231), then here is the ultimate Sikh rebuttal. Of course there were many classes of Indians – notably clerks and bureaucrats – who had taken to English dress and for whom the dress was an additional subjugation, but they were not Sikhs – hardly any Sikhs were employed in this capacity – and their racial grouping was not ambiguous like that of the Sikhs whom I have shown. The British found them genuinely difficult to situate. These other Indians' efforts could be dismissed as parody since they could never hope to pass off as Britons. It was an entirely different matter when a racial consanguine – or as near to one as the British believed it was possible to find in the sub-continent – took to the British form. Here was scope for real anarchy and the breakdown of the ethnological schema that made India comprehensible and govern-able to the British.

To conclude, the Victorians who disguised Dalip Singh in the form of the other did so not only because the Sikhs could be unmenacingly disguised as such, but because they wished to see the other reflected in themselves – an other on its own would not have been granted the kind of intimacy given Dalip Singh in royal circles. For the very same reasons, one might say, the Sikhs have taken to heart Bhagat Singh's picture since they too can – at one level – appreciate the paradoxical truth communi-cated by it; the British can be seen in the Sikh self-reflection. In the Bhagat Singh image, however, the Sikhs have cast off the 'burden of representation' with which they were shackled and which is so vividly conveyed by Winterhalter's image. Having been reduced to existing as 'outer' selves by the British, they can at last have the satisfaction of representing the British as such, as external beings comprised of form and hollow in content. In Bhagat Singh's representation as an Englishman, he has achieved his final and most complete subversion of the imperial state.

James Morris, in his book *Pax Britannica*, writes of the colonial repugnance of the aggressively Anglicized Indian: 'Nothing irritated the British more than a veneer of Western education without as they thought any real understanding of the values it represented. The emergence of Western-educated Indians, speaking a flowery English of their own, casually failing to recognize their own preordained place in the order of things – the arrival on the scene of these bouncy protégés did nothing to draw the British closer to their wards, but only exacerbated their aloof-ness' (Morris, 1968, p. 140). If it was the 'sly civility' (Bhabha, 1994) of the native that produced discomfort in the eyes of the British, signifying as it did, the appropriation of British form which revealed no essence, then it seems that the Sikh perception of Winterhalter's image, and indeed appreciation of Dalip Singh's character, is a direct counterpart.

CHAPTER FIVE

Race and the social plot in *The Mystery of Edwin Drood*

Tim Dolin

'Two things, great things, dwell … in all thinking heads in England,' wrote Thomas Carlyle in 1839: 'Universal Education [and] general Emigration' (Carlyle, 1969b, p. 192). Throughout the 1840s and 1850s, as sectarian resistance to education reform mounted and emigration schemes were attacked, Victorian social fiction and academic art vigorously took up the promotion of these two middle-class causes. Countless scenes in novels and Royal Academy exhibitions depicted poorly educated children as victims of institutional abuse or as imaginary creatures in village schoolyard idylls, and many others depicted poorly educated men and women gazing upon the last of an England that had seen the last of them – and, it was argued by social critics like Carlyle, the last of disease, crime, poverty and vice.[1] Few writers so powerfully mythologized Victorian childhood or so poignantly described the patriotic spectacle of emigration, as Charles Dickens.[2] It is all the more significant, then, that there are also characters in Dickens's fiction who prove consistently troublesome to both these two 'great things'. These characters are English exiles who turn out not to have seen the last of England at all, but travel home against the tide of settlers, colonial officials and transported convicts. The homecoming in Dickens sometimes signifies narrative and social resolution, as in Martin Chuzzlewit's return from America or Walter Gay's journeys back from the West Indies and China in *Dombey and Son*. More commonly, however, these travellers are guilty, watchful and secretive. When Alice Marwood lands, in *Dombey and Son*, or Arthur Clennam, in *Little Dorrit*, Magwitch and Compeyson, in *Great Expectations*, or John Harmon, in *Our Mutual Friend*, they find themselves (for a time, at least) unwelcome strangers in their own country. Even the innocents, Clennam and Harmon, creep back like convicts who 'cannot be allowed to "return" to metropolitan space' (Said, 1994, p. xvi). They are awkward interlopers in the class system, and Dickens uses them to expose the deceit and hypocrisy that drives English social relations. They triumph in the end, of course, restored to the social order – even Magwitch, who dies with dignity, tended by a gentleman-in-the-making. But they remain repatriates, English natives marked by exile, and their fortunes cannot be explained in social terms alone, but must also be read through emergent discourses of empire, and through mid-Victorian writings in which class and race are treated as 'interchangeable or at least analogous' (Brantlinger, 1986, p. 201).[3]

The significance of education in the plot of the returning native is explored most fully in Dickens's last novel, *The Mystery of Edwin Drood* (first published 1869–70). In an unpredictable twist to the theme, a pair of orphan twins from British Ceylon,[4] aptly named Helena and Neville Landless, are brought 'home' on the death of their tyrannical stepfather to an England they have presumably never seen. They turn up in the Trollopian cathedral town of Cloisterham, a claustrophobic backwater which preserves pathologically a delusion of unitary English-ness.[5] In 'the confines of its oppressive respectability' (Dickens, 1985, p. 51) the Landlesses look conspicuously 'un-English', in the catch-word of the mayor Mr Sapsea. But at the same time, the novel does not say exactly what they are, if not English. Cloisterham's Minor Canon, Septimus Crisparkle, fantasizes, like one of Rider Haggard's later he-roes, that they are 'beautiful barbaric captives brought from some wild tropical dominion' (Dickens, 1985, p. 85). Their dark complexion and Neville's familiar manner of the 'self-hating hybrid' (Perera, 1990, p. 106) suggest that they are of mixed race, but in his working notes Dickens was undecided: 'Mixture of Oriental blood – or imperceptibly acquired mixture in them' (Dickens, 1985, p. 286). As Neville explains it, they have simply been 'brought up', like Kipling's Kim, among an 'inferior race' (Dickens, 1985, p. 90). They are at once exemplars of that familiar Dickensian institution, orphanhood, and forerunners of the familiar orphans of empire. They are landless – without parents, estate, or nation – and their ambivalent homecoming is imagined by Dickens as a new version of the old story of an orphan's social advance-ment, unencumbered by family.

Edwin Drood is Dickens's condition-of-England-in-the-age-of-empire novel.[6] It draws upon themes and plots of education to explore links between race, class and the capacity for social transformation. Jenny Sharpe has shown that the Victorian discourse of race was founded in Enlightenment ideas of social progress in which biological explanations for racial degeneration articulated 'the impossibility of social transfor-mation by binding human types to racially marked bodies' (Sharpe, 1993, p. 5). The newly wealthy Victorian middle classes later found in these biological explanations a corresponding scientific rationale for prohibiting social mobility to those below them. According to Robert Young, in the 1850s and 1860s there was an 'increased emphasis on racial difference, on the permanence of the intellectual capacities, or incapacities, of the different races, and the similar differentiations that could be made between the classes' (Young, 1995, p. 96). *Edwin Drood* encodes these complementary theories of inherency in a double plot of social mobility and racial degeneration in which the thwarted class rehabilitation of the racially marked Neville Landless (but not Helena, who is marked for gender, as I explain a little later) is balanced by John Jasper's traumatic social descent, a reciprocal story of expatriation, racialization and degeneration.

This descent was to be unrelenting, for Dickens planned to set the last chapters of the novel in prison, where Jasper would review his career 'as if, not he the culprit, but some other man, were the tempted' (Forster, 1928, p. 808). Dickens even advised his illustrator Luke Fildes that 'his concluding illustration must outvie Cruickshank's ... "Fagin in the condemned cell" in *Oliver Twist*' (Fildes, 1968, p. 16). Because Jasper's split personality is manifested as the xenophobe's obsession with the hated unknown, it is significant that Dickens should so expressly figure his villain's unconscious self as Fagin. *Edwin Drood*, which Forster considered 'quite free from the social criticism which grew more biting as Dickens had grown older' (quoted in Johnson, 1952, p. 1124), alludes furtively to the social plots of the heyday of reform fiction, and to the angry novels of the post-reform 1850s. This 'elegiac' last work (Johnson, 1952, p. 1116), which Dickens sets in the very years dominated by 'the question of the Working Classes', looks back anxiously from the brink of empire and the brink of the 'Great Depression' of the 1870s. Precisely when attention was being 'directed to a newly identified social grouping with special characteristics: the unemployed and/or the unemployable' (Donald, 1992, p. 26), Dickens returns to what had always been a problematic issue for him: 'doing' and 'working'. Racial infection is repeatedly implicated in 'not getting things done' in earlier novels: the influence of Fagin in *Oliver Twist*; the distracting Borrioboolans in *Bleak House*; and the crisis of will Arthur Clennam contracts in the Orient before the opening of *Little Dorrit*.[7] In *Edwin Drood*, Dickens draws upon analogies between race and social change in early Victorian ideologies of education and public health, and juxtaposes them with topical controversies over colonial rule and racial determinism. In what follows, I argue that *Edwin Drood* also recalls other related cultural texts in which social relations are conceived (problematically) as interracial encounters on English soil: Thomas de Quincey's *The Confessions of an English Opium Eater* (1971; first published in 1822–56), and two works by the early Victorian artist William Mulready (1786–1863).

'I believe in the immense influence of that fixed hereditary transmission which constitutes a race,' wrote T. H. Huxley in January 1870 (Biddiss, 1979, p. 168). But Huxley did not believe, as other Victorian ethnologists in the 1860s did, that 'physical, mental, and moral peculiarities go with blood' (Biddiss, 1979, p. 160). For him, 'the character of a man depends in part upon the tendencies he has brought with him into the world, and in part upon the circumstances to which he is subjected'. Sometimes 'one group of influence predominates, sometimes the other' (Biddiss, 1979, p. 168). Education and upbringing is therefore integral to the formation of 'racial' characteristics:

> by diligent and careful education you may help a child to be good and wise and keep it out of evil and folly. But the wisest education cannot ensure its being either good or wise; while, on the other hand, a few years of perverted ingenuity would suffice to convert the best child that ever lived into a monster of vice and wickedness. The like applies to those great children, nations, and the rulers, who are their educators. (Biddiss, 1979, p. 168)

However enlightened this qualified essentialism may have been, Huxley none the less sidesteps one of the fundamental arguments of his opponents: that the very capacity or incapacity for education is also racially determined. If European nations were 'great children', so too, it was claimed, were primitive cultures: 'Unlikeness between the juvenile mind and the adult mind ... typifies the unlikeness between the minds of savage and civilized,' argued Herbert Spencer (1876, p. 259). Political resistance to western expansion (the Muslim resistance to English education in India, for example) was rationalized as a constitutional incapacity for education and influence. These were not children in the Godwinian sense of immature minds, 'well regulated, active, and prepared to learn' (Godwin, 1965, p. 5), but minds incapable of and indifferent to learning and development. With such notable exceptions as the 'indigenous elite within colonial production' (Spivak, 1994, p. 77) and the Hindu middle classes trained for the Indian Civil Service,[8] primitive races were doomed to evolutionary stasis or degeneration.

Only when basic education became an economic imperative for the empire in the last quarter of the century were these conceptions of the uneducable primitive modified. Macaulay's fantasy in 1833 of the profits that could be yielded by 'the diffusion of European civilisation' in the East – 'To trade with civilized men is infinitely more profitable than to govern savages'(Macaulay, 1952, p. 717) – soon gave way to the more predictable economic relationship which cast the empire as a vast labour force to be exploited by British capital.[9] By 1902, the Victorian jurist, historian and politician, James Bryce, could write: 'It is hardly too much to say that for economic purposes all mankind is fast becoming one people, in which the hitherto backward nations are taking a place analogous to that which the unskilled workers have held in each one of the civilized nations' (Bryce, 1979, p. 9). Such was the worth to colonial administrators of the example of the British labouring classes' education in the values of non-violent reform. The 'immense Problem of Organising Labour, and first of all of Managing the Working Classes' (Carlyle, 1969a, p. 270) provided for the new volatile and unreliable labour force, an ideal model of successful social control. Imperialists traced forward the development of the worker from an uneducated, undisciplined, and insurgent 'primitive' to a civilized, responsible agent of prosperity in the free-trade era, and superimposed this narrative on the 'hitherto backward nations'.

In the 1830s and 1840s, analogies between the urban poor and the savage races can be found in the 'moral environmentalism' (Donald, 1992, p. 23) of Benthamite reformers like James Kay-Shuttleworth, author of the pioneering *The Moral and Physical Condition of the Working Classes of Manchester in 1832*, and the sanitarian Edwin Chadwick, whose *Sanitary Report* (1842) was enormously influential in 'the creation of a "literary" poor' (Childers, 1994, p. 406). The living conditions and habits of the lower classes were constantly being compared with those of savage races, but the racial analogy, as well as carrying infectious and miscegenous implications, undermined the very idea of social reform. To counter this, the moral environmentalists attributed the degradation of the English poor to their very pliability, and used the omnipresent 'white chimpanzees' (Kingsley, 1883, p. 111), the Irish, as counter-examples of the unreformable savage.[10] Taking up the common Victorian stereotype of the prognathous Paddy, Carlyle, too, blamed the 'uncivilised Irishman' who with his 'Berserkir rage' (Carlyle, 1969a, p. 140) and 'laughing savagery' (Carlyle, 1969a, p. 138) drives the Saxon from his home.[11] Significantly, Dickens also assimilated the Irish with the 'noble' savage ('a something highly desirable to be civilised off the face of the earth' [Dickens, 1853, p. 337]); and even more significantly, in *Oliver Twist* he displaced the racial contaminant from 'the lowest orders of Irish ... wrangling with might and main' (Dickens, 1982, p. 49) to a single Jew.

But though the Saxon may be ignorant and corruptible, 'he has not sunk from decent manhood to squalid apehood: he cannot continue there' (Carlyle, 1969a, p. 139). Kay-Shuttleworth, though he likewise feared that a 'debilitated race would be rapidly multiplied' (Kay-Shuttleworth, 1973, p. 51) by 'the natural progress of barbarous habits' passed on, like cholera and typhus, through the medium of an environment morally polluted by idleness, dissolution and sexual promiscuity, would not concede that the labouring classes were 'condemned for ever, by an inexorable fate, to the unmitigated curse of toil, scarcely rewarded by the bare necessities of existence, and often visited by the horrors of hunger and disease'. The only historical evidence of this, he maintained, derived from 'the history of uncivilised races, and ... feudal institutions', was invalid, since even the 'most wretched cabin of the poor' was infinitely more advanced than the living conditions of the 'unsheltered, naked savage' (Kay-Shuttleworth, 1973, pp. 49–50). Education, hopelessly inappropriate for the 'ultra-savage ... in the midst of civilisation' (Carlyle, 1969a, p. 140), was the key to discipline of the masses, and educated children were the key to the continued purity of the race.

So powerful was this idea of the child-like poor that the injustices and ills of an entire class came to be expressed in the abused body of the child. In Oliver Twist and his successors, Dickens used these bodies as a powerful pathetic focus for the middle-class will to carry out reform. Any ambivalence he felt towards the idea of an educated proletariat – which was considerable, as Lillian Nayder has shown – was deflected into vehement attacks on corrupt institutions or sentimental tableaux of elementary instruction such as Kit's writing lesson in The Old Curiosity Shop.[12] These tableaux owe their affective immediacy in part to the flourishing genre of child painting and its subgenre, the scene of education.[13] The most important painter of education pictures in England before 1850 was the Irish-born William Mulready, whose distinctive and often disturbing images of the playground can be traced back to his early association with William Godwin.[14] Mulready's paintings 'stressed the role of social example in the education of the child' (Pointon, 1986, p. 108), characteristically balancing the benefits of formal education and social interaction (Pointon, 1986, p. 129). These paintings – The Fight Interrupted (1815–16), A Sailing Match (1831/1833), The Last In (1835), and many others – anticipate the emphasis in Dickens's fiction on social experience which culminates in the great novels of education, David Copperfield and Great Expectations.

Unlike Dickens's fiction, though, Mulready's paintings seem almost wilfully to ignore topical social issues. His only depiction of mendicancy – Train Up a Child in the Way He Should Go, and When He Is Old He Will Not Depart from It (1841; see Figure 5.1) – deals not with the English poor, but with three lascar sailors begging off two women and a child against a vague picturesque backdrop. Mulready has been criticized, like Mrs Jellyby, for 'concentrating on these exotic subjects' while ignoring 'the plight of the everyday English poor' (Heleniak, 1980, p. 102).[15] But viewed in the context of the pervasive analogy between primitive races and the indigent, this painting's universalist fable of education and charity gives way to other fables; those of an imaginary Orient and an imaginary poor.

5.1 William Mulready, *Train Up a Child in the Way He Should Go, and When He Is Old He Will Not Depart from It.* Oil on panel, 25¼" × 30½"

When first exhibited at the Royal Academy *The Art-Union* found the subject of *Train Up a Child* disagreeable and 'not easily intelligible':

> We supposed the scene to be laid in Italy; and the wayside beggars to be a trio of bandits, watching for their prey; and marvelled, therefore, why it was that the fair young maidens did not 'make off' as rapidly as their delicate limbs could bear them – following the example of the little boy in their company, who, though he seems a stout lad, shrinks back with instinctive dread from contact with the rascal-looking fellows who are asking charity. The subject is unfortunately chosen; we venture to assert that not one person out of twenty who examine it, will comprehend that the painter designed to picture three weather-beaten Lascars making their 'salam' to the gentle ladies who offer them relief. (*The Art-Union*, 1841, p. 77)[16]

Marcia Pointon contends that *Train Up a Child* encouraged 'mis-recognition of its subject' (Pointon, 1986, p. 126), by veering between 'sets of conventions that invoke the non-temporal, the permanent and the true' (Pointon, 1986, p. 126) and topical images of lascars; and by providing 'for Mulready by displacement the possibility of working on a representation of those dominated and impoverished Irish which for reasons psychological and political he could not overtly or consciously address' (Pointon, 1986, p. 125). The conspicuous presence of abandoned East India Company sailors in England at this time – the subject of considerable discussion, as Visram (1986, pp. 48–9) and Pointon (1986, pp. 121–5) have shown – intrudes the conventions of social realism into an image which otherwise draws upon an iconographic tradition in which exotic beggars are expected to be gypsies or Italian *banditti*. This unexpected introduction of the social mode was every bit as troubling to the picture's early reviewers as the implied infiltration of exotic races into England. The lascars were unintelligible precisely because they were at once incidental figures in a moral allegory of English upbringing, colonial subjects in an allegory of 'imperial beneficence' inexplicably played out 'on English rural soil' (Heleniak, 1980, p. 100), and allegories of the reform ideal.

These uneasy shifts become more obvious if we compare *Train Up a Child* not with its usual companion piece, the unfinished *The Toyseller* (1857–63),[17] but with Mulready's small drawing of a chimney sweep (see Figure 5.2). In this sketch, which repeats the motif of the child's outstretched hand and the arrangement of groups of black and white figures, the social subtext of *Train Up a Child* becomes patent, while overlaying the boys' irritation and disgust at the sweep with broad hints of racial revulsion. They recoil at the infectiousness of poverty, which represents a profound threat to the moral and bodily uprightness of English boyhood. The nervous boy in *Train Up a Child* likewise betrays

5.2   William Mulready, *Chimney Sweep*. Pen and brown ink, $2^{3}/_{4}$" × $2^{1}/_{2}$"

a hint of aggression in his tentative approach. Trained up in the way he
should go, he will surely outgrow his dismay and come into the authority that is present already in his rigid, almost martial, body. His anxiety
is evidence of a developmental stage; it is a part of his education.
Indeed, this little group, protected from their antagonists by the *cordon
sanitaire* of the conspicuous wedding ring, do not look worried at all, as
the decidedly unruffled attitude of the dog suggests. The family group
are composed as if completely self-contained, and as if the beggars are
simply a happy opportunity for an impromptu lesson. That lesson is
also implied in the title: if a boy is taught industriousness and charity he
will be secure from poverty, a virulent affliction that sinks its victims in
abjection, indolence and submissiveness, and, once caught, can reduce
him to a creature essentially non-English. But like the 'not easily intelli-

gible' narrative, and like the middle classes in dread of the cholera their money could cure, his hand is suspended between competing impulses. Resolute in his role of alms-giver but watchful of the corrupting touch, he embodies the fortitude and pragmatism of the architects of reform and the future architects of empire. It is all the more remarkable, then, that a picture so ideologically precarious was so successful as an expression of the national idea in the 1850s and 1860s, when the myth of a coherent English vernacular tradition was being so vigorously promoted.[18] Clearly, with growing economic prosperity and an increasingly expansive outlook, it came to describe a safe pastoral space from which virtually all social meaning could be excluded, and in which myths of social order and racial hierarchy were protected from local insurrections and rebellions in the colonies, and protected from the painting's own confused memories of reform ideology and interracial encounter.

Just such a space – part pastoral, part social allegory, part imaginary Orient – was created by Thomas de Quincey in *The Confessions of an English Opium Eater*, to which *Train Up a Child* clearly alludes. The 'little incident' of the visiting Malay in the *Confessions* describes a benign sailor arriving, as it were, from nowhere: 'What business a Malay could have to transact amongst English mountains, I cannot conjecture,' de Quincey writes, 'but possibly he was on his road to a sea-port about forty miles distant' (De Quincey, 1971, p. 90). His description of this incident is pointedly pictorial, a kind of embedded tableau in which time seems almost suspended:

> In a cottage kitchen, but panelled on the wall with dark wood that from age and rubbing resembled oak ... stood the Malay ... he had placed himself nearer to the girl than she seemed to relish; though her native spirit of mountain intrepidity contended with the feeling of simple awe which her countenance expressed as she gazed upon the tiger-cat before her. And a more striking picture there could not be imagined, than the beautiful English face of the girl, and its exquisite fairness, together with her erect and independent attitude, contrasted with the sallow and bilious skin of the Malay, enamelled or veneered with mahogany, by marine air, his small, fierce, restless eyes, thin lips, slavish gestures and adorations. Half-hidden by the ferocious looking Malay, was a little child from a neighbouring cottage who ... was now in the act of reverting its head, and gazing upwards at the turban and the fiery eyes beneath it, whilst with one hand he caught at the dress of the young woman for protection. (De Quincey, 1971, pp. 90–1)

This Malay later returns as the 'fearful enemy' of de Quincey's extravagant and violent laudanum visions of the Orient; but worse, he brings 'other Malays with him worse than himself, that ran "a-muck"' (De Quincey, 1971, p. 92). John Barrell has pointed to the displacement in de Quincey of 'the "mass society" of the industrial nations, and an idea of Asia as "*swarming* with *human* life" – with human beings who are evoked only to be dehumanised' (Barrell, 1991, p. 5), and in *Train Up a Child* Mulready also channels the threat of spreading working-class agitations in the late 1830s and early 1840s into a portentous scene of pastoral visitants. Like the Malay, these lascars will return in later popular imagery of the 1857 Indian Mutiny as rampaging sepoys, demonically white-eyed and triumphantly usurping the place of Mulready's thrusting child. And as Lillian Nayder has shown, Dickens's direct response to these flagrant defilements of English homes, women and children, 'The Perils of Certain English Prisoners' (1857), was a tale as much about 'working class *ressentiment*' as racial conflict (Nayder, 1992, p. 693).

But in *Edwin Drood* social alienation and working-class revolution is a distant memory eclipsed by nostalgia for the great enterprise of middle-class reform which, as Patrick Brantlinger (1977) has established, had weakened considerably as a political force after 1850. In this novel, the self-reliance and boundless energy of Samuel Smiles's exemplary autodidacts and engineers of the mid-century is replaced by the futile labours of a half-caste and the pompous self-importance of a boy going 'to wake up Egypt a little' (Dickens, 1985, p. 96). *Drood* signals its distant provenance in the social novel by opening upon that most familiar of Dickensian spaces, 'the meanest and closest of small rooms',[19] but this is no longer the reassuring space at the heart of the labyrinth of London. It is a volatile material world, vulnerable to neurological flukes and pathologically unfixing of space, time and identity. The destitute opium den with its broken bedstead could be Jacob's Island or Tom-all-Alone's – it is the province of Chadwick and Mayhew – except that it instantaneously dissolves into a provincial cathedral spire and an exotic scene of a Sultan's procession. In Jasper's vision Dickens 'touches the key note' of the novel: its alarming social and racial displacements. In this room the sentimental contrast between a starving, neglected, uneducated poor and John Chinaman or Mrs Jellyby's distant Borrioboolans – the stridently asserted division between a socialized self and a racialized other in *Bleak House* – no longer makes sense. The Orient has found its way to England, most obviously in the persons of Helena and Neville (hell and the devil to the natives of Cloisterham), in Jasper's association with the Hindu Thuggee cult, and in the related prehistories of the main protagonists and their families in Egypt.[20] But the novel also depicts an England already profoundly marked by an entrenched culture of imperialism – complacently superior, predatory, violent and, ironically, already profoundly orientalized – against which the fortunes of Edwin Drood, Neville Landless and John Jasper are cast.

Cloisterham itself is the epitome of this paradox. The 'purest Jackass' in the town (Dickens, 1985, p. 62), the xenophobic Sapsea, would 'reduce to a smashed condition all other islands but this island' (Dickens, 1985, p. 147). He is Cloisterham's representative example of what Dickens had called 20 years earlier 'the true Tory spirit' that 'would have made a China of England, if it could' (Stone, 1969, p. 322). Cloisterham harbours this Tory spirit like an Oriental enclave within England's growing expansionist ambitions: 'A drowsy city, ... all its changes lie behind it, and ... there are no more to come' (Dickens, 1985, p. 51). It is understandable, then, that in this backward place extreme xenophobia should mingle with anachronistic Enlightenment ideals of the noble savage, ideals ridiculed by Dickens in an extraordinary attack in *Household Words* (Dickens, 1853). When Neville is accused of murdering Edwin, stories circulate of his 'vindictive and violent nature': before coming to England 'he had caused to be whipped sundry "Natives" – nomadic persons, encamping now in Asia, now in Africa, now in the West Indies, and now at the North Pole – vaguely supposed in Cloisterham to be always black [and] always of great virtue' (Dickens, 1985, p. 198). But the Cloisterham gossips are themselves described like mad Malays, beating up 'the wildest frenzy and fatuity of evil report' (Dickens, 1985, p. 198).

Another unexpected Malay materializes in the town in the shape of the bellicose philanthropist Honeythunder, who coerces new subscribers to his Haven of Philanthropy by ferociously claiming brotherhood with them, ironically appropriating the abolitionist slogan in the process: 'whether you like it or not ... I am your brother' (Dickens, 1985, p. 84). When the gentleman amateur boxer and 'unprofessional philanthropist' Crisparkle engages him in a violent verbal bout, the mild minor canon accuses Professors of Philanthropy of running amuck 'like so many mad Malays' (Dickens, 1985, p. 207). This epithet lends Honeythunder's berserk denunciations a distinctly un-English complexion, complicating the novel's racial tensions by alluding, as Suvendrini Perera points out, to the still-topical rhetoric of the Governor Eyre controversy of 1865 (Perera, 1990, pp. 115–16).

Many of the virtuous characters in the novel also participate in the confusion of English and un-English, private and public, domestic and imperial. It is signified in the ambiguous colour coding of the browner than brown-faced Tartar, white below his shirt, and the whiter than white-haired Datchery, with his black eyebrows. The knightly Grewgious, too, ostensibly one of Dickens's innocent bachelors, conceals an air of ruthless self-possession more typical of the imperial big-game hunter. Indeed, the 'passion *for hunting something*' which, as Dickens declared in *Oliver Twist*, is 'deeply implanted in the human breast' (Dickens,

1982, p. 61), is dominant in *Edwin Drood*. Grewgious coolly fells his victim Jasper (another hunter, with gunsights for eyes [Dickens, 1985, p. 152]), rendering him 'nothing but a heap of torn and miry clothes' (Dickens, 1985, p. 192), skinned like a trophy from the jungle and laid before the fire.

By contrast, the dark Helena Landless, though she 'came into the world with the same dispositions' as her twin brother, and passed her 'younger days surrounded by the same adverse circumstances' (Dickens, 1985, p. 130) is instantly assimilated into the novel's informing idea of Englishness. There is 'a slumbering gleam of fire' in her eyes, but they are 'softened with compassion and admiration' (Dickens, 1985, p. 96), transforming her into a Dickensian paragon of homely virtue remade for the public school ethos of Cloisterham and empire: a kind of Amy Dorrit for the 1870s. In Ceylon, where as Charles Dilke discovered, it was safe to 'set down everybody that was womanly as a man, and everybody that was manly as a woman' (Dilke, 1985, p. 168), Helena dressed as a boy and showed the 'daring of a man' (Dickens, 1985, p. 90), but in Cloisterham she is automatically set down as one of Mrs Ellis's women of England. She effortlessly transcends the anguished posturing of her brother and the agonistic, 'boysy' world of the novel. Her role (as his twin) is simply to show Neville a version of himself made English, reinforcing the novel's persistent association of privacy, domesticity, femininity and national character.[21]

Under Helena's influence, and with Crisparkle's patronage, the eager new fag from the colonies is to be rehabilitated into the class system via a brisk Christian socialist regime, and, until Edwin Drood disappears, Neville seems set to succeed. But things do not go well, for his dark passion sets him apart from his own cool English blood, an other to himself. Both the hunter and the hunted (Dickens, 1985, p. 85), he displays erratically the aggression and disgust of the colonial administrator, and the cowed and embittered civility of the colonized race. Trying to explain himself to his patron, Neville attributes this volatile temper to the perverted ingenuity of his autocratic stepfather, whose strong hand held him down. But he also fears that he may have 'contracted some affinity' with the natives of Ceylon, 'abject and servile dependants, of an inferior race … "Sometimes, I don't know but that it may be a drop of what is tigerish in their blood"' (Dickens, 1985, p. 90). A drop of blood: Neville's explanation merges the rhetoric of social contagion and miscegenation, recalling the 'drop of Tom's corrupted blood' in *Bleak House* and Carlyle's dying Irish widow in *Past and Present* who proves her sisterhood by spreading typhus. But Crisparkle will not accept this explanation. Ironically, he follows Honeythunder in identifying Neville's problem as 'defective education' (Dickens, 1985, p. 81), and he sets out to remedy it.

Neville's grim, systematic project of self-reform recalls to us those exemplars of the Dickensian meritocracy, David Copperfield and Pip, and the individualistic model of social change which runs through all of Dickens's work. But Neville is placed in the curious position of having to relearn his nativity, so that his social advancement and the trajectory of his self-knowledge – the conventional materials of the *Bildungsroman* – converge with an enterprise of internal racial unification. The ideal of emotional self-government and social integration which underwrites the English novel of education is finally to be denied to him, however. In purchasing a walking-stick, Neville had decided to emulate Dickens's successful meritocrats; heavy with heterosexual potency and ready to be wielded heroically against injustice, this stick was to have been the sure instrument of his repatriation. But when he is hunted down and escorted back to Cloisterham, and then to London, his confidence deserts him and he becomes paranoid and defensive, like Charlie Hexam in *Our Mutual Friend*. Finding himself next door to Tartar, who is at once the landless sailor and the landed gentleman, Neville can only try to fulfil Macaulay's ambition, expressed in 1835, for an India educated in the Western tradition: 'The languages of Western Europe civilised Russia. I cannot doubt that they will do for the Hindoo what they have done for the Tartar' (Macaulay, 1952, p. 724).

Inevitably, though, Neville is excluded from the myth of the self-made man and is left only with the rather desperate alternative of hiding himself away from the social world with his books, like a dogged autodidact. By connecting these bookish aspirations with his fate as the 'beautiful barbarous captive' locked in a tower away from the sunlight, Dickens reworks the familiar narrative of the primitive who is caught and unsuccessfully civilized, and who sickens and dies. In fact, Dickens supplies a comic counterpoint to this narrative in Stony Durdles's 'sort of a – scheme of a – National Education' (Dickens, 1985, p. 74) for the violent urchin Deputy, with his missiles and his fearsome talisman, 'Widdy widdy wen!'[22] As Durdles explains it, Deputy is 'own brother to Peter the Wild Boy' (Dickens, 1985, p. 73), and like Neville the wild boy, he is given an 'object', something to 'aim' at: the drunken Durdles, who is perpetually moved on, like Jo in *Bleak House*, by this appalling disciplinarian with his truly Benthamite code of surveillance.

Edwin Drood himself is also in many ways reminiscent of a *Bildungsroman* hero about to take the obligatory fall. Like Pip, Edwin is a noticeably indolent 'doer'. In the end, Dickens's enigmatic preliminary note 'Dead? Or alive?' (Dickens, 1985, p. 283) remains unanswered. Instead, the novel, as if recognizing that the culture of the English *Bildungsroman* is passing, suspends its eponymous hero at what suddenly seems a clichéd moment, just as he is about to launch himself into work and society. In the unfinished text, Edwin's fate is linked closely with Neville's; they both end up in a kind of landless space between boyhood and manhood, a space of arrested development, at once Cloisterham and the Orient.

Victorian imperialists and ethnologists often attributed arrested development in savage races with the onset of sexual passion at puberty, so Neville's illicit feelings for Rosa and Edwin's secret attraction to Helena – the novel's most explicit expression of what Robert Young (1995) calls colonial desire – can also be implicated in their suspended youth. But what of Jasper's undisciplined body? Dickens imagined his villain as a moral hybrid, a Jekyll-and-Hyde personality split between the English Lay Precentor with the angelic voice and the devilish Thug. The characteristic 'mixing and compounding' (Dickens, 1985, p. 100) with which he is associated informs his sensational descent into this muddy coloured hybrid, traumatized by his own susceptibility to the 'unclean spirit of imitation' which infects him via the 'spasmodic shoots and darts that break out of [the Princess Puffer's] face and limbs' (Dickens, 1985, p. 39). In many ways Jasper's development is as fatally arrested as the boys'. As static as any of Dickens's villains, he also shows a primitive's 'lack of self-control' (Bryce, 1902, quoted in Bolt, 1971, p. 72) – most conspicuously in his dealings with Rosa and Grewgious – and an Irishman's 'false ingenuity, restlessness, unreason, misery and mockery' (Carlyle, 1969b, p. 138). But confronted with his own reflection in the haggard old English face of a woman 'who has opium-smoked herself into a strange likeness of the Chinaman' (Dickens, 1985, p. 38), he recognizes too the full horror of his social descent. His essential Englishness, his power to remake himself, is threatened by the affinity he has contracted not merely with the East, but with the East End.[23] Like the labouring poor in Chadwick and Kay-Shuttleworth, and like Herbert Spencer's primitives, Jasper is pulled between 'two extreme states' (Dickens, 1985, p. 49) of privation and profligacy. He must 'subdue' himself in what he bitterly calls his vocation: the 'cramped monotony' of his 'daily drudging round' (Dickens, 1985, p. 48). Beneath his idyllic existence, his work is as alienating as that of a machine operator. A 'poor monotonous chorister and grinder of music' (Dickens, 1985, p. 49), he talks like a disaffected factoryhand. Without even Neville's ill-fated promise, Jasper is 'troubled with some stray sort of ambition, aspiration, restlessness, dissatisfaction' (Dickens, 1985, p. 11) which he is powerless to satisfy legitimately. His bitter pronouncement on the Princess Puffer is therefore all the more grimly prophetic of his own lowly prospects: 'What visions can *she* have? ... Visions of many butchers' shops, and public-houses, and much credit? ... What can she rise to, under any quantity of opium, higher than that!' (Dickens, 1985, p. 38). His desperate resistance to this fate is expressed in his fierce grip on the arms of the chair in chapter one, but this ultimately ineffectual gesture only foreshadows the somatic crises which are to come. Prostration, the most telling symptom of Jasper's moral decline, is as suggestive of the two curses of the poor, typhus and indolence, as it is of his feminization and orientalization by opium addiction. Literally unable to remain an upright Englishman, his mesmeric personality works its corruption on the upward training of his youthful charges like the deadly influence of the Irish in Manchester.

Jasper's body, then, only expresses in extremity the crisis of social renovation latent in what is a national crisis of identity.[24] His disgusted cry of 'Unintelligible!' reverberates ironically back across the years, echoing the qualms of Mulready's disquieted critics; across the novel; and across the England of these texts, a place suddenly unintelligible to itself. Implicated in Jasper's deterioration is the enervated national will to social reform so crucial to the rhetorical force of Dickens's fiction; no longer is it possible for him to resort to the rallying strategies of the earlier novels to wake up England a little, and no longer is it possible with any certainty to train up a child in the way he should go. With *Edwin Drood* unfinished, however, this threat of unintelligibility is happily diverted into the superficial mysteries which keep scores of armchair detectives absorbed, anxious, as the novel itself is, to stave off the new world order which awaits imperial and post-imperial Britain, in which Malays wandering among English mountains is not the half of it.

Notes

1. Images of emigration include Ford Madox Brown, *The Last of England* (1855), Richard Redgrave, *The Emigrants' Last Sight of Home* (1859), and Thomas Faed, *The Last of the Clan* (1865). For images of education, see note 13 below.
2. See Dickens's 'A Bundle of Emigrants' Letters', *Household Words* 1, 30 March 1850; and the scenes of farewell in *David Copperfield*.
3. For more general discussions of this imperative, see, for example, Said (1994), Spivak (1986), and Perera (1990).
4. British rule in Ceylon began in 1796.
5. Many early critics of the novel likened Cloisterham to Trollope's Barchester: see Collins (1971) pp. 542–3. Septimus Crisparkle's name also recalls the Minor Canon of Barchester, Septimus Harding.
6. Perera (1990) describes it as a turning point in Victorian fiction, after which empire is no longer 'a suggestive hidden presence' but 'an explicit force' (p. 122).
7. On the problem of 'doing' in Dickens, see Yeazell (1991).
8. On Indian education see McCully (1966).

9. The 'metropole-colony relationship is essentially the same as that between capital and labor' (JanMohamed, 1983, p. 2).

10. 'Debased alike by ignorance and pauperism, [the labourers] have discovered, with the savage, what is the minimum of the means of life, upon which existence may be prolonged. The paucity of the amount of means and comforts *necessary for the mere support of life*, is not known by a more civilized population, and this secret has been taught the labourers of this country by the Irish' (Kay-Shuttleworth, 1973, p. 6).

11. On the representation of the Irish in Victorian England, see Curtis (1971).

12. See Collins (1964) especially pp. 70–97 and 209–21.

13. *Kit's First Writing Lesson* was exhibited by Robert Braithwaite Martineau at the 1852 Royal Academy. Other images include Thomas Brooks, *The Captured Truant* (1854); Alfred Rankley, *The Village School* (1855); and William Bromley, *The Schoolroom* (1863).

14. Mulready illustrated Godwin's *Fables Ancient and Modern* (1805) and many other children's books. See also Pointon (1986) pp. 102–21. Godwin also published an exemplary story of Mulready's youth, *The Looking Glass: A True History of the Early Years of an Artist* (1805).

15. Cf. Pointon (1986) p. 99ff.

16. Pointon (1986) also notes other misreadings (p. 126).

17. *The Toyseller* depicts a white child in its mother's arms turning away in fear from a black African pedlar who benignly holds up a rattle.

18. See West (1990).

19. On de Quincey's influence, see Herbert (1974), Perera (1990), and Jacobson (1986).

20. On Jasper as probable Thug, see Aylmer (1964), Sedgwick (1985) and Perera (1990). On the prehistories, see Aylmer's complicated speculations on the Droods, Buds and Jaspers.

21. There are compelling similarities between Helena and Neville's relationship and some of Dickens's most successful marriages, especially that of David Copperfield and Agnes Wickfield. In 1854, Dickens published an article about the Eastern custom of betrothed sibling children: 'The Betrothed Children', *Household Words* 10, 124.

22. The Forster Act, a first tentative legislative step towards compulsory national education, became law in 1870.

23. Barry Milligan discusses the Contagious Diseases Act of 1864 and the idea of 'dangerous East End women' in *Edwin Drood* (1995, pp. 94–102).

24. Milligan concludes: 'There seems to be no example in *Edwin Drood* of British identity that is unalloyed with the Orient, and no place where the ubiquitous and insidious Oriental contagion does not pose a threat to British femininity' (1995, p. 109).

CHAPTER SIX

The half-breed as Gothic unnatural[1]

H. L. Malchow

In 1831 there was a meeting in the Town Hall of Calcutta of those members of the Eurasian (or, as they preferred, 'East Indian') community who had petitioned against a rising prejudice toward half-castes, and particularly against their exclusion from military and government office. One of those attending, a Mr J. Welsh, seized upon the obvious irony: 'It is absurd to see our rulers starting at shadows of their own creation' (*Report*, 1831, p. ix). Though unintended no doubt, his image of the half-caste as shadow – as an inescapable, following/pursuing, guilt-inducing, distortion of its creator – has a kind of spectral, Gothic quality. Indeed, the British denial of paternity and responsibility that this so vividly invokes recalls precisely the dilemma confronting Mary Shelley's Frankenstein *vis à vis his* Creation.

Important elements of literary Gothic, tightly woven into racial discourse throughout the nineteenth century, are particularly dense in the language used to describe and define those of mixed blood. For example, in 1845 Walt Whitman's youthful exploration of a mixed-race theme, 'The Half-Breed', portrays a deformed Irish-Red Indian hunchback, malignantly evil but 'not very bright', in language that appears to be lifted almost verbatim from Mary Shelley: 'this strange and hideous creature ... I almost shrieked with horror at the monstrous abortion! ... Scorned and abhorred by man, woman, and child, the half-breed ... fled' (Whitman, 1963, pp. 257–91).[2]

This study explores one aspect of the creation of a popular vocabulary by which racial and cultural difference could be represented as unnatural – a 'racial Gothic' discourse which employed certain striking metaphoric images to filter and give meaning to a flood of experience and information from abroad, but which also thereby recharged itself for an assault on domestic social and physical 'pathology'. Such an exploration sends one back and forth between the imagined world of literature and the 'real' world of historical experience, between literary fiction and what Sander Gilman has called the 'parallel fictions' of the human sciences, of anthropology and biology (Gilman, 1985b, pp. 27–8), between popular representations of the 'unnatural' at home and of those abroad. 'Race', it has become a commonplace to observe, is an inherently fluid idea, with a meaning that, like class or nationality, shifts over time, and seems at once concrete and intangible. Rac*ism* required a 'demonization' (I do not use the word casually here) of difference, and from the late eighteenth century onwards the Gothic literary genre offered a language that could be appropriated in a powerful and obsessively reiterated evocation of terror, disgust and alienation.

Clearly, nineteenth-century racial discourse – with its prurient obsession with torture and cannibalism, sexual exoticism, and miscegenous pollutions – was deeply indebted to the themes and language of popular late-eighteenth and early-nineteenth century domestic Gothic fictions, from Matthew Lewis's *The Monk* down to the salacious pot-boilers of 'James Rymer' and G. M. W. Reynolds in the 1840s. Following David Punter's influential study (Punter, 1980, pp. 1–6), one may define this genre by characteristics that resonate strongly with racial prejudice, imperial exploration and sensational anthropology – themes and images that are meant to shock and terrify, that emphasize chaos and excess, sexual taboo and barbarism, and a style grounded in techniques of suspense and threat. If the archaic settings of many early Gothic romances do not seem to have much significance here (though of course archaism may evoke primitivism), other elements, such as highly stereotyped characters and an insistence on the readable signs of depravity and the demonic concealed in physiognomy, dress and mannerism are strikingly apt. Both the Gothic novel and racist discourse manipulate deeply buried anxieties, both dwell on the chaos beyond natural and rational boundaries, and massage a deep, often unconscious and sexual, fear of contamination, and both present the threatened destruction of the simple and pure by the poisonously exotic, by anarchic forces of passion and appetite, carnal lust and blood-lust. In fact, as the century progressed, there was a mutual exchange – a concurrent gothicization of racial discourse and a racialization of Gothic fiction.

The ground has been well broken in the digging out of such connections, at least with regard to late nineteenth-century fiction and its context of a general *fin-de-siècle* malaise over cultural and sexual identity, empire, race, and nation. In particular, Patrick Brantlinger (1988) and Elaine Showalter (1990), from different perspectives, have fuelled a general re-examination of a literature that Brantlinger has christened 'imperial Gothic'.[3] My debt to this scholarship will be obvious. The themes and texts I search range, however, beyond and beneath the 'imperial Gothic' fiction of Haggard, Kipling and Stevenson, and the chronological limits of the *fin-de-siècle*. In fact, it may be that the excellence of a decade or so of scholarship on this period has somewhat overburdened it as *the* critical era of crisis.

The racial and sexual cross-boundary confusions implicit in the idea of 'the half-breed', the problem of secret identities betrayed by readable signs of difference, of fated, unstable natures torn between two worlds, of a violent contradictory combination of opposites – of villain and victim, masculine and feminine – makes the mixed race as constructed in nineteenth-century British popular culture an *essentially* Gothic type. It acquires what it did not commonly possess in eighteenth-century Britain – a close affinity with such fictional monsters torn between antithetical worlds as vampires and werewolves. There was, in fact, a progressive gothicization of the half-breed over the course of the nineteenth century, ending in a pre-war representation of the dangers of 'bad blood' and cultural-cum-racial pollution as a kind of threatened vampirism.

My object here is not to engage the reality of mixed-raced culture beyond Europe, but to examine the representation of the half-breed, half-caste, or mulatto in popular science, the press and literature. The idea of the half-breed as unnatural is of course an arbitrary construction of the imagination in an era that saw race and nationality emerge as the essential qualities of European identity. Earlier there had prevailed a more sanguine opinion, common at the beginning of the century, that traces of blackness were likely to disappear over time into the larger pool of more vigorous European blood. The half-breed had been often viewed sympathetically not as a racial danger to whites, but as a superior – and useful – class of black or, alternatively, as an object of sympathy, a 'victim of class and colour', unfairly rejected, martyred, by both worlds. Either way the half-breed was here the true inheritor of the image of the passive ex-slave crafted by the evangelical abolitionist. An eternal victim raised from the bestial, not merely by evangelical exhortation, by the blood of the lamb, but by the actual blood of the white paternalist. One can still see this sentimental, sympathetic mode of representation at mid-century in Mayne Reid's novels *The Quadroon* (1856), *Oçeola* (1859), or *The Wild Huntress* (1861).

But a double process was already under way by which the 'pure-blood' non-white became romanticized and safely relegated to the past as a vanishing Mohican or to the reservation or kraal, while it is the half-breed who becomes the threatening creature of the boundary between white and non-white, a living sign, an emblem of shame. Either innocent and sympathetic or deformed and demonic, they were visible reminders of what came to be felt as a white fall from grace, a perpetual witness against the weak or dissolute natures that created man. As the French missionaries in southern Africa, Arbousset and Daumas, declared in 1846: 'wherever Europeans have carried their civilization and their industry, there they have also carried their vices ... In every country colonized by Europeans we find a mixed race, – a living testimony to the sin of their fathers' (Arbousset and Daumas, 1846, p. 9). While such an observation draws from a well-established Christian moral discourse on bastardy, it takes on added force in the context of the developing reification of 'race' and the presumed boundaries of biological affinity. Such a heightened sense of the sexual 'unnaturalness' of interracial union especially resonates with the language generated in the mid-nineteenth century to stigmatize other sexual misconduct – like masturbation and sodomy – as 'acts' of social and biological as well as moral 'degradation'.

Where, earlier, liaisons abroad with native women among traders, officials and military men had often been blessed by marriage or at least a customary social approval and even official encouragement, by the early nineteenth century, Ronald Hyam has argued, racial inter*marriage* in much of the British Empire 'was virtually at an end' (Hyam, 1990, p. 201). It was assaulted by Protestant missionaries, the growing number of memsahib, and an officialdom that needed to displace the half-caste in order to find jobs for the superfluous sons of the English middling and upper classes. 'Instead of stable unions, native women were reduced to the status of temporary mistresses and even prostitutes' (Hyam, 1990, p. 98), and their progeny, the half-breed, took on the added stigma of the prostitute's bastard.

It will be clear that language employed to define interracial genealogy inevitably also fixes a certain negative reading of individual character. The progeny of parents of different 'races' – already arbitrary abstractions – becomes not merely something different, but are themselves confined by the very words used to name them. The terms 'half-breed' and 'half-caste' are double, hyphenated constructions resonating with other linguistic inadequacies and incompletes – with 'half-wit' or 'half-dead', with 'half-naked' or 'half-truth', and of course with 'half-civilized'. The half-breed is, by the word that defines him or her, not a true or authentic being, not a member of a 'race' for which there is a word. In this may lie some explanation of the long and insistent effort to deny the fertility of the mulatto, the full ability of the half-breed to replicate his or her self, for a shadow cannot cast a shadow.

One might note in passing that this odd insistence on the infertility of the human 'hybrid' resonates strongly with a charge laid against the homosexual in modern European culture – that such unions were unproductive and therefore, especially in a world dominated by the language of political economy and the reproductive imperatives of the financial and industrial system, by definition unnatural, inefficient and fated. There was inevitably a back-and-forth dialogue between domestic and imperial stereotype. If at mid-century the mulatto male was often represented as inherently effeminate, Edward Carpenter could later write of European homosexuals as 'half-breeds' of the Inner Self (Somerville, 1994, p. 259).

It is clear, to employ the analysis popularized by Elaine Showalter, that domestic, middle-class fears of uncontrolled sexuality and the violation of the boundaries of class and gender played an important role in shaping a negative image of the half-breed. But social and political changes in the empire also served to marginalize and devalue those of mixed race parentage – earlier the natural 'collaborating class' in an expanding imperial enterprise. This clearly encouraged the evolution of a less-favourable reading of the half-breed, not as an improved (and useful) species but as a curious, unstable and inconvenient, perhaps dangerous, anomaly.

In 1864 the French anthropologist Paul Broca's loose and impressionistic speculations on human hybridity were published in London under the aegis of the Anthropological Society. *On the Phenomena of Hybridity in the Genus Homo* owes perhaps as much to Gobineau as to Darwin, but its use of animal analogy locates it within an evolutionary discourse that approached the study of variation in mankind through the lower animal world. In Broca's view, half-breeds ('mongrels') were a 'eugenesic' type, that is, though able to reproduce, they were marked by a diminished degree of fertility. This biological shortcoming serves to confirm a 'common knowledge' of the moral, intellectual, and physical failings of the half-breed that Broca cites: a lack of 'vigour or moral energy', and a tendency to produce 'stammerers, [the] blind, hunchbacks, and idiots' as well as criminals (Broca, 1864, pp. 6, 29, 30–40). It will be evident here how closely his language parallels that often used to describe the effect of habitual masturbation. The masturbator and, at one remove, the half-breed are both suffering from the physiological effects of a shameful and unnatural sexual indulgence.

Broca's favourite eugenesic parallel in the animal world was, significantly, the cross between a dog and a wolf. It will be seen that this depends at least as much on an implied character analogy as it does on a biological parallel. The dog is an owned and mastered thing, fawning, loyal and grateful; the wolf is a red-eyed savage and threatening creature of folk-myth, and the cross is suggestive, not of a tamed wolf but of a demonized dog. The wolf or half-wolf became, in fact, a common trope for the threatening half-breed in the nineteenth century, just as the earlier image of mule (mulatto) had been appropriate to a slave-labour society.

The negative image, in late Victorian popular culture, of the half-breed also draws from an older tradition in which the mixed-race person was often represented as an ambivalent creature torn between different cultures and loyalties, an outcast, a misfit – as well as, latterly, a biological unnatural. In the colonial empire he or she had long been an object of condescension, when loyal and useful, and of fear and hatred when rebellious. After mid-century whatever positive aspects of representation there may have been are in fact overwhelmed by a growing sense of, first, the effeminate inadequacy of the half-breed or half-caste as intermediary and facilitator of colonial rule (as dramatically proved to be the case in India in 1857). Elsewhere, as among the Jamaican mulattos or the *métis* in Canada, concern for the unstable race-loyalty of the half-breed comes to predominate – that is, a fear of his 'reversion' to the dangerous side of his nature. After mid-century stories of rebellion in whatever imperial theatre – in Africa, Asia, the South Pacific or America – frequently carry a subtext of half-breed disloyalty. They are figures of disorder and opportunism, no longer useful tools in the spread of British rule and culture but, at best, marginal and irrelevant, and at worst dangerous instruments of pollution and subversion.

Eight years after the Indian Mutiny an 'uprising' of blacks confined largely to the parish of St Thomas-in-the-East in Jamaica triggered a savage campaign of retribution throughout the island. Fuelled by Governor Eyre's own exaggerated dispatches English newspapers dwelt on the horrors with a gory, *anatomical* detail reminiscent of their Gothic reportage of, say, the Cawnpore massacre during the Indian rebellion. But where the Eurasian community in India had been portrayed as loyal, if largely ineffective, the Jamaican mulatto received a more ambiguous reading. As in the Reconstruction South in America, in post-abolition Jamaica there were mulatto 'rogues' whose allegiance seemed to be shifting from white to black, who saw themselves as advocates of the rights of the freed slave and looked to become leaders of the majority mixed-race and Negro community. Prominent among these in Jamaica was the self-taught illegitimate mulatto, George William Gordon – the son of a white planter and a Negro slave, who was himself married to an Irish woman. And it is Gordon, summarily hanged by Governor Eyre as the diabolical instigator of atrocity, whom the press first seized upon in their lurid accounts of massacre and torture.[4]

Though, as in India, property-owning, respectable mixed-race people rushed to affirm their loyalty to the white establishment during the crisis, public attention was inevitably focused on Gordon as *mulatto* trouble-maker[5] and, as he was himself a propertied (if self-made) member of the House of Assembly, as class traitor as well. Gordon had long been a thorn in the governor's side, and Eyre took advantage of the violence in St Thomas's hastily to seize, prosecute and execute him as 'the chief cause and origin of the whole rebellion' (*The Times*, 20

November 1865). Before Gordon's cause was taken up by Exeter Hall (he was also a lay Baptist preacher), correspondents from Jamaica and the English press that reproduced them simply echoed Eyre's representation of Gordon's 'deep-dyed wickedness'.

What is of interest is the way these reports commonly turn from Gordon's undoubted political radicalism to what they construct as Gordon's *secret* character. In this, his presumed 'hypocrisy' – in serving the Crown as legislator and magistrate while fomenting treason, in preaching love within his Baptist chapel while inspiring race hatred outside, and in enjoying his own wealth and comparative privilege while encouraging the propertyless to seize the wealth of others – is explained by invoking a deep contradiction in his inherent character: 'Mr. G W Gordon,' *The Times* reported, 'was a singular compound of opposites ... Such a mixture of strange contradictions leads to a suspicion that he could not have been a man of sound mind' (16 December 1865). It is clear that the buried message here goes beyond speculation about Gordon's own aberrant psychology. It draws directly from, and helps reinforce, the common image of the unstable, contradictory mind and character of the half-breed generally. Five years after Gordon was hanged in Jamaica, another half-breed rebel, Louis Riel, the mixed blood (French Canadian, Red Indian and Irish) leader of the Red River *métis* in western Canada, was presented in strikingly similar terms.

The heated debate in England over Gordon and Riel as either victims or villains conforms to the familiar problem of racial construction, the view of the half-breed generally as both victim and villain, a 'compound of opposites'. The 1860s and 1870s are, however, an important period of transition, a working out of the contradiction in which the light-skinned mulatto or half-breed collapses into his or her blackness or otherness – often allowing the full play of Gothic stereotype without the restraining element of the half-breed as near-white. This seems to happen in the evolution of Louis Riel's image in the English-language press. When he reappears in his fated, quasi-farcical second rebellion, Riel has floated free from his role as the spokesman for the *métis*, in any event a failed and unstable community and, instead, like Dr Jekyll, has declined into the more primitive side of his own duality. His character has shifted from one side of his double nature to the other, and his campaign appears as hopeless and as primitive as that of the dying tribes of plains Indians with whom he is now identified. According to *The Times*, 'Half-Indian in blood', Riel has become 'wholly Indian in character and sympathies ... one of themselves'. When captured, Riel had 'let his hair grow long, and is dressed more shabbily than most half-breeds'. He was 'beyond hope of mercy' and, *The Times* professed to know, had been abandoned by loyal French Canadians as 'wholly Indian' (18 May and 17 November 1885).

In the years following the rebellion in Jamaica, prosecutions of servicemen sent to England for trial and of Eyre himself (1867–68) failed because juries refused, against the instructions of the bench, to indict them. At the same time the case mounted by the defending barristers, well-reported in the metropolitan and local press, kept alive the most lurid details of the early reports of atrocity, the wildly exaggerated stories of murder, rape, and mutilation, and of Gordon's probable culpability. It was in this context that the issue of the character of the mulatto generally, and in the Caribbean in particular, was taken up in the pages of the *Anthropological Review* and elsewhere. Shortly before a grand jury refused, finally, to indict Eyre in June of 1868, Charles Napier Groom, an amateur ethnologist with West Indian connections, read a paper before the Anthropological Society (most of whose members were, of course, strong supporters of the governor) that examined some 40 case studies of 'coloured' (mixed-race) people of West Indian origin. While he detailed an instance or two of 'noble characters', cases of dissipation, disease and immorality were 'far more common' (Groom, 1868, p. lvii).

Groom's most colourful example, the centrepiece of his presentation, was an educated young man who had become a successful West Indian merchant (Gordon had made his money as a merchant). This 'child of quadroons' was 'vain and proud', 'addicted to display and frippery', with 'the manners of a French hairdresser or man-milliner' (Groom, 1868, p. lvii). As often in the literature of the half-breed, the mulatto is depicted as living a double life, an inherent hypocrisy.[6] He seems respectable but only his careful concealment, his 'prudence', prevents public scandal.

Groom leaves little doubt about the particular secret immorality that parallels the mulatto's racial unnaturalness: 'Like coloured men in general he is more than half a woman, without the tenderness and chasteness which becomes the better examples of European females.' Reproducing a discourse familiar in African exploration literature, that of black gender reversal, he completes the image by observing that the mulatto women he has observed 'have strong passions which in Europe are characteristic of the male sex' (Groom, 1868, p. lvii). Finally, there is significance in the fact that both Groom and the commentators on his paper dwell on a presumed predilection of the mulatto for the crime of forgery. This deceit, the attempt to 'pass' bad checks, of course suggests the light-skinned Negro's attempt to 'pass' as white, as it does generally the half-breed character as a kind of biological fraud. In the context of Groom's portrayal of the man-milliner merchant it also suggests the effeminate man, white or black, as a kind of self-forgery.

It will be clear that the image of the half-breed, like that of the cannibal, beginning as largely an act of imagination, took on confirming, corroborating reality in popular readings of imperial events in the nineteenth century. Mixed-race people were freed from their special places on the red map of empire, invested by means of a spurious empiricism with a common character, and as powerfully reified abstractions were then drawn back into the world of literary fantasy, to Patrick Brantlinger's 'imperial Gothic' that flourished in the 1880s and 1890s.

To return to the Eurasians of the Raj with whom we began, to the 'shadows of their own creation' whom the British found loyal but inadequate in the crisis of the Mutiny, here too more densely negative representations characterize the end of the century. Not only in the familiar Kipling stories but also in a whole range of sensational/popular fictions of the time 'miscegenation' is a reiterated theme in which its monstrous product, the half-breed, becomes both a symbolic and physical threat to empire and race. And so to the 'parallel fictions' of ethnology. In 1898 Edgar Thurston (Superintendent of the Madras Government Museum) compared a sample of poor Eurasians unfavourably with the physique of the 'average Sepoy' (Thurston, 1898a, pp. 69–114). The badly nourished pauper half-castes he examined were (not surprisingly) thin-chested. He also noted something else: 'The Eurasian body being enveloped in clothes, it was not til they stripped before me, for the purpose of anthropometry, that I became aware how prevalent is the practice of tattooing among the male members of the community.'[7] And there was yet another 'sign' of difference. The dark colour of their 'pudenda' was 'very conspicuous in many cases which came under observation' (Thurston, 1898a, pp. 78–9). These 'observations' are of course packed with meaning; from beneath his or her European clothes the half-caste emerges, not as a near-European, but as a secret 'other'.

And so by the end of the century the Eurasian as impotent victim (the dominant mid-century image, which itself had replaced that of the Eurasian as, like the men of Skinner's Horse, imperial assets) yielded to a *fin-de-siècle* Eurasian as either despicable parvenu – vulgar and sycophantic – or (like Gordon and Riel) treacherous and an unstable threat, prone to contradiction, disguise and secret vices, to feminine hysteria and a vengeful sense of grievance. A violent tale published in 1913 by Henry Bruce, historical biographer and sensational minor novelist, graphically illustrates this latter, Gothic style.[8]

The Eurasian is the story of a half-caste clerk, Robert Slow, who is obsessed by his belief that he is the illegitimate son of the province's governor. He is a 'weakling', unmanly, 'the truest sort of Eurasian', and the District Collector, Mr Atkins, vainly tries to discourage Slow's intended bride, the English servant-girl Cherry, from making a tragic mistake:

> Because he hasn't a chance in nature, my girl! Because he connects
> with a world full of corruptions and of obscure dangers, which is
> antipathetic to ours! Because, in short, he's a Eurasian, a mixture!
> ... The Eurasian as such is a man of streaks, all striped, like a
> barber's pole. He's not a whole man. Many mixtures are good, but
> not this one. The only certainty about a Eurasian is his uncertainty.
> (Bruce, 1913, pp. 90, 206)

Though he marries Cherry, Slow gradually and fatally declines into the
Hindu half of his nature, and what respectability he has in his junior
post is destroyed, not only by his resentful illusion of upper-class parentage, but by a 'secret vice'. He becomes a 'ganja fiend' and, having
given up wearing boots, he was 'no longer the man of streaks, the
striped barber's pole ... He was an Indian now' (Bruce, 1913, p. 234).
For Cherry, the white woman who abandoned her own kind, there can
only be a miserable entrapment among people she despises. She has a
'puny', 'yellow' daughter who 'would perpetuate the faults, and the
grotesque weaknesses, of its father. There was no escaping the doom of
mixed blood.' Her 'little alien eyes ... were pools of shadow' (Bruce,
1913, pp. 243–5).[9]

Bruce's conclusion returns to the familiar Victorian theme of the
ultimate instability of the half-caste and his suspect loyalties, but focused by the contemporary *fin-de-siècle* obsession with European decline and loss of empire. Robert Slow's self-destructive rage at his own
fantasized dispossession, his constitutional and emotional weaknesses
and, finally, his Asiatic abandonment to narcotic illusion draw him into
a Hindu conspiracy to 'bring down the Empire'. Now thoroughly Indian, disguised in a long white cloth and 'crazed' with ganja, he assassi-
nates the Governor of the Northern Provinces, as he thought, his white
father – stabbing him 'deep in at the throat, twisting [the blade] round
savagely several times' (Bruce, 1913, p. 320).

Notes

1. The material in this chapter will appear in *Shadows of their own Creation:
   Gothic Images of Race in Nineteenth-Century Britain*, by Howard L.
   Malchow, forthcoming from Stanford University Press. No portion of this
   text may be reproduced without the express permission of the publisher.
2. For racial imagery in *Frankenstein* itself, see Malchow (1993) pp. 90–130.
3. Also see Arata (1990) and McBratney (1990) and (1992).
4. The best treatment of the Jamaican rebellion and its aftermath in England
   is still that of Semmel (1962).
5. Carlyle, no friend of the Negro in Jamaica, called Gordon an 'incendiary
   mulatto' and a 'half-brutish type' (quoted in Semmel, 1962, pp. 106–7).
6. Even a scholar like the French anthropologist Quatrefages who, unlike

Broca, took a strongly positive view of the physical and mental characteristics of mixed-race people, contrasted these merits with contradictory vices: the half-breed is 'almost everywhere indolent, passionate, and addicted to gaming, *always ready to foment civil discord*' [emphasis mine] (Quatrefages, 1869, p. 24).

7. Significantly, perhaps, the professional tattooers whom Thurston interviewed were females, and of a gypsy-like tribe notorious, he claims, for robbing and begging. The first woman he questioned 'arrived in a state of maudlin intoxication' (Thurston, 1898b, pp. 115–18).

8. Bruce began his literary career in the early 1890s with biographical studies drawn from American history (a *Life of General Ogelthorpe* [1890] and a *Life of General Houston 1793–1863* [1891]). In the Edwardian period he followed a visit of some months to India with a travel memoir (*Letters from Malabar and on the Way* [1909]), and subsequently turned to writing highly sensational novels, mostly about the Raj (*The Native Wife; or, Indian Love and Anarchism. A Novel* [1909]; *The Residency. An Indian Novel* [1914]; *The Song of Surrender. An Indian Novel* [1915]; *The Temple Girl. An Indian Story* [1919]; *Bride of Shive* [1920]).

9. In Kipling's well-known tale of miscegenation, 'Without Benefit of Clergy' (1890), the 'impossibility' of such race-mixing is confirmed in the death of both native mother and half-caste child, and the washing away of their mud-brick house by an angry deluge.

CHAPTER SEVEN

The colonized in the colonies: representation of Celts in Victorian battle painting

Joseph A. Kestner

In *Be a Man! Males in Modern Society*, Peter Stearns (1990, p. 68) observes that 'for men, the nineteenth century, effectively launched and ended by major wars, was a militant, indeed military century. A greater percentage of European men served in the military, even in peacetime, than ever before'. This militarism was part of what Stearns denominates as the 'self-conscious assertiveness about nineteenth-century masculinity' (Stearns, 1990, p. 78) manifested ,in myriad dimensions of the culture. In Victorian battle painting, *Machtpolitik* intersects with formation of ideologies of masculinity.

In the representation of masculinities in Victorian painting, one of the most prominent elements was the reification of racialist theories of polygenesis. As Biddiss (1979, p. 17) observes, 'confrontation centred on competing ideas of monogenesis and polygenesis', that is, whether 'all mankind ultimately descended from a single union' or whether 'the major races each [had] an independent point of origin'. The effect of polygenist thought was to delineate certain races and/or ethnic groups as inferior in a hierarchical construction of races. 'Prominent among those who fared rather less well were the Celts'; Biddiss affirms: 'Their inferiority to Anglo-Saxon or Teutonic stock was a recurrent theme in much Victorian writing, especially by historians' (Biddiss, 1979, p. 28). Among the anti-Celtic were Thomas Carlyle in *On Heroes, Hero-Worship, and the Heroic in History* (1841), Charles Kingsley in *The Roman and the Teuton* (1864), and 'that Teuton of Teutons, the Celt-hating Dr. [Thomas] Arnold' (Faverty, 1968, p. 76). The representation of Celts in Victorian battle painting constitutes an emphatic manifestation of the paradoxical nature of Victorian racial ideas.

This construction of masculinity is particularly conflicted in the representation of 'the colonized in the colonies', that is, the representation of Scottish and Irish rankers in Victorian battle art. As Stearns (1990, p. 108) notes: 'If we understand masculinity as a constant contradictory struggle rather than just the privileged position within a power disequilibrium, we come closer to a full definition of gender studies.' Kaja Silverman (1992, p. 42) in *Male Subjectivity at the Margins* contends that the 'dominant fiction calls upon the male subject to see himself ... only through the mediation of images of an unimpaired masculinity ... by believing in the commensurability of penis and phallus, actual and symbolic father'. Victorian battle iconography would appear to necessitate the premise of the commensurability of penis and phallus, of possession of the penis with automatic inscription into the symbolic order and the Law of the Father. For males in Victorian England, the ideology of the dominant masculinity posited that to possess the penis inscribed men into positions of power, control and authority. While according to Jacques Lacan (1978, pp. 89, 102–3) neither men nor women possess the phallus – that is isomorphism with the Law of the Father – because males possess the penis it was a functional ideological inference to equate maleness with dominance and superiority.

The act of gazing at the male in artistic representations could empower 'males with assurances of control, affirmation, hierarchy, and [power of] surveillance during the nineteenth century' (Kestner, 1995, pp. 26–7). For example, representations of victories are posited on the assumption of the commensurability of penis with phallus, as in depictions of battles such as Kandahar, Ulundi, or Omdurman. As Silverman (1992, pp. 44–5) contends: 'The phallus/penis equation is promoted by the dominant fiction, and sustained by collective belief ... The dominant fiction offers a seemingly infinite supply of phallic sounds and images within which the male subject can find "himself".' Richard Caton Woodville's *Kandahar* of 1881 (see Figure 7.1) depicts the 92nd Highlanders storming the village of Gundi Mullah Sahibdad during the Second Afghan War on 1 September 1880. Ayub Khan and his army were defeated, with the loss of 2 000 men, while the British lost less than 250 soldiers. Woodville completed this canvas in eight months, surely to reaffirm the symbolic masculine code after the defeat at Maiwand on 27 July in the same campaign. Vereker Hamilton's canvas of the same incident shows the line of Highlanders in a charge just prior to entering the village, deploying the kilts to dramatize motion. To stress the notion of victory and to legitimize imperialism, the clasped rifle forms a cross with the protruding bayonet, elements reinforced by the bagpipe silhouetted farther down the line.

In both these canvases, the artists deploy the Scottish soldier for several reasons. Scottish soldiers were renowned for their tenacity. But of equal importance for artists was the fact that the kilt provided opportunities for colour tonalities and also for motion in paintings which might otherwise appear static in the manner of *tableaux vivants*. As Kandahar was a victory, these canvases serve the ideological purpose

7.1   Richard Caton Woodville, *Kandahar*, 1881, 52" × 73"

of reinforcing the penis/phallus equation of the dominant fiction of masculinity.

The representation of Celts in Victorian battle imagery, however, reveals the conflicted nature of the dominant fiction. The Irish and Scots in such canvases constituted 'the colonized in the colonies' in imperial battle art, where soldiers from groups which have lost independence (the Act of Union 1707 in the case of Scotland, the 1800 Act in the case of Ireland) fight to maintain British hegemony over other colonized groups. Serge Leclaire (1979, p. 46) observes that 'the possession of the penis ... serves as a screen denying the fundamental character of castration. Man comes to believe that he has not been castrated'. The representation of Scottish and Irish rankers in Victorian battle iconography exposes the conflicted nature of the dominant fiction, the 'phallus/penis equation' in Silverman's (1992, p. 44) conception. Instead, as she argues, the dominant fiction is exposed as dependent upon a *méconnaissance*, 'the misrecognition upon which masculinity is founded' (Silverman, 1992, p. 42). In particular, war as historical trauma implodes this equation: 'History may manifest itself in so traumatic and unassimilable a guise that it temporarily dislocates penis from phallus, or renders null and void the other elements of the dominant fiction' (Silverman, 1992, p. 47). Scottish and Irish soldiers, therefore, are in an extremely conflicted situation in Victorian battle art: their Caucasian race permits them to be dominant over the dark colonized other, whether that be an Afghani, a Sudanese, or a Zulu. As Poliakov (1971, p. 272) has observed, 'On close inspection the true Aryan appeared to be a Westerner of the male sex, belonging to the upper or middle classes, who could be defined equally by reference to coloured men, proletarians or women.' On the other hand, the soldiers' ethnicity, their Celtic birth, renders them inferior in terms of a hierarchy of Caucasians, above all inferior to those of Anglo-Saxon or Teutonic heritage. It is this conflicted element which is constantly being negotiated in Victorian battle art when it concentrates on Scottish or Irish soldiers.

No image from the nineteenth century so encapsulates this conflicted equation as Elizabeth Butler's 1879 RA exhibit *Listed for the Connaught Rangers: Recruiting in Ireland*, representing a 'sergeant, private, and two drummer boys' with two Irish recruits (Usherwood and Spencer-Smith, 1987, p. 74) in the 1870s. The canvas is striking in her work for the prominence of the landscape and for the ruined cottage at the picture's left. During the agricultural disasters of the 1830s and 1840s, many Scottish and Irish peasants had been forced to enlist in the army to avoid starvation and unemployment. As Spiers (1980, p. 48) notes, 'In 1830 and 1840 over half of the noncommissioned officers and men came from Scotland and Ireland.' In 1878, the year in which Butler painted *Listed for the Connaught Rangers*, her husband William Butler, an ardent nationalist and friend of Parnell, wrote his essay 'A Plea for the Peasant', in which he indicated the British government for forcing Irish men to enlist because of the gross brutality of British policy in Ireland. Although over 50 per cent of NCOs and rankers came from Ireland and Scotland in the 1830s and although their proportion decreased as the century progressed, the Irish contingent still 'kept pace with Ireland's share of the United Kingdom population' (Skelley, 1977, p. 131) albeit the Scottish did not. Butler's indictment of 1878 is therefore directed at pervasive discriminatory policies of the British government which transcended the military.

The private soldier, Butler (1881, p. 284) wrote, was 'thrown to our service by the hazard of his social condition, that social condition being poverty or disgrace', concealing 'the great secret that the cradle of an army is the cottage of the peasant' (Butler, 1881, p. 288; on recruiting, see Skelley, 1977, ch. 5). About the victories in the Napoleonic Wars or the Crimea or the colonial campaigns, Butler asserts 'that it was only through the assistance of our Celtic peasants, Irish and Scotch, that our armies were able to achieve victory' (Butler, 1881, p. 291). Recruits were automatically commodified since 'recruiting officials received a fee for every man they enlisted' (Skelley, 1977, p. 240), already a manifestation of *méconnaissance*.

About these Scottish and Irish troopers, Butler asks, 'Were they men on whom the nation had lavished the benefits of civil law, the blessings of good government, the privilege of a free faith? Alas! the answer must be, No' (Butler, 1881, p. 300). He continues: 'While abroad over the earth Highlanders were thus first in assault and last in retreat, their lowly homes in far-away glens were being dragged down ... [by] the cold malignity of a civilised law ... Celtic blood had freely flowed to extend the boundaries of our Indian Empire' (Butler, 1881, pp. 301–2, 306). *Listed for the Connaught Rangers* demonstrates Silverman's (1992, p. 62) contention about 'the centrality of the discourse of war to the construction of conventional masculinity ... how pivotal that discourse is to the consolidation of the penis/phallus equation ... The discourse of war works not only to solicit civilian belief in the dominant fiction, but to shape the subjective experience of battle'. In Butler's canvas, the juxtaposition of ruined cottage with remote mountain and especially the contrast of the two recruits, one looking back with regret on the historical circumstances which have driven him to enlist, presents the conflicted construction of masculinity present in the Celtic subject in battle iconography. This incommensurability was given particular point in the 1860s and 1870s when Scottish regiments were posted in Ireland to counter Fenian revolt.

It was, however, Scottish troops which drew the focus of Victorian battle artists, especially because of their exotic dress – from mid-century the kilt – and their haunting bagpipe music. Scotland by the nineteenth century, however, had undergone a metamorphosis in the public imagination from a variety of events, among them the visit of George IV to Edinburgh in 1822, the Eglinton tournament in 1839, the impact of Scott's novels, the visit of Queen Victoria there in 1840, her purchase of Balmoral in 1847 and her close relationship with Napoleon III's wife, Eugenie, who had a Scottish grandfather (see Hichberger, 1988, pp. 108–9; Wood, 1987, p. 76). More overt political events were: the formation of the National Association for the Vindication of Scottish Rights in 1853, the creation of a Secretary for Scotland in 1885, and the growing cult of Mary Queen of Scots from the 1850s onward (see Hanham, 1967; Smailes, 1987, *passim*; Strong, 1978, pp. 162–3; Trevor-Roper, 1983) a cult evoked in canvases by Victorian artists such as Robert Herdman, John Callcott Horsley, Henry Andrews and William Allan.

In the final two decades of the century, Lady Butler often used images of Celtic soldiers for two other ideological reasons. As the century advanced, England often found it difficult to police the boundaries of the Empire. This situation was aggravated by the rise of Germany, which lacked imperial possessions. The result was English anxiety about German predatory activity, particularly in Africa. In addition, during the final two decades of the century, the culture experienced what became known as a 'crisis of masculinity', one cause of which was the inadequate supply of recruits for the army, who were often too short, too ignorant and too physically inadequate to serve. This situation in its turn gave rise to theories of 'race degeneration' undermining Caucasian superiority.

Lady Butler's particular contribution to reinforcing ideas of military supremacy was to invoke great exploits of the Napoleonic or Crimean wars, which she often did using Celtic soldiers as paradigms of valiant masculinity to reinforce conceptions of white superiority. The evocation of past glories sought to inspire belief in heroic militarism during decades of doubt. Thus, Butler painted a number of canvases of Scottish regiments, nearly always in the context of global rather than small/colonial/imperial wars. These canvases, however, become conflicted representations of masculinity through their construction of the incommensurability of penis and phallus by representing the sacrifice of Scottish rankers for British military supremacy. In *Scotland for Ever!* (1881), showing the Scots Greys at Waterloo in the charge of the Union Brigade, the representation of what appears a victory (only two men are shown shot) is in fact equivocal; although Sergeant Ewart managed to capture the French eagle, 'a counter-attack by French cavalry while [the Greys] were returning from this mad-cap venture led to their being cut to pieces and reduced to little more than a squadron in number' (Usherwood and Spencer-Smith, 1987, p. 82), in Wood's (1987, p. 50) terms a 'Pyrrhic achievement'.

Butler's 1895 exhibit *The Dawn of Waterloo* shows the Irish members of the Scots Greys at reveille prior to the charge in *Scotland for Ever!*, but again this representation of Celts is intensely conflicted if one recalls William Butler's 1878 essay. A similar evocation of past glory appears in *The Colours: Advance of the Scots Guards at the Alma* of 1899, recording an incident during the battle 20 September 1854 in the Crimea. For bringing order to the line, Captain Lloyd Lindsay was awarded the Victoria Cross. In *Scotland for Ever!*, *The Dawn of Waterloo*, and *The Colours*, Butler deploys Scottish and Irish soldiers of the Napoleonic and Crimean conflicts to reinforce imperial ventures during the 80s and 90s, even though ascendant nationalism was evident in both Scotland and especially Ireland during the same decades.

The conflicted situation of Celtic rankers is given particular point in an imperial context in Butler's *A Lament in the Desert: Cameron Highlanders 1885*, painted only in 1925. Set during the Sudanese War of 1883–85, the colonized Scots bury one of their own in the campaign against the Dervishes or what Kipling in 1890 called the Fuzzie-Wuzzies. In his 1880 essay 'The Zulus' in which he attacks the British government for its abuse of this nation, William Butler had said that 'nothing is more natural' than that blacks should revolt against British white occupation and conquest. He notes: 'All these long centuries of crime are still unpaid for. The slaves set free by us fifty years ago were not a thousandth part of those we had enslaved ... Notwithstanding the wide gulf which we fancy lies between us and this black man, he is singularly like us' (Butler, 1881, pp. 178, 189–90). Here Scottish troopers, themselves driven to enlist because of the Clearances and other abuses, become the oppressed oppressing the oppressed.

An artist whose work is crucial to examining the representation of Celtic soldiers in battle painting is Robert Gibb. Gibb constructs a range of imagery in his depiction of Scottish soldiers, like Butler invoking the past exploits of Scottish soldiers to reinforce ideologies of Caucasian superiority. At the same time, however, Gibb's paintings emphasize their Scottish subjects and reflect a Scottish nationalist agenda by concentrating on Scottish heroism, much of it a result of the comradeship associated with Scottish regiments and derived from conceptions of clan loyalties in Scottish history.

In his most famous canvas, *The Thin Red Line* of 1881 (see Figure 7.2), Gibb depicts the 93rd (Sutherland) Highlanders receiving the charge

7.2 Robert Gibb, *The Thin Red Line*, 1881, 42" × 83³/₄"

of Russian cavalry at Balaclava on 25 October 1854, an 'action immortalized by William Howard Russell's phrase "that thin red streak topped with a line of steel"' (Usherwood and Spencer-Smith, 1987, p. 171). Drawing on Alexander Kinglake's *Invasion of the Crimea*, Gibb depicts the Scottish troops, only some 550 augmented by 100 sick troopers, at the moment when Turkish battalions had deserted before the attack. Although it is disputed whether there were two or four lines of troops, Gibb selects the former to emphasize the heroism of the rankers. Crucial to the success of this famous work is the topos of the 'last stand' or 'backs to wall'. *The Thin Red Line* reflects elements which became signatures of Gibb's work, especially his preference for infantry rather than cavalry. Gibb concentrates on the psychologically tense situation of the combatants, and emphasizes the line rather than the defensive square, which was the usual formation used to repel cavalry.

The same line formation appears in *The Alma: Forward the 42nd* of 1889, showing Sir Colin Campbell leading the Black Watch to scale the Russian fortifications. The Scots at the Alma, according to Kinglake, were living embodiments of Victorian masculinity: 'These young soldiers, distinguished to the vulgar eye by their tall stature, their tartan uniforms, and the plumes of their Highland bonnets, were yet more marked in the eyes of those who know what soldiers are by the warlike carriage of the men, and their strong, lithesome, resolute step' (Harrington, 1898, p. 590). Nevertheless, the ostensible heroism of both canvases is conflicted: the engagement of the 'thin red line' with the Russian cavalry was a minor episode; and, of course, the Battle of the Alma was extremely equivocal because the Allies did not demolish the Russians forces but in fact 'allowed the Russians to retreat to Sebastopol and to refortify the town, thus prolonging the War until 1856' (Woosnam-Savage, n.d., p. 1).

Gibb is particularly famous for painting images of comrades on the battlefield, in the 1885 *Letters from Home* or especially in his first battle picture, the 1878 *Comrades*, showing 'a young soldier, dying amid a snowstorm' (Gilbert, 1897, p. 27) during the Crimea. The emphasis on comradeship is crucial for the maintenance of the dominant fiction, as Silverman (1992, p. 63) notes: 'As long as the soldier remains on the battlefield, he is fortified to some degree by his comrades; the "binding" which can no longer take place at the level of the ego occurs instead at the level of the group.' Gibb's three soldiers of the Black Watch have left their column as one of their number has collapsed in the snow. The artist constructs a military pietà as the dying confidences are exchanged. The role of Kipling's *The Light that Failed* (1891) in emphasizing this comradeship among soldiers and 'specials' supports the ideology constructed in Gibb's *Letters from Home* and *Comrades*.

The comradeship of Scottish forces is particularly important in two representations of the Gordon Highlanders scaling the heights at Dargai on 20 October 1897 during the Tirah Expeditionary Force campaign against the Afridis in northwest India. In Gibb's *Dargai* of 1909 (see Figure 7.3), the Gordons, commanded to take the position at all costs, succeeded. Gibb uses the landscape to suggest the brutal circumstances in which the charge occurred; the rough terrain magnifies the achievement. Woodville's *The Storming of Dargai Heights* of 1898 emphasizes the famous element of the charge, Piper George Findlater continuing to play even though both his legs were wounded. Findlater's action is the very icon of comradeship, the importance of which was key to the 'pals' battalions' mode of conscription during the First World War (Reader, 1988, pp. 108–9). In both these representations of Dargai, the imagery of the Scots abroad eliminates the stigma of their ethnicity, which would be felt in England; the penis/phallus equation abroad could be maintained as their Celtic ancestry was subsumed by racial superiority.

The Scots as heroic rescuers is a focus of Joseph Noel Paton's *In Memoriam* of 1858, which has a history both combat- and race-inflected. As the picture exists today, it represents a group of English women, one of whom holds a bible, praying for divine intervention at the moment that Highlanders enter to effect their rescue during the Indian Mutiny, probably a scene at Cawnpore. When first exhibited, the picture had in fact depicted a group 'of maddened Sepoys, hot after blood' according to *The Times* (Bayly, 1990, p. 241). However, the picture was engraved not with murderous Sepoys but with the revised Highlanders, demonstrating – and circulating – the idea of British Caucasian superiority over the lustful dark natives. Hichberger (1988, p. 175) notes that 'the depiction of ladies in the power of black soldiers was deeply offensive'. Thus, a canvas that contested the heroic code of white male militarism by *not* showing a rescue – and thereby exposing the incommensurability of the penis/phallus equation – was reconfigured to affirm that equation.

This incommensurability, however, is not camouflaged in Frank Holl's *A Deserter* of 1874, in which Highlanders have caught a deserter/labourer, his 'heavy, split boots and ragged attire ... in obvious contrast to the brilliant red clothing of the Highlanders' (Casteras, 1988, p. 51). When one considers Butler's essay on the factors driving men to enlist – famine, the Clearances, unemployment, starvation (the last signalled by the loaf in the man's hand) – the issues of class, ethnicity, and imperialism are conjoined, especially since in the 1870s the recruit would be destined for a colonial campaign.

Particularly because of its setting, questions of incommensurability and the misrecognition underlying the dominant fiction also conflict

7.3 Robert Gibb, *The Dargai*, 1909, 61" × 91"

Robert G. Hutchinson's *Under Orders* of 1883, depicting the Black Watch in a barrack room of Edinburgh Castle prior to embarking for the Egyptian War which led to Tel-el-Kebir. Hutchinson shows the families gathered with their individual loved ones, with elderly relatives counselling the young soldiers. In the background of the painting, a reproduction of Millais's *Cherry Ripe* (1879) symbolizes the reason why the troops are fighting; it is to preserve white womanhood. The canvas has affiliation with Paton's *In Memoriam*, as Scots become defenders of Caucasian racial superiority whether that be in Africa or India.

This racial superiority, emphasized by the ethnicity of the Scot, appears in George Joy's *The Last Stand of General Gordon* of 1893 (see Figure 7.4), commemorating the death of Gordon at Khartoum on 26 January 1885, when the Sudanese capital fell to the Mahdi's forces. Although born in Woolwich, commentators emphasized Gordon's Scottish heritage, including William Butler (1887, p. 84), who described Gordon in *The Campaign of the Cataracts* as 'the solitary figure of the great Celtic soldier' at his death. Gordon epitomizes the Scot caught at the very moment exposing the *méconnaissance* upon which the dominant fiction of the commensurability of penis and phallus rests. In this representation, the Celt in Victorian battle imagery, himself colonized, confronts another 'other' in the form of an alternative, non-Caucasian masculinity. Gordon admitted that 'one black face looked like another to him' (Johnson, 1982, p. 301). Johnson notes that a 'saint cult' (Johnson, 1982, p. 304) was built around the figure of the Celtic Gordon, the motive of which was to justify the imperial idea: 'A man without imperfection, [Gordon] justified the winning of an empire by men of more mortal stature' (Johnson, 1982, p. 307). Thus, this ultimate example of Celtic valour constructs white masculinity in imperial contexts. Caton Woodville's *The Gordon Memorial Service at Khartoum* of 1899, painted expressly for the Queen, is the iconographic memorial to this construction of Gordon. The Catholic, Anglican, Presbyterian and Methodist chaplains are shown before the ruins of the palace. Steevens (1990, pp. 314–16) recorded the event as follows: 'We buried Gordon after the manner of his race ... He was an Englishman doing his duty, alone and at the peril of his life ... We left Gordon ... alone in majesty under the conquering ensign of his own people.' Steevens summarizes that 'the vindication of our self-respect was the great treasure we won at Khartoum, and it was worth the price we paid for it' (Steevens, 1990, p. 318).

The attempt to reassert the dominant fiction of masculinity is most difficult in the representation of the wounded male body, particularly in the case of the returned veteran. It is striking that representations of

7.4   George Joy, *The Last Stand of General Gordon*, 1893, 120" × 84"

veterans from imperial campaigns were relatively few after mid-century. Silverman (1992, p. 63) offers an explanation of this anomaly: 'Once removed from the battlefront, the traumatized veteran no longer enjoys the support of his comrades-in-arms ... For the society to which he returns ... he represents a sorry travesty of "our fighting men and

boys", a living proof of the incommensurability of penis and phallus.'
Hichberger (1988, p. 141) notes that 40 paintings of veterans were
exhibited at the Royal Academy between 1815 and 1914, 18 of which
involved Chelsea pensioners. This small number is not surprising if one
considers that the wounded body of the male becomes the signifier not
of masculinity but of the other, the resourceless, passive, non-aggressive
paradigm associated with the feminine or the colonized.

Few of these veteran depictions were of imperial war campaigns.
Rather, the best known involve the Crimea. In Joseph Paton's *Home:
The Return from the Crimea*, exhibited in 1859, a corporal in the Scots
Fusilier Guards is embraced by his kneeling wife as his aged mother
hovers over him. He has lost his left arm and is still bandaged about the
head. As Christopher Lloyd (1991, p. 202) notes, 'the painting can ...
be interpreted as an implied criticism of the war', the 'anti-heroic sentiments' of which disturbed reviewers. The wounded and incapacitated
male body exposed the fragility of the penis/phallus equation. The
disabled veteran, in fact, guaranteed that the prevailing order was *not*
sabotaged. Hichberger (1989, p. 62) observes that the public feared 'the
dangers of radicals "subverting" soldiers and veterans'. Located in a
domestic setting, and disabled as well 'the veteran of the Crimea became an unthreatening patriot' (Hichberger, 1989, p. 55).

The Scottish soldier was of interest to other artists who were not
principally known as battle painters. One such example is the Pre-
Raphaelite John Everett Millais. In *News from Home* of 1857, Millais
depicted a Highland soldier in the Crimea reading a letter as he stands
in a trench. The figure was construed to be a member of the Black
Watch, later painted by Robert Gibb in *Forward the 42nd*. Millais's
painting demonstrates the strong attraction of Scottish costume for
artists. Frank Holl, who had already demonstrated an interest in the
Scottish battle subject with *A Deserter*, painted two canvases in the
1880s of Scottish soldiers. In *Ordered to the Front* of 1880, soldiers of
the McKenzie Highlanders are being shown off to a campaign of the
1870s, such as the Second Afghan War. In the companion piece, *Home
from the Front* of 1881, Holl shows these soldiers returning as veterans.
The welcoming citizenry accord the veteran acceptance and status in a
civic ceremony to camouflage the much more certain neglect, unemployment and poverty experienced by many veterans during the century.

The context in which to evaluate the representation of Celts in Victorian battle art is the intense debate about the nature of Celtic populations
which occurred during the nineteenth century, an issue complicated
because, although the Celts were construed as Aryans, they were not
Anglo-Saxons. In an essay in the *Anthropological Review* John William

Jackson, for example, declared in 1866: 'There is obviously more indi-
viduality in the Teutonic than the Celtic type' (Jackson, 1979, p. 132).
In the *Contemporary Review* in 1877, Edward A. Freeman was more
moderate: 'My present point is that no existing nation is … purely
Celtic, Teutonic, Slavonic, or anything else. All races have assimilated a
greater or less amount of foreign elements' (Freeman, 1979, p. 223).
Thomas Huxley (1979, p. 165), in 'The Forefathers and Forerunners of
the English People' in the *Pall Mall Gazette* of 1870, advocated the
removal of ethnic distinctions, stating: 'I think that the sooner we leave
off drawing political distinctions between Celts and Saxons the better
… I deny that there is sufficient proof of the existence of any difference
whatever, except that of language, between Celt and Teuton.'

In 1880 the monogenesist Grant Allen (1979, p. 248) in his essay,
'Are We Englishmen?' for the *Fortnightly Review*, argued that not only
were there strong Celtic populations in England, but that it was the
Celtic groups which constituted the strength of British industrialism:
'Students of early English history … always over-estimate the importance of the Teutonic element … They forget that, while Teutonic
Britain has been sinking to the position of a simple agricultural country,
Keltic [*sic*] Britain has been rising to that of a great manufacturing
region.' And if the Celtic populations drive industrialization, they also
catalyse the processes of colonization, according to Allen: 'It is common
to speak of the "Anglo-Saxons" as the great colonizing race, but …
such pretensions will not for a moment hold water. It is the Kelt who
colonises' (Allen, 1979, p. 252). Allen concludes by observing that
through intermarriage, the Celts and the Anglo-Saxons have merged.
Then he adds significantly: 'Out of Britain the Kelts have it all their
own way … In the colonies [the Kelt] has certainly gained the upper
hand in every case … Most true British people are not "Anglo-Saxons",
but Kelts … Coal, not blood, is the true differentiating agent' (Allen,
1979, pp. 253, 255). Allen denounces 'this unhappy prejudice of race'
(Allen, 1979, pp. 255–6) existing at his time. The Celts in Victorian
battle painting are thus part of a larger national discourse about race,
ethnicity, and imperialism.

The appropriate literary gloss on such canvases is the series of tales
about Terence Mulvaney, Stanley Ortheris and John Learoyd written by
Rudyard Kipling from 1887 through 1899, the most important of which
were collected in *Plain Tales from the Hills* (1888), *Soldiers Three*
(1888) and *Life's Handicap* (1891). Kipling's focus on an Irishman, a
Cockney, and a Yorkshireman for his three rankers demonstrates the
complex process of ethnic negotiation occurring in both war literature
and battle painting. This ethnic conflict is epitomized in Arthur Conan
Doyle's tale 'The Green Flag' of 1893 in which Jack Conolly of the

Royal Mallows first incites rebellion among the Irish rankers of the regiment. Then, as race intervenes, Conolly cannot see blacks (here the Dervishes) as allies of the Irish, so he arouses his comrades to fight the Dervishes by displaying the Irish flag. In Kipling and Doyle, the Celtic soldier is both integral and marginal: as a Celt he is often cannon-fodder, as in William Barnes Wollen's *The Black Watch at Quatre Bras* of 1894 or Alphonse DeNeuville's *The Highland Brigade at Tel-el-Kebir* of 1883; as a white man he is a colonizer and imperialist, as in Louis Desanges's *The Third Highlanders Winning the VC at Lucknow* of 1859–62 or Skeoch Cumming's *Drummer Roddick at Afghanistan* of 1890.

The pictorial epitome of this incommensurability of the Celtic soldier is constructed in Robert Gibb's *Backs to the Wall, 1918*, exhibited in 1929. Khaki-clad Scottish troops stand 'defiantly with their bayonets at the ready' (Harrington, 1898, p. 595). The title derives from Sir Douglas Haig's famous Order of the Day, 12 April 1918: 'Every position must be held to the last man. There must be no retirement. With our backs to the wall and believing in the justice of our cause, each one must fight on to the end' (Fussell, 1975, p. 17). As one corporal remembered: 'We never received it [the Order of the Day]. We to whom it was addressed, the infantry of the front line, were too scattered, too busy trying to survive, to be called into any formation to listen to orders of the day' (Fussell, 1975, p. 17). The paradoxical situation of the Celtic ranker in Victorian battle iconography is illuminated by this stunning irony of the actual historical event.

CHAPTER EIGHT

'Principle, party and protest': the language of Victorian Orangeism in the north of England

Donald M. MacRaild

There is broad agreement among historians that the Orange Order in Britain was little more than a raucous side-show to the real stuff of Victorian politics. For John Vincent, the movement occupied a vague position on the political right and only surfaced intermittently and opportunistically (Vincent, 1968, p. 113). In similar fashion, D. G. Paz states that Orangeism never rose above the status of an ineffectual, northern diversion, being marginal, 'geographically, politically and socially' (Paz, 1992, p. 4) throughout the middle decades of the century. Indeed, a considerable literature on working-class political organization, in which the Order fleetingly appears, commonly supposes that Paz is right, and that the Orange Order was little more than the 'proletarian face of Protestantism' (Joyce, 1980, pp. 153, 256-8; Lowe, 1990, p. 153).

Such a view of British Orangeism is shaped by two related factors. First, by the fact that the Orange movement in Ireland was consistently stronger and persistently more aggressive than British versions, with the result that historians presume, not unsurprisingly, that the odd bout of sectarian squabbling in Liverpool or Glasgow constituted but a pale imitation of activities across the Irish Sea. Secondly, this belief in the marginality of the organization has been shaped by historians' readings of contemporary attitudes. A general mistrust and loathing of Irish settlers in Britain led many Victorians to dismiss the Orange Order as a quirky aberration outside of its Irish context. However, in sharp contrast to these wider perceptions of the Order, one leading Orangeman, Colonel William Blennerhasset Fairman, claimed that, as early as the 1830s, northern lodges were just as English as they were Irish. This was certainly the case in Liverpool from an early point in the Order's history. Indeed, by the mid-1870s the Cumbria movement was neither purely proletarian nor completely Irish (Lowe, 1990, p. 153; Neal, 1988, p. 71). The true place of Orangeism in Victorian England, then, is less unambiguous than its dismissal to the ethnic margins of social inquiry might suggest. The language of Orangeism – with its allusions to the Protestant settlement and its defence of quintessentially English political institutions – was too broadly understood by too many sympathetic Britons for Orangeism to be cast to the periphery. Moreover, as we shall see, later nineteenth-century political and intellectual developments increased the relevance of the Orangeman's peculiar brand of religious bigotry and strident patriotism.

As the Home Rule question rose to prominence in the 1880s, the religious and historical dimensions of Orangeism were reforged by the Order's increasing association with Conservatism. While Orangeism had always been about defending the Protestant state, the threat from Irish nationalism encouraged Orangemen to invigorate their archaic brand of loyalism with a zealous Unionism that encapsulated the languages of nation and race which were being brought to bear on Irish affairs with increasing passion in the later Victorian era. This mix of politics and patriotism was openly encouraged by Tory MPs whose desire for electoral leverage led them to voice deep-seated Orange prejudices. Indeed, throughout the years covered in this chapter, Orangemen proudly displayed a curiously blended religious, political and, later, racial identity – an identity which others were quick to utilize. Orangeism was something of a world-view which was essentially constructed from the lodgemen's consideration of themselves as defenders of church and state, and upholders of what they saw as the politically mature and racially superior Ascendancy which had been enshrined in the Act of Union. Moreover, an unshakeable belief in one Britain, but two Irelands, united Orangemen on both sides of St George's Channel and connected them to the groundswell of popular Tory Unionism which dominated political discourse, at both national and local levels, in the 1880s and 1890s.

It is clear from the nineteenth-century press, as well as periodical literature and the parliamentary debates of the day, that ideas generic to the Orange society drew in widespread support in defence of the Union and the British Empire. It is also important to notice, however, that provincial Orangeism was contoured by local issues and by the nature of local communities (e.g. Lowe, 1990, pp. 152–62; MacFarland, 1990, *passim*). It is the purpose of this chapter to contribute to that regional dimension, in Lancashire and Cumberland. Particular consideration will be given to the consistency of the Orange Order's language and to the stability of its position within the spectrum of national, religious and political, and racial beliefs. It is hoped that the following discussion will demonstrate enough of the texture of Orangeism to explain how the movement managed to manoeuvre, during the course of the nineteenth century, from plebeian Irish radicalism to mainstream British party politics by developing close links with Toryism. This chapter is also intended to demonstrate that, while Orangeism clearly appealed to Ulster Protestants, it was more than a 'mere Irish faction' (McFarland, 1994, p. 80) and that its message held sway across national boundaries. It is hoped, therefore, that the issues raised will lead us to understand something of the complex nature of Irish immigration by considering the common language that the Irish Protestant community shared with indigenous Britons.

The foundation of an Orange identity

The Orange Order first appeared in Ulster in 1795 during the turmoil which led to the United Rebellion of 1798, although its brand of popular conservatism quickly attracted a broader compass of support. By the late 1790s, the combined efforts of British troops returning after the rebellion and Irish Protestant immigrants introduced the Order to Britain; thereafter, it spread rapidly across the north of England, especially around Manchester and the central lowlands of Scotland. After one or two earlier fits and starts, the Order was, by the 1840s, a movement of increasing importance in areas of concentrated Irish settlement, especially across north-west Britain between the Clyde and the Dee.

While it has been argued that although Orangeism was a vital strand of popular Tory ideology, its first and most important context was Irish. In many ways the nineteenth-century Orange Order was, like the various nationalist movements it paralleled, an emblem of one side of a divided Ireland. As English imperialist aspirations and Irish nationalist resistance rose to prominence in the aftermath of the Act of Union (1801), so the nature of socio-cultural divisions in Ireland grew more intense. While the English traditionally viewed the division between Catholicism and Protestantism as part of the fabric of Irish society, these socio-cultural alignments assumed a much greater, deeper complexity in the Victorian period. So great did these divisions become that historians of Ireland and the Irish cannot ignore them. Indeed, Donald H. Akenson justifiably describes the cultures of Catholicism and Protestantism as 'cosmologies', by which he means 'two over-arching psychologics, two complex networks of ideology, faith, social practice, and economic arithmetic' (Akenson, 1988, p. 127). Moreover, few groups were more ardent, or more blinkered, in upholding these cosmological division of Irish society than the Orange Order. Despite the obvious importance in the nineteenth century of these varieties of Irishness, many English observers still preferred to frame their own perceptions of the Irish in what Conor Cruise O'Brien calls the 'pejorative singular' (Curtis, 1968, p. 22). For Victorians who witnessed mass Irish settlement in Britain, or who read of agrarian violence in Ireland, there was only one kind of Irish – an indistinguishable mass of violent, disloyal and dangerous 'Paddies' and 'Biddies'. In this sense, the Irish suffered from what G. S. Goschen, the Liberal Unionist, described in 1886 as 'a double dose of original sin', damned as they were by their class and their race. Thus, the perceived inferiority of the Irish was seen as an almost natural product of their being proletarian Celts (Curtis, 1968, pp. 23–4). In an age when the ruling élite generally feared the levelling tendencies of the working class, the Irish stood out as either agrarian rebels, nationalist conspirators or industrial militants. Condemned as Catholic, Celtic and lower class, they came to be seen as a people who, like any other colonial tribe, required the firm hand of Anglo-Saxon government. Questions about Home Rule and empire were discussed in the sinister language of the day which was then being popularized by Anglo-Saxonist historians like Kingsley, Freeman, Stubbs and Froude. Given the generally anti-Irish disposition of the English, the rough culture of Orangeism, before the 1870s, threatened to drag Protestant as well as Catholic Irish under this blanket of racially inspired opprobrium. Thus, it is little wonder that, in an attempt to divorce themselves from their Catholic-Celtic countrymen, Orangemen from the 1870s came increasingly to echo the language of Anglo-Saxonism which seemingly gripped the Victorian middle and upper class.

However, if seen from a slightly different perspective, it is possible that, rather than condemning the Order to some kind of Celtic fringe, the movement's undoubted Irish element might instead help us to understand something of that variety of Irishness which Victorian Britons failed to distinguish. Much has been written about Irish immigrants as an outcast people, as a nation within a nation and as a stark reminder of the tensions of Anglo-Irish relations, for this kind of Irishness dominates the historiography of immigration to Britain (Swift, 1987, pp. 264–76, 1992, pp. 52–81). However, to regard this as an accurate generalization is to concur with the Victorians who themselves tended to see 'Irishness' and 'Catholicism' as the same thing. Quite simply, not all Irish settlers were Catholic; nor were they all marginal. Perhaps, then, the term marginal is better applied, as Boyce does, to Catholic Ireland at large (Boyce, 1986, pp. 230–53). Under the terms of the union, Irish Catholics were a people cast to the periphery in both British and Irish contexts, first, by the inferior status of all Catholic citizens before emancipation and the restoration of the hierarchy, and secondly, by the Protestant Ascendancy in Ireland. Therefore, marginality may well have been the lot of Irish Catholics, home and abroad, but how could those of the Orange tradition – with its mystical allusions to patriotic duty – share the fate of their Catholic countrymen? A failure to acknowledge Irish Protestant self-perceptions helps partly to explain why contemporary observers seem confused in their observations of Irish typologies.

Despite the fact that the English in general may have confused the nature of Irishness, the Irish themselves did not. Northern Irish Orange-men, for example, knew very well that, by the late nineteenth century, they were not Irish in the same way that Southern Catholics were. That this was the case, one historian contends, can be explained by the fact that Catholic and nationalist Ireland hijacked the term 'Irish' in one of the 'greatest imperialist coups of the nineteenth century', and he quotes an Anglo-Irish observer, whose sentiments support this argument con-cerning the cultural imperialism of Irish Catholics: 'When I was a boy, the "Irish people" meant the Protestants; now it means the Roman Catholics' (Akenson, 1988, p. 134). Akenson sees this transformation as fundamental in shaping the twin cosmologies that dominated Irish life, as integral to what he calls the development of a 'sacred-profane' dichotomy wherein one group cherished what the other abhorred. Thus, whereas Daniel O'Connell could talk about both 'Catholic Ireland' and 'Protestant Ireland', by the mid-to-late nineteenth century 'an equation developed of Catholic = Irish and, perforce, non-Catholic = non-Irish' (Akenson, 1988, p. 134). It is this aspect of Akenson's convincing thesis which explains the Orangemen's claims to a wider British identity.

In general terms, therefore, it might be possible to argue that if one Irish population, the Catholic, resided on a cultural, socio-economic and psychological margin, the other, the Protestant, is correctly located at the vanguard of a shared British identity. Indeed an American fron-tier-type spirit washed over Ulster's Protestant population, as they de-fended their belief system. Their historic connection to planted fore-bears, and a pride in the hardiness of this breed, were common themes in defence of Orange beliefs, as they were in fierce opposition to Home Rule, and in remembrance of the 'Glorious Twelfth'. Yet, the ritualized belligerence of Orange Day brings us full circle in any attempt to understand perceptions of identity, for it was the 'Twelfth', and its promotion of sectarian conflict in British cities, which, more than any-thing else, caused Victorians to dismiss the Orange tradition as a mar-ginal Irish or working-class movement.

A struggle from the margins

One of the central beliefs of Orangeism was that William III enshrined the Protestant constitution and rescued the principles of bible Christianity from papal domination. The debt to King William was never forgotten, and formed the centrepiece in every annual celebration of the Glorious Twelfth in the Victorian north-west. The Battle of the Boyne and the deeds of King Billy were firmly cast in Orange folklore, and many of the songs aired each year were themselves rousing reminders of those distant days. Orangemen believed themselves akin to the Israelites – a bonded people set free – as one song, *When Pharaoh Reign'd*, illustrates (Anon., 1815):

> When Pharaoh sat on Egypt's throne,
> And Israel in their bonds did groan,
>   And Israel, &c.
> The great I AM, to Moses gave command.
> To lead them to the promis'd land;
> And all the proud, the proud Egyptian host,
> Pursuing, in the sea were lost.
>
> So when oppress'd by papal pow'r,
> With death and plunder every hour,
>   With death, &c.
> The brave King William, Prince of Orange-men,
> Restor'd us to our rights again;
> Hail! mighty William, conquerer [*sic*] of the Boyne,
> Our voices in thy praise we join.
>
> Our constitution we'll maintain,
> Gainst ev'ry foe on land or main,
>   'Gainst ev'ry, &c.
> With loyal hearts, our hearts both firm and true,
> We'll never stain the orange or blue;
> We love our King, our country, and its laws,
> For ever live the Orangemen's cause.

This victory over the Catholic King James was one of the great connections for all Orangemen. Each year might throw up specific issues to confront them, but an image of William of Orange and his putatively heroic deeds, went unchanged over time. Each year from the 1870s, in Cumbria as elsewhere, Orangemen donned their Orange lilies and sashes, hoisted their painted banners and marched around the local towns, fife and drum bands playing as members sung the words which recounted William's deeds, while denouncing popery and the priesthood. Throughout the Victorian era and beyond, the sight of these garish and raucous gatherings excited variously fear and awe. James Connolly's words are surely representative of the mixed emotions invoked by the marching

season: 'Viewing the processions as a mere league, ... I must confess
some parts of it are beautiful, some of it are ludicrous and some of it
exceedingly disturbing' (McFarland, 1990, p. 70). It was this public
face of Orangeism, the annual procession, that prompted hostile on-
lookers to comment on the difference between what might be termed
'rough' and 'respectable' culture:

> Processions, whatever their character, are costly pageants, interest-
> ing to childhood and adolescence, but a nuisance or an absurdity
> to men of sense. Gee-gaws, show trumpery, dazzling colours, bad
> music and meretricious ornaments captivate the senses of the half-
> savage, and in any country they will attract a multitude of unedu-
> cated sight lovers. (*Liverpool Mercury*, 18 July 1851, quoted in
> Lowe, 1990, p. 155)

Although Orange leaders vehemently denied their ranks were 'the dregs
of society' (*Barrow Herald*, 14 July 1877), the public posturing and
defiance of the 'Glorious Twelfth' led contemporaries to comment,
perhaps too easily, on the Irishness of the rank and file. As the *Glasgow
Herald*'s observation of just one marcher demonstrates: 'The face is
curiously Irish ... but not all the sombre vicissitudes of navvydom have
quenched the Celtic fervour in this old Orangeman's soul ... the Orangemen's walk is essentially the pageant of the proletariat' (11 July
1908, quoted in McFarland, 1990, p. 110). These two assertions, that
Orangeism was both working class and Irish, are crucial. If the *Glasgow Herald*'s observation was correct, then the Scots might exculpate
themselves from any associated blame by reference to the marginality of
the movement. There was a tendency for moderate Protestants to distance themselves from Orangeism by reference to its perceived Irishness.
For example, one writer in Barrow, 'An English Protestant', dismissed
the movement as a suspicious, foreign body:

> It is a dangerous exotic, a weed of foreign growth, and a most
> noxious one; like the Colorado beetle it should be kept out, or
> crushed as soon as found. The Orange Party may, on occasions,
> make use of some compliant minister, but it merits the contempt
> and aversion of every honourable and peace-loving citizen. (*Bar-
> row Herald*, 19 July 1879)

It cannot be denied that Orangeism attracted a proportion of Irish
adherents, or that it comprised a rank and file that was overwhelmingly
working class. But it was the ribaldry attached to the annual gatherings
in July which shaped these rather contemptuous views of the Order.
From the earliest example of Orange Day violence, in Manchester in
1807 (Neal, 1988, p. 15), the nineteenth century was regularly punctu-
ated by sometimes serious communal strife. The antipathetic response
to the Papal Aggression of 1850 was particularly acute in this respect,

as was the heated atmosphere of the years from 1866 to 1872, when the Fenian threat and the peregrinations of William Murphy proved more than sufficient to light the Orange and Green touch paper in countless towns, from Plymouth to Tynemouth and Wolverhampton to Whitehaven (Arnstein, 1975, pp. 51–71; Hanham, 1978, pp. 84–5, 303–8; MacRaild, 1993, pp. 44–52). Indeed, it is no coincidence that these years witnessed the Orange reawakening.

Although sporadic outbreaks of violence were a feature of many towns in this period, the depth of feeling in Liverpool was clearly atypical. As one observer noted: 'The peculiar hatred which Christians feel to Christians ... burns nowhere so devouringly as it does in our religious town' (*Porcupine*, 10 March 1866, quoted in Lowe, 1990, p. 161). The role of the Orange Order in fanning the flames of sectarian hatred in Liverpool was also noticed by the local press: Orangemen, the *Liverpool Mercury* asserted, 'claim to be Protestants of the purest type, yet the conduct of many of these would disgrace pagans' (quoted in Lowe, 1990, p. 160). Although Liverpool was evidently regarded as unique in respect of Orange–Green tensions, it would be quite wrong to dismiss Orange affrays elsewhere. West Cumbria, for example, also harboured Irish and non-Irish communities who often found themselves divided by allegiances to a dead king or a live pope. Indeed, few riots outside Liverpool were as serious as that which erupted in Cleator Moor, near Whitehaven, in July 1884, when one young man – a 17-year-old Irish nationalist named Henry Tumelty – was shot dead (Arnstein, 1975, pp. 51–71; MacRaild, 1993, pp. 47–52, 56–60; Neal, 1988, pp. 54–64).

The Liverpool press, given Orange propensities to violence, was understandably contemptuous of the purpose of the 'Twelfth'. Moreover, Liberal journalists elsewhere would generally have agreed that 'Altogether, a fair summary of the "glorious anniversary would be – much heat, dust, dirt and drink"'(*Liverpool Mercury*, 13 July 1871, quoted in Lowe, 1990, p. 160). The authorities in Britain broadly subscribed to the view that Orange Day was little more than an excuse to drink heavily. Few, however, made the point as wittily as the author of this eyewitness account: 'The great festival of St William III was observed with special devotion – and drunkenness – by the Liverpool Orangemen ... and something much stronger than the Boyne water was imbibed' (*Catholic Times*, 16 July 1870, quoted in Lowe, 1990, p. 162). Generally speaking, pleas for sobriety from the Orange platform echoed wider concerns about the drinking habits of the working man, though no amount of Boyne or Liffey water could excuse the depth of feelings occasioned by the 'Twelfth'. Indeed, the view of Orangeism as simply a drunken reaction to Irish Catholicism is slightly misleading. There is plenty of evidence to suggest that some Orangemen drank heavily; but the institution on both sides of the border consistently attracted temperance supporters whose abstinence was announced in their lodge-names, and whose self-professed sober respect for law and authority echoed wider claims for respectability.

The politics of nation and race

The Irish question, in all its manifestations, transformed north-west politics in the mid-Victorian period, and so increased the importance of Orangeism, not least in relation to Toryism. While the Orange Order has traditionally been seen as strongest in traditional Tory areas, like Whitehaven, it was also an important force in Liberal towns, like Barrow, where the local Tory élite struggled to gain a niche in the working man's political consciousness (Lowe, 1990, pp. 153–4). In a local, political sense, therefore, the utility of Orangeism centred on its bellicose, patriotic, church and state Toryism, for this provided Tories with a way to persuade the working-class voter to subjugate the cause of class to that of nation and, ultimately, race. Thus, in the late 1860s and early 1870s the spectre of Fenianism and the insidious Catholic threat were effectively mobilized to transform utterly the political culture of Lancashire. While other factors, such as working-class antipathy to the Liberalism of mill-owners, were important in promoting the lurch to Toryism, 'Irish' factors were probably decisive. In the 1868 election the Liberal ascendancy in the county was overturned, and in 1874 the Tories triumphed comprehensively by 26 seats to seven (Kirk, 1980, p. 92). With the rise of the Home Rule crisis in subsequent decades, the Orange Order's particular role in both national and regional politics seemed assured.

While Orangeism was intimately connected to the populist political desires of local Tory élites, the movement was not democratic; nor were Tory designs upon the Order's constituency in any sense emancipatory. Orangemen mobilized their most vehement religious and political language for the battle over Home Rule, not in support of legislation for the working man. The Irish question provided a unique opportunity for the Tory–Orange alliance to harness working-class support by playing upon fears of an eroding empire. Thus, Cumbrian Tories, in uniting with Orangemen over the Home Rule issue, were merely sounding a faint echo of their peers' activities in Ulster. Like the maverick Randolph Churchill, local Tories were convinced that if the Liberals 'went for Home Rule, the Orange card would be the one to play'. Like him, they also prayed 'Please God it may turn out the ace of trumps and not the two' (Stewart, 1977, p. 18). However, the role of Cumbrian Orangemen, unlike their Ulster peers, was never critical enough to be the ace or the two, yet neither were they the joker in the pack that some contemporaries liked to think. The appeal of their language, particularly over Home Rule, was too widely understood for that. None in their ranks disagreed with the Tory MP for Barrow, Sir Charles Cayzer, who told local Orangemen that 'Home Rule for Ireland, ... meant the dismemberment of the United Kingdom' (*Barrow Herald*, 4 January 1906). In fact, Orange views of the Union spread beyond the United Kingdom. Home Rule was simply a threat to empire; hence, Cayzer argued, 'Orangemen ... had always voted solid for the unity and the integrity of this Empire, on which it depended for its peace and prosperity' (*Barrow Herald*, 6 January 1906). And it was because of this view that, during the heated years after Gladstone's conversion to Home Rule in 1886, much energy was expended by Orange-Tories in defiance of the popular will of a growing majority of the Irish people. In an echo of politics in Ireland, where Home Rule threw differing types of Irishness into sharp relief, local battle lines were also clearly drawn between Irish Protestants and Irish Catholics. Also in common with the awakening Unionism in Ireland, Cumbrian Orangeism lent heavily on analogies between the defence of Ireland in 1798 and preparedness to fight Home Rule in the 1890s. 'To these ardent supporters of the constitution', argued one Orangeman, 'the safety of Ulster might be confidently entrusted' (*Barrow Herald*, 30 May 1893).

The activities of the Orange Order in Britain during the 1880s and 1890s must be seen as part of a wider train of events, within a deeper set of entrenched attitudes. Opponents of Home Rule in this period came increasingly to see the Irish question as a racial struggle fought between superior Anglo-Saxons, on the one hand, and inferior Celts on the other. At the same time, the wider, perhaps more nebulous, idea that Home Rule presented a threat to empire was also woven into the political broadcloth and age-old fears about sinister 'Romish' plots were dusted down and brought into play against the Irish nationalist cause. When linked to the questions of nationhood, race and empire, the Ulster Unionist cry of the 1890s that 'Home Rule meant Rome Rule' (Curtis, 1968, p. 26) evoked a powerful image of mythical status. The fierce debates of 1886 and 1893–4 deserve detailed treatment themselves, but for now it is fair to say that the tone of these engagements was one of extreme anti-Irish prejudice, in which anti-Catholicism, a denial of Irish nationhood and the equation of self-determination with Teutonic, rather than Celtic, peoples came to the fore time and again (Boyce, 1986, pp. 232–9; Curtis, 1968, pp. 98–107). Lord Salisbury's opposition to Home Rule was seen in this racialist way, as a question of fitness to rule when he remarked in May 1886 that 'You would not confide free representative institutions to the Hottentots for instance' (quoted in Curtis, 1968, p. 102).

It is against a background in which race and nation were closely identified that the Orange Order in Britain played its part. In Ireland, the closeness of Ulster Orangemen to the event, or non-event, of Home Rule serves to lessen somewhat the comparative impression of its English counterpart, as does the immensely strong and growing power-base of the Irish Order and its hardening links with British Toryism. However, it would be wrong to see Orangeism as only important in a purely Irish environment, though it was stronger on that side of St George's Channel. Equally, it misses the point to ask, as one writer does, 'what meaning, other than an Irish one, could the Loyal Orangeman's toast have for mainland Britain?' (Colls, 1986, p. 40). During the Home Rule crisis the language of 'margins' and 'frontiers' came to the fore, and the differences between Catholic- and Protestant-Irish became clearer, perhaps, than ever they had been. The idea of Ulster as the frontier of British civilization was explicit in the language of Irish Orange traditions; their alleged protection of the soft underbelly of the United Kingdom, and the marginalism of Irish Catholics were viewed as mutually supporting truisms. Additionally, in the heated atmosphere of the 1890s, Orangemen parroted the tenets of social Darwinism in the fierce campaign against Home Rule. The language of Anglo-Saxons versus Celts trickled down all the way to the grass-roots, entering the discourse which devoured countless column inches in local newspapers. It is perhaps in these debates that we can see most clearly how questions of race and nation were inscribed as local as well as national issues. In April 1893 one Unionist, Sir Ellis Ashmead Bartlett, claimed to oppose Home Rule because it meant 'placing the best part of … [Ireland] under the control of the worst' (Curtis, 1968, pp. 26–7). Men like Bartlett were followed by local Unionists who tried desperately to articulate the essence of their own vision of Ireland. When viewed adjacent to Bartlett's bile, the following extracts from letters by two Orangemen clearly demonstrate the conflation between national and local opinion:

> In the north of Ireland and part of Leinster, … the wealth, the moral character, and hence the moral influence of the kingdom might be considered as being concentrated; and as it will ever be, the intelligence of the minor sections of the Irish people overbalances the physical superiority of the other. (*Barrow Herald*, 30 May 1893)

> my kinsman in Ireland have done more by the indomitable energy and industry common to the Anglo-Saxon towards building the

British Empire than Irish Celts can ever hope to, even if they were willing, which I emphatically deny. (*Barrow Herald*, 16 June 1893)

Here we see evidence of the defining logic of Orange-Irish unionism. Orangemen were a people planted from Britain in the seventeenth century who never forgot the allegedly superior culture of their antecedents. Contained in these words was an acceptance of the numerical inferiority of Protestant Ireland; this, after all, added to their heroism. Moreover, Orangemen believed this handicap was offset by a redoubtable spirit and by a central role, not merely on British frontiers, but at the vanguard of the British Empire. Their arguments were not sophisticated, but Orangemen advanced a myopic view of history and politics. Anything could be stood on its head if it helped Orangemen win an argument. For example, when Irish nationalists claimed Ireland's island status strengthened arguments for independence, Orange critics could easily overlook the fact that this very point helped to define the English nationhood evinced in Shakespeare's 'Sceptered Isle'. As 'A Corner Boy' argued: how does 'the roar of the Ocean around Ireland's sea girt shore proclaim her a nation ... is there a nation occupying Walney Island just now and also how many nations are there in America? Shure, the ocean roars around both of them' (*Barrow Herald*, 30 May 1893).

Conclusions

Orangeism was a paradox even when viewed as part of a complex Victorian political arena. The movement claimed to uphold key liberties; but it also descended frequently into the mire of racial and religious hatred. Liberal Britons could not remove themselves from the view that the Order was simply an expression of Irish bigotry, a by-product of mass immigration. The *Glasgow News* summed up the problem:

> [Orangemen] disgrace society and originate evils of a particularly far reaching kind. They pander to ignorance and intolerance and excite political animosity and sectarian hate. They are at best a mischievous anachronism alike degrading and disgraceful – a splendid testimony to our perfect freedom but a sad example of the way even freedom can be abused. (*Glasgow News*, 27 July 1878, quoted in McFarland, 1990, p. 147)

Liberal newspapers in northern England saw things in similar fashion, questioning the claim that Orangemen had a monopoly interest in the protection of Protestantism. Yet, despite tensions such as these, and perhaps because of them, the language of Orangeism proved to be remarkably hardy throughout the nineteenth century. Of course, those

English who understood Ireland a little better might well have seen Orangeism in a different light. In 1886, for example, Joseph Chamberlain argued that Ireland consisted of two races, two nations and two religions, with little hope of ever bringing them together (Curtis, 1968, p. 103). With the problem seemingly so intractable, Curtis is right to say that 'It would be hard to exaggerate the importance of Protestant prejudice, tinged with an Orange hue, to the Anglo-Saxonist image of Ireland and the Irish' (Curtis, 1968, p. 26). Although the Victorian vision of Ireland as universally Celtic served at times to marginalize the Order, these arguments about the gulf between two Irelands also explains how Orangeism worked out a common ground with Toryism in the north-west where politics was regularly overcast by a curiously Irish and sectarian cloud.

Furthermore, it was the unyielding pugnacity of the Orange tradition – still present in Belfast today – which enabled Orangemen to bat back their critics' epithets without a flicker. During all the years of Victoria's reign Orangemen believed they held some kind of moral high ground by intertwining, almost imperceptibly, vague notions of civil and religious liberty, anti-Catholicism, bible Christianity, loyalty to the Crown and constitution, and political Toryism. Furthermore, it was during the Home Rule campaigns of the 1880s and 1890s that the race dimension was dovetailed with these issues. At its roots Orangeism was something Irish, yet its survival and growth in Britain was ensured because it encapsulated an idea beyond sectarianism. In this sense, Cumbrian Orangeism was typical, for it combined broad-based support for the union of Britain and Ireland with strident religious bigotry and unflickering assertions of loyalism which attracted English and Irish alike into a movement with clear echoes of other forms of populist, conservative nationalism that rose to prominence in Europe in the years before the First World War.

CHAPTER NINE

Reinventing origins: the Victorian Arthur and racial myth

Inga Bryden

Back to the sunset bound of Lyonnesse –
A land of old upheaven from the abyss
By fire, to sink into the abyss again;
Where fragments of forgotten people dwelt,
And the long mountains ended in a coast
Of ever-shifting sand. (Ricks, 1987, vol. 3, p. 551)

From the sixteenth century onwards a conviction had gradually formed in the Englishman's mind that he was peculiarly manly, honorable, apt for leadership and that his social institutions, of ancient Saxon pedigree, were superior to those of any other people. (MacDougall, 1982, p. 89)

Hugh MacDougall's description is of the English national myth of origin known as Anglo-Saxonism, Teutonism or Gothicism. In the nineteenth century this particular strain of racial myth, partly facilitated by the development of historiography, was culturally dominant. Myths of national origin work to reinforce social identity by rooting a belief system which sanctions a society's attitudes. The basis of this myth-laying, though, is the assumption of a uniform, or at least integrated, society. For industrialization to be successful the pretence of a homogenized culture needs to be maintained and this is expressed in the form of nationalism (Gellner, 1983).

In the context of the Victorian Arthurian Revival (part of the Medieval Revival which conceived the Middle Ages as both historical and mythical) the figure of Arthur (Christian Worthy, Patriot King and Once and Future King) came to typify, indeed embody, the components of manliness, honour, heroic leadership and liberty which comprised the Teutonic notion of Englishness. Nineteenth-century Arthurians fashioned the Caucasian, Christian Arthur as a social model for the young knights of the nation and as a Darwinian type of the modern gentleman; for Alfred Tennyson, Arthur was 'like a modern gentleman/Of stateliest port' (*The Epic: Morte d'Arthur* in Ricks, 1987, vol. 2). The very reasons for the popularity of Arthurian legends among Victorian writers and artists could be located in the Arthurian Revival's generating discourses of chivalry, manliness and heroism (the military, the spiritual and the domestic).

The English myth of racial origin which defined Anglo-Saxonism in terms of the freedom of social and political institutions and purity of race (thought of as an inheritance from Germanic ancestors) was constantly being adapted and reinforced.[1] Yet 'Teutomania' dyed the cultural fabric of mid-Victorian Britain to an unprecedented extent.[2] The historical Arthur was shaped in the context of substantial histories of the Anglo-Saxons. The historian Sharon Turner, for example, has Arthur take his place among the Anglo-Saxons:

> a nation has, in the course of twelve centuries, been formed ... inferior to none in every moral and intellectual merit, is superior in every other in the love and possession of useful liberty: a nation which cultivates with equal success the elegancies of art, the ingenious labours of industry, the energies of war, the researches of science. (Turner, 1823, vol. 3, pp. 1–2)

Turner is here describing the British nation at the start of the nineteenth century in terms which had a common currency. The language of liberty, progress and civilization, indeed of moral and intellectual superiority, is linked to the time of Arthur's supposed reign; the development of qualities which constitute a national but also a racial identity is dated from the sixth century.

Nineteenth-century historians wrangled over the issues of Arthur's historical and mythical status, yet they found common ground in stressing his importance as the founder of a civilized and just social order.[3] In this capacity Arthur became the (frequently Anglo-Saxon) representative of a golden age of racial harmony, of a political 'state' to be measured against alternative social models. However in nineteenth-century Arthurian fiction the King is not necessarily depicted in Teutonic terms (in legend he is victorious over the Saxons). Rather he functions as a sign of ethnic marginalization, textually appropriated as defender of one form of regional identity against multiple identities according to a tangled web of political, religious and topographical considerations. In Henry Alford's *The Ballad of Glastonbury* the region of Somerset and Anglican politics determine Arthur's identity, in the Reverend Hawker's *The Quest of the Sangraal* Arthur is first and foremost a Cornishman, and in Charlotte Dempster's novel *Iseulte* Arthurian lineage has connections with France. In other words, within the Victorian Arthurian corpus Arthur signifies ethnic diversity rather than homogenized culture.

The 'restless relativism' of nineteenth-century historicism ensured that Victorians persisted in a kind of perpetual quest, 'the search for an authenticating ancestor who would redeem their parvenu age' (Gilmour,

1993, p. 31). As Gillian Beer has suggested Victorian writers' fascination with race is 'essentially a fascination with class' since both are concerned with descent, genealogy and the possibility of transformation (Beer, 1983, p. 202). With regard to the legendary Arthur, William Camden's topographical survey *Britannia* (a key source for Victorian Medievalists and Arthurian Revivalists alike) had cleared the ground for the planting of a historic myth which crucially integrated racial and dynastic aspirations.[4] Specifically Camden's account of the supposed discovery of Arthur's grave at Glastonbury precipitated Victorian speculation about the sites and natures of Arthur's birth and death, enabling the recreation of other myths of origin. In the context of an emerging ideology of symbolic monarchy it is unsurprising, then, that the poet laureate should fashion Prince Albert as Arthur, 'Ideal manhood closed in real man' (Ricks, 1987, vol. 3, pp. 561–3).

The questions concerning Arthur's illegitimacy/legitimacy and his own 'childless' state allowed writers such as Tennyson and Christiana Douglas to explore notions of inheritance and interclass, interracial marriages. In Douglas's contemporary novel *Arthur* (1870) the heroine Meta (bearing obvious similarities to Guinevere) has to choose between the chivalric, educated Arthur Caldicot (whose child by Meta dies) and the self-made millionaire Duncan Black. The novel ends with a union of classes and ethnic identities; the Scotsman Duncan marries the well-travelled house-servant Grace Lockie. In Tennyson's epic *The Idylls of the King* Arthur is unable to propagate his line, to perpetuate history as patrilineal authority and racial purity.[5]

By the 1840s when knowledge of the Arthurian legends was well established (Simpson, 1990, p. 221) there was widespread cultural acknowledgement that a search for the nation's historical origins necessarily involved questions of racial identity. Race was increasingly being viewed as 'the principal determinant of personal character and social progress' (MacDougall, 1982, p. 91). Similarly the literary and antiquarian quest to resurrect the historico-mythical Arthur remodelled the legendary king in the light of contemporary ethnological and ethnographical discourses.[6]

Having discussed the relevance of racial and dynastic issues to the Victorian Arthurian Revival, I want to focus on one text – Edward Bulwer-Lytton's 12-book epic poem *King Arthur* (1848) – in the context of the emerging sciences of ethnology and geology. In 1848 the first issues of *The Ethnological Journal*[7] were published, a year in which (as Robert Knox was to articulate in his influential *The Races of Men* of 1850) European revolutions had jolted people into realizing that racial identity was inseparable from national history. Additionally, 1848 witnessed the publication of *King Arthur* and Bulwer-Lytton's novel *Harold, or the Last of the Saxon Kings. King Arthur* is the central text in the formation of a nineteenth-century Arthurian ethnography. In offering complex reading strategies based on the juxtaposition of contrasting racial strains and cultural practices it reflects the contemporary 'scientific' discourses concerning racial and ethnic identities. Indeed it is as much an ethnographical text as it is a substantial reinvention of Arthurian legend.

Catherine Hall has suggested how 'otherness' is a historically specific site of struggle. In the 1840s the figure of the working man (rather than the slave of the preceding decade) was the significant 'other'. The myth of an Anglo-Saxon constitution may have justified looking to the past, but industrialization posed threats to liberty, too, in the form of the causes taken up by Chartism.[8] When Bulwer-Lytton (who combined belief in a landowning class with support of radical political causes) allows the people into the epic framework of *King Arthur* we see a picture of youth 'labour-bow'd, with wither'd look' (Bulwer-Lytton, 1853, vol. 2, p. 253), described by Roger Simpson as 'the gloomy, pauperised, and famished creatures of the hungry 1840s' (Simpson, 1990, p. 48). Carlyle's 1843 essay *Past and Present* had addressed the Condition of England question, asserting in the chapter 'The English' that the nation gained honour through deeds not words: 'if his Epic be a mighty Empire slowly built together, a mighty series of Heroic Deeds, – a mighty Conquest over Chaos' (Carlyle, 1888, p. 196). Carlyle hints at racial unity as a solution to social disunity – the Epic is the Empire. In the form of a literary Arthurian epic Bulwer-Lytton, I would argue, imagines a similar 'Conquest over Chaos' achieved via ethnic harmony, only the Chaos is in the natural, rather than in the social, world.

Edward Bulwer-Lytton's Arthurian epic is concerned with ancestral qualities and with the relationship between the individual man and his descendants. Within a framework which recasts Arthurian legend as a fable of race and dynasty, myths of racial purity and national origin are reinterpreted in terms of dynastic origin. Bulwer-Lytton's scholarly work is primarily concerned with the distinguishing of Saxon and Cymrian nationalities. The author envisages himself writing in the tradition of the Romance of the North, employing elements of the chivalrous, the marvellous and the mystical: 'a Romance, like the Northern mythology, full of typical meaning and latent import' (Bulwer-Lytton, 1853, vol. 2, p. 2). This 'mysticism', or textual symbolism, which characterizes early Cymrian literature, is the main feature of the Gothic Romance, and is traceable in Anglo-Saxon poetry. Moreover it is visible, the author tells his reader, 'wherever a tribe allied to the Goth, the Frank, or the Teuton, carries with it the deep mysteries of the Christian faith' (Bulwer-Lytton, 1853, vol. 2, p. 3). Literary lineage is here transformed into a tribal and religious type.

The author hopes he has captured 'the native air of our National Romance' (Bulwer-Lytton, 1853, vol. 2, p. 5) by writing about the Great North and the chivalry which sprung from it. In offering a vindication of 'northernness' Bulwer-Lytton is aligning himself with a distinctive tradition of Britishness (in which Arthurian lore figured prominently) which emerged in the eighteenth century in opposition to the Roman legacy (Lucas, 1991, p. 47). As Richard Jenkyns points out, 'as northerners, the Victorians felt themselves inferior to the south; as moderns, to the past' (Jenkyns, 1980, p. 171). It is the Arthur of Romance though, rather than the historical Arthur, who is the catalyst for Bulwer-Lytton's resurrection of 'national' identity in textual, racial and geographical terms.

Geographical location as an index of racial identity is an important aspect of *King Arthur* – South Wales is the country of Arthur, the Prince of the Silures, and the 'polished Christianity' of the Cymrian Knighthood is contrasted with the 'rudeness' of the heathen Teutons. This in itself seems an inversion of the Teutonic myth of national origin, or at least the element which equates civilization with Teutonism. Arthur is defending the Cymrians *against* the Saxons. It should be remembered, though, that for Bulwer-Lytton's purposes both groups are embraced by Northern mythology and chivalry.

Arthur himself dominates Bulwer-Lytton's epic. In keeping with the heroes of literary epics he must complete a series of tasks; to achieve the sword, the shield and the virgin guide. Eventually Arthur is victorious at the Siege of Carduel; the conflict of Saxons and Cymrians which the reader expects and which forms a high point in the poem's narrative structure. Above all Arthur is destined to beget a race of kings. However, as Bulwer-Lytton states in the Preface, Arthur is not Sovereign of Britain and conquering invader of Europe (as represented by Geoffrey of Monmouth), he is the patriot Prince of South Wales, 'resisting successfully the invasion of his own native soil, and accomplishing the object of his career in preserving entire the nationality of his Welsh countrymen' (Bulwer-Lytton, 1853, vol. 2, p. 5n). This he thinks to be a reconstruction 'such as it really appears to have been' of the historical Arthur. If Arthur is represented as the champion of Britain against the Saxons his life would have been a failure, but as the 'preserver of the Cymrian Nationality' Arthur 'has a claim to the epic glory of success' (Bulwer-Lytton, 1853, vol. 2, p. 5).

Interestingly an influential ethnographical essay given as a paper to the British Association six years after the publication of *King Arthur* (and published in 1861) challenged Bulwer-Lytton's view of the racial make-up of Arthur's time. In 'On the Ethnology of South Britain at the Period of the Extinction of the Roman Government in this Island' the renowned antiquary Thomas Wright attempts to disprove the 'popular notion' that uniformity of race existed in Britain during and immediately after the period of Roman rule.[9] The essay is concerned with identifying the Britons (who were confronted with the Saxon invasion) as an amalgam of Teutonic and Celtic races, rather than with reading the situation as a more straightforward opposition between the Celts (Bulwer-Lytton's Cymrians led by Arthur) and the Saxons. According to Wright, Bulwer-Lytton accepts the popular story that the Saxons were resisted by a population of Celts who took refuge in Wales. Whereas Bulwer-Lytton sees this story as to some extent historically accurate Wright dismisses it as a 'mere fiction'.

Wright examines the social structures of sixth- and seventh-century Britain, locating there the development of the 'feeling of a new nationality' before tackling the core of his argument. In the context of the formation of an Arthurian ethnography 'On the Ethnology of South Britain' parallels and usefully informs what Bulwer-Lytton aims to achieve with *King Arthur*. Wright uses ethnographical arguments to explain the formation of a nation's mythology, which he terms 'mythic genealogy'. The Arthurian legends represent the 'mythic genealogy of the Celtic race as preserved in Armorica'. These legends, together with their subsequent assimilation of historical traditions, 'form what is usually called the fabulous or heroic period of a nation's history' (Wright, 1861, p. 82). It is exactly the historical and mythical 'materials' of their science that Wright urges ethnologists to study. Furthermore Wright's thesis exemplifies Victorian attitudes to Arthurian oral, textual and archaeological remains: the legends surrounding Arthur were both the matter (geophysical evidence) and Matter (corpus of stories) of Britain, fossilizing clues to the nature of the nation's ethnic identity.

Published in the same year as Wright's essays was the collection *Essays Ethnological and Linguistic*, a series of papers read before the Ethnological Society. The author, James Kennedy, did indeed demonstrate the use and examination of historical and mythical materials as specified by Wright, just as Bulwer-Lytton was remodelling the historico-mythical Matter of Britain as a literary epic. Ironically the methodical approach Kennedy adopts is employed to argue the existence of the renowned Cimbri as an ethnic group of distinct identity who defended Britain, thus endorsing Bulwer-Lytton's fictional representation of an Arthurian breed. In 'On the Ethnology and Civilisation of the Ancient Britons', read before the Ethnological Society in July 1857, Kennedy first elucidates his intertextual and 'scientific' method and, then, implements it in a discussion of Cymric oral and written records.

For Bulwer-Lytton a crucial factor of the nation's 'mythic genealogy', and a reason for that myth's emergence, is that Arthur signifies civilization and progress. As I have suggested, in *King Arthur* the King is represented as the vanguard of 'polished Christianity' against 'rudeness'. It is again Kennedy in 'On the Ethnology and Civilisation of the Ancient Britons' who 'scientifically' defends what Bulwer-Lytton images in fiction. The essay is formed as a response to 'those English writers' and 'the most popular of our modern historians' (Kennedy, 1861, p. 26) who Kennedy considers depict Arthur's people as savages. Kennedy aims to show that the ancient Britons at the time of, and immediately after, the Roman invasion 'must have been already considerably advanced in civilisation, or at any rate far above being the miserable savages they are generally depicted' (Kennedy, 1861, p. 43). Significantly the 'Arthurian' past is constructed according to Victorian notions of the Medieval past: in Kennedy's eyes chivalry, bravery, learning and worship of women are markers of a civilized society.[10]

In Bulwer-Lytton's epic King Arthur functions typologically as an icon of Northern Chivalry and civilized values. In book one, following a traditional invocation to the Muse to sing 'Our land's first legends', the reader is given a picture of Arthur, King of the 'Dragon Race', at the centre of a pastoral idyll: 'Safe, in the sun-light, royal Arthur stood' (Bulwer-Lytton, 1853, vol. 2, p. 20). The King sees in a pool a vision of Britain as slave to the Saxon. Yet Merlin prophecies the begetting of a race of kings and an empire 'broader than the Caesar won' which will 'clasp a realm where never sets the sun'; both have Arthur as their progenitor (Bulwer-Lytton, 1853, vol. 2, p. 36). Interestingly Arthur's empire is described in terms of geographical and historical boundaries which exist beyond our concept of time, like the paradoxical substantial and insubstantial nature of Tennyson's city of Camelot in *The Idylls of the King* ('Gareth and Lynette' in Ricks, 1987, vol. 3). This can be read as an allegory of the creation of Victoria's empire, though one which sublimates the more unpleasant aspects of racial imperialism. Merlin addresses Arthur in Tennysonian riddling mode:

> And thou, thyself, shalt live from age to age,
> A thought of beauty and a type of fame; –
> Not the faint memory of some mouldering page,
> But by the hearths of men a household name:
> Theme to all song, and marvel to all youth –
> Beloved as Fable, yet believed as Truth. (Bulwer-Lytton, 1853, vol. 2, p. 37)

Here the image of Arthur himself is envisaged as boundless and almost solid, not 'faint', in memory. Indeed Arthur is referred to as an eternal 'type' throughout *King Arthur*, as if his figure is replicated many times like the multiplying races in Bulwer-Lytton's epic; a phantom haunting the visionary procession of monarchs in book seven. 'Type' in the sense of 'breed' of non-human races was to be a leitmotif in Tennyson's *In Memoriam*, published two years after *King Arthur*. Both texts attempt to describe a universe transformed by contemporary geology.

In *King Arthur*, Arthur learns from the different races he encounters during his quest, just as the nineteenth-century reader is invited to compare the various fictional social set-ups to contemporary society. At the court of the Vandal King Ludovick, Arthur sees much 'for king to imitate and sage to praise' (Bulwer-Lytton, 1853, vol. 2, p. 66). Ludovick seeks to gain power and influence through marrying off his son to a Saxon princess, which prefigures the creation of a new dynasty at the poem's end. In book three Arthur spends time in the Happy Valley, the history of which is given in the book's opening argument. The colony in the valley is strangely secluded and safe from the changes of the 'ancient world'. It has a law which forbids daughters of the Lartian or ruling family to marry into other clans – now only the queen, Aegle, survives and the male line is extinct. The colony's Augur, through man-made rather than supernatural means, has ensured the continuance of the royal house; a stranger (Arthur), whom the valley dwellers have been deceived into believing is a god, will be lured into the valley and marry the queen. Following the birth of a son the stranger will 'vanish again amongst the gods' (Bulwer-Lytton, 1853, vol. 2, p. 86), or in other words he will be secretly bundled away. In effect Bulwer-Lytton is offering a parody of Arthur's supposed mythical and childless status; Arthur's manhood must be proved at all costs if patrilineal history is to survive. Bulwer-Lytton himself was inordinately proud of his lineage and a great believer in the need for an aristocracy.[11] As I have indicated he charts this extension of the Arthurian race, the creation of an Arthurian dynasty, at a time of shifting social structures and the forging of new dynasties in nineteenth-century Britain.

King Arthur, then, is an exploration of both kingship and kinship, and kinship was a central concern of ethnologists from the 1840s onwards. *Hereditary Genius: An Inquiry into its Laws and Consequences*, the influential and best known work of the scientist Francis Galton, was published in 1869. Galton turned to studying heredity, psychology and eugenics after being involved in geographical expeditions to south-west Africa, a change of investigations brought about by the publication in 1859 of Charles Darwin's *Origin of Species*.[12] The effect of this publication on Galton was 'to arouse a spirit of rebellion against all ancient authorities' (Galton, 1908, p. 287). D. W. Forrest suggests that Galton's religious faith was in effect 'replaced by a programme for the eugenic improvement of mankind as a future article of faith' (Forrest, 1974, p. 85). After 1860, with the increasing acceptance of the evolutionary theory of human origins, science became more of an imperialist mission.

Hereditary Genius examines the kindred of about 400 men from different periods of history. Galton's list includes musicians, poets, divines, judges, oarsmen and, curiously, north-country wrestlers. Victorian 'Britons' are seen as the forgers of a new civilization, having the power, Galton argues, to indirectly improve the natural gifts of future generations: then 'the Utopias in the dreamland of philanthropists' become 'practical possibilities'.[13] The discourse of freedom and civilization being secured for future generations of Britons is that informing Bulwer-Lytton's reworking of Arthurian legend. Here, though, the emphasis is on the practical, rather than on the magical or mythical, means of ensuring liberty. Bulwer-Lytton's Arthurian epic invokes the spirit of a 'new religion' in a way which prefigures the establishment of eugenics as an 'article of faith'.

Although the narrative structure seems unwieldy and rambling at times, the cumulative effect of *King Arthur* is that of a montage of cultures, races and dynasties. Arthur is 'the knightly Caesar of the Christian North', an ethnico-religious identity which finds expression in 'The Christian Funeral Hymn', juxtaposed with 'The Etrurian Naeniae' as the culmination of book five. The importance Bulwer-Lytton has Arthur place on language mirrors a broader cultural concern for national identity. The nineteenth century witnessed the professionalization of philology; the English language itself was to become part of the Victorian myth of national origin. As MacDougall states, 'language became a test of race' (MacDougall, 1982, p. 119).[14] With *King Arthur* Bulwer-Lytton demonstrates that the recovery of the Arthurian literary past is paralleled by the Victorian reconstruction of the English linguistic past. Arthur's language is apposite for the establishing of an empire and for the nation's cultural destiny.[15]

The picture of an Arthurian world painted by Bulwer-Lytton in *King Arthur* is one of warring races. Outside the safety of the Happy Valley the chief pursuit of life, as Arthur mournfully tells the Augur, is war: 'Amidst a storm we snatch our troubled breath/And life is one grim battle-field of death' (Bulwer-Lytton, 1853, vol. 2, p. 129). This 'storm' engulfs all, ensuring that 'Age rolls on age' and that 'As tree on tree, so race succeeds to race' (Bulwer-Lytton, 1853, vol. 2, p. 108). The landscape of this world is formed from the remains of cities and empires, the relics of ancient 'giant' races.[16] It is elemental and timeless, qualities more evident than any spirit of the Middle Ages employed by the author as colouring.

Books nine and ten of *King Arthur* invoke the North, describing the Polar Spring, the Boreal Lights and the apparition of a double sun. As Arthur journeys in this territory he witnesses the 'lurid skeletons of vanished races' and 'earliest reptile spectra' (Bulwer-Lytton, 1853, vol.

3, p. 12), scenes which mark his 'fair face' with 'solemn change' (Bulwer-Lytton, 1853, vol. 3, p. 21). On confronting a Fiend he is rendered 'corpselike'. His knights arrive to raise him, and although his mail is all crushed and hewn, his face retains a 'rigid beauty'.[17] Arthur's 'rebirth' prompts the narrative voice in *King Arthur* to comment on the freedom of all Britons. The charter of freedom and Britain's shield of empire have been achieved through a gradual process which stems from the 'graves of earth's primaeval bones' (Bulwer-Lytton, 1853, vol. 3, p. 23).

The dawn of a 'new era' meant, for the later Victorians, simultaneously confronting the notions of pre-history, evolution and the questioning of religious faith. The degenerist myth of human origins had been replaced by a progressionist myth, an evolutionary doctrine which implied that complex forms developed from simple forms (or that 'advanced' was superior to 'simple', an assumption which could be applied to the study of race).[18]

Bulwer-Lytton's epic chivalric romance expresses this evolutionary attitude, binding national identity with the notion of the progress of civilization.[19] It is concerned with a multiplicity of origins, examining not only national, racial and dynastic origins, but the origins of the physical world. As such it is inextricably linked with the broader pursuit of the origin *per se* which underscores nineteenth-century historiography. Arthur's quest in *King Arthur* involves set heroic tasks, but is also for him a metaphysical quest among fossil evidence of the earth's beginnings and an educational quest for the reader, indeed a test of faith for both. One of Bulwer-Lytton's sources for his epic was Gideon Mantell's *Wonders of Geology* (1838), itself a popularization of Charles Lyell's *Principles of Geology* (1830–33). Beer suggests that Lyell's work emphasized the ability of the imagination 'to recuperate the staggeringly extended time-scale of the physical world' (Beer, 1983, p. 44); this insistence is borne out in Bulwer-Lytton's text.

Yet any sense of disorientation at the new perspectives offered by scientific discovery which the first readers of *King Arthur* might have experienced is balanced, and to a degree assuaged, by Bulwer-Lytton's placing of Arthur in the context of British history. Uncertainties are deflected by certainties: evolution signifies constant modifications in nature and the progression of British history.[20] The poem reveals many pasts; a nation's past (and its future projected through Arthur) and nature's past. It suggests a perspective beyond narrative time (Simpson, 1990, p. 39). In book seven Arthur, faced with a choice of three arches, sees himself in the third arch as a corpse. The king's image itself is refracted, mirroring the epic's multiplicity of pasts, just as Arthur is a 'type of fame' and 'race succeeds to race'. Arthur asks if his death will be in vain and is answered by the rising of the corpse-like king and a vision of the future. The visionary procession of monarchs includes Henry VII, Henry VIII and Elizabeth, and culminates in the union of Cymrian and Saxon under the banner of 'Crowned Liberty'. After witnessing and learning from this, Arthur, the 'Type of the Hero-age', chooses the arch of death: 'for in death I seize the life of fame/And link eternal millions with the dead' (Bulwer-Lytton, 1853, vol. 2, p. 264). The linear view of British history ends in Queen Victoria's land with the prophesied return of Arthur. Here Victoria is seen to extend the glory of Arthur's rule: 'Britannia's Issue'[21] maintains racial as well as dynastic continuity.

Roger Simpson suggests that with *King Arthur* 'Lytton is intent on fusing the individual into a moral type, a social class, a nation or, finally, mankind' (Simpson, 1990, p. 166). This is in accord with the poem as an ambitious representative of nineteenth-century allegory and with Bulwer-Lytton's own awareness of writing in the 'epic' tradition. In fact *King Arthur* was the first Victorian epic on Arthur to be published, since Tennyson had temporarily abandoned his planned Arthurian epic. The Preface explains the design of *King Arthur* in terms of the three divisions of epic fable – the probable, the allegorical and the marvellous – as defined by Pope. Bulwer-Lytton refers to Milton's unfulfilled 'original idea of founding a heroic poem upon the legendary existence of Arthur' and hopes that his own poem is not without originality (Bulwer-Lytton, 1853, vol. 2, p. 2).[22] A true epic, he believes, 'ought to embody the whole learning of the period in which it is composed' (Bulwer-Lytton, 1853, vol. 2, p. 10), although he is aware of his readership, not wishing to demand an erudition from the ordinary reader. Nevertheless the narrative is bolstered by scholarly notes, a development from the practices of the antiquarian treatment of Arthurian legend. It is also self-referential; in book two the narrator 'suspends the course' of the epic and questions if 'That kind of poem be not out of date?' (Bulwer-Lytton, 1853, vol. 2, p. 53), a preoccupation which can be seen in the context of the Victorian cultural quest for new ways of recasting the old.

King Arthur not only attempts to blend historicist detail with allegory, it combines topographical interest with concerns about race, nationhood and 'discovery' in the Carlylean sense of invention. In addition it provides a critique of early nineteenth-century politics by means of an allegorical subplot. Published in the year of European revolutions *King Arthur* presents the Vandal court as that of Louis Philippe, while selected Cymric knights represent British parliamentary figures of the 1830s: Geraint is the Duke of Wellington; Cadwr (Cornwall's chief) is Hardinge of Lahore, a Waterloo veteran.

Bulwer-Lytton's epic remodelling of Arthurian matter, then, is characterized by contemporary political allusion, by a representation of the

British state as evolutionary (expressed in the form of a procession of monarchs) and by a concern for dynastic and racial triumph; the eventual unity of Celt and Saxon. In this, *King Arthur* encapsulates the dominant preoccupations of nineteenth-century Arthurian literature and, more particularly, of Arthurian texts published in the 1830s.

John Parker, in *The Celtic Annals* (1831), places Arthur in the contexts of Celtic culture and British history until the Norman Conquest. *The Celtic Annals* forms part of *The Passengers*, a series of conversations between three characters touring in North Wales adapted for aiding the tourist. Parker traces the origin of the Welsh nation and in stressing the Cymric nature of Arthur and depicting him initially as a Celtic hero pitched against the Saxons he anticipates the Celtic triumphalism of Bulwer-Lytton's epic.

Yet if Parker anticipates the language of glory and liberty employed by Bulwer-Lytton, the picture he presents of the emergence of a particular racial myth of origin is rather different. In *The Celtic Annals* it is the Celtic nations which are seen to nurture the seed of Arthur's, and thus their own, downfall. The victorious Arthur is destroyed not by foreign invasion but by a 'home-born strife', a threat to the purity of the Celtic race.

Discord and a sense of the nation's decline are notes struck by John Walker Ord in *England: A Historical Poem*. The Dedication to the King suggests that the 'indomitable spirit of our ancestors' is evident in contemporary society's 'untiring enterprise' and 'household virtue'. Yet Ord employs the past–present dialectic characteristic of nineteenth-century Medievalists to lament the decline of the English race; England is, paradoxically, a slave to 'seditious and revolutionary measures', to 'new fangled notions of liberty' (Ord, 1834–35, vol. 1, pp. vii–viii). Given that Ord was writing in the England of 1833 and 1834 it is likely that his poem is an expression of Tory regret at the passing of the 1832 Reform Bill and the influence of radical politics. To restore a sense of patriotism Ord invokes his myth of national origin (firmly rooted in the concept of English constitutional liberty) in the form of a procession of monarchs, great writers and military triumphs. Arthur is, as in Bulwer-Lytton's poem, the link between past and present, connecting the 'first race of giants' with the inhabitants of Victorian Britain.

Bulwer-Lytton's *King Arthur* attempts to negotiate the question of Arthur's ethnic identity through textual representation of that which evades representation; the immeasurability of both the past and 'deep time'. One effect of this is that race is lost in space; that the political immediacy of contemporary ethnological issues is defused by the vertiginous perspectives opened up by the poem. Bulwer-Lytton ultimately comes to the conclusion that the world's history, not Arthur's history, is the greatest Epic. Contemporary geological theories which saw the universe as a continuum find expression in the legendary life of Arthur which also had 'no vestige of a beginning, no prospect of an end' (Hutton, 1795, p. 200). Today post-colonial cultural critics speak of narratives and nations in similar terms: as Homi K. Bhabha has argued, nations too can 'lose their origins in the myths of time and only fully realize their horizons in the mind's eye' (Bhabha, 1990, p. 1).

Notes

1. For accounts of the historical development of Teutonism, see MacDougall (1982) and Kliger (1952).
2. The Anglo-Saxons' 'finest hour' was in 1867, one year after the publication of Charles Kingsley's *Hereward the Wake, 'Last of the English'* and two years after John Earle's publication of *Two of the Anglo-Saxon Chronicles Parallel*. Kingsley's *The Roman and the Teuton: A Series of Lectures* (1864) casts 'Romantic Teutonism' as the racial heritage of the Protestant manly ideal, contrasting Protestant manliness with Roman decadence. *The Anthropological Review*, the journal of the Anthropological Society of London, was established in the 1860s. The year 1867 witnessed the publication of the first volume of E. A. Freeman's *History of the Norman Conquest* and the placing of William Theed's statue of Queen Victoria and the late Prince Albert in Anglo-Saxon dress in the Royal Mausoleum at Frogmore.
3. J. A. Giles's discussion of Arthur is paradigmatic of the nineteenth-century historical dilemma surrounding Arthur (Giles, 1847, vol. 1, p. 393).
4. Graham Parry (1989, p. 167) argues that '*Britannia* set the model for antiquarian studies for the next century, and sustained an enduring interest in the early history of Britain'. In successive editions Camden allowed a broader appreciation of Saxon culture.
5. Elliot L. Gilbert (1989) sees this as contributing to the 'feminization' of Arthur.
6. Ethnology (1842) is the science which deals with the relations of races and peoples, 'their distinctive physical and other characteristics'. Ethnography (1834) is the 'scientific description of nations or races of men with their customs, habits, and points of difference'. Ethnicity signified at this time heathenness as much as ethnic character (*OED*).
7. Subtitled *A Magazine of Ethnography, Phrenology and Archaeology, Considered as Elements of the Science of Races, with the Applications of this Science to Education, Legislation, and Social Progress* (June 1848 to March 1849). A new series was issued in 1854. The Ethnological Society had been founded in 1843. The review *The Anglo-Saxon* was established in 1849.
8. Hugh Cunningham (1981, p. 16) points out that in the 1840s the language of patriotism (as opposition to the Government) was still being used 'in defence of liberty against tyranny and slavery'.
9. Wright was a pioneer in the study of Anglo-Saxonism, British archaeology and Medieval remains.

10. 'On the Ethnology and Civilisation of the Ancient Britons' is similar to Bulwer-Lytton's *King Arthur* in its celebration of Celtic wisdom, affirming northernness in the tradition of antiquarian interest in Celtic history. For a contrasting view of Druidic society see Herbert (1836).

11. The Bulwers claimed Norman blood. Bulwer-Lytton inherited the Lytton family house at Knebworth in 1844. His interest in chivalric themes increased in the 1840s, partly due to the influence of the painter Daniel Maclise (who painted Bulwer-Lytton's portrait in 1850).

12. Galton had submitted the plans for his expedition to south-west Africa to the Royal Geographical Society in 1850. Southern Africa came to symbolize for Victorians the exploration of the unknown; the territory of the 'other'.

13. Preface to the 1892 edition of *Hereditary Genius*. At this time measurable data from two generations of a human population did not exist and Galton had to speculate on the hereditary mechanism. In his paper *On Blood Relationship*, written in 1872 and sent to Darwin, he attempts to explain the concept of kinship, that individuals can transmit ancestral qualities (in a latent form) to their descendants.

14. Kennedy, who stressed in the context of Arthurian ethnography that the history of a nation is often best read in its language, presented *Hints on the Formation of a New English Dictionary* before the Philological Society in May 1858. The compilation of the *Oxford English Dictionary* had been proposed to the society in 1857 by Richard Chevenix Trench. The first volume was eventually published in 1888.

15. The movement which came to be known as 'Romantic Philology' (stressing language as 'the outward expression of the inner essence of a nation or people') and how it contributed to the high Victorian ideal of civilization is discussed by Dowling (1986).

16. The geophysical relics mentioned here are indistinguishable from the historical and mythical 'relics' which Bulwer-Lytton has unearthed in rewriting Arthurian legend, and which are discussed in Wright's 'On the Ethnology of South Britain'. Ethnologists, Wright argues, should be concerned with the collection and display of such evidence or material which is both actual and mythical. 'Many Saxon cemeteries ... will pour in their contributions to our ethnological museums' (Wright, 1861, vol. 1, p. 84). Significantly both Bulwer-Lytton and Wright are writing during the peak period (1830s to 1850s) of museum building in Britain.

17. An image reminiscent of, and possibly influenced by, the depiction of Arthur 'like a shatter'd column' in Tennyson's epic fragment *Morte d'Arthur* (1842).

18. Charles Darwin's theory relating to constant modifications. Pre-1850s evolution theory was mainly associated with the French naturalist Jean-Baptiste Lamarck.

19. An attitude expressed by E. B. Tylor in *Researches into the Early History of Mankind and the Development of Civilisation* (1865). Edward Tylor was a contemporary of Galton and Huxley. See also Lord Avebury (Sir John Lubbock), *The Origin of Civilisation and the Primitive Condition of Man* (1870).

20. Nineteenth-century histories of the nation published during the Teutomania of the 1860s stressed the concept of a continuous Englishness, of an unbroken national consciousness. E. A. Freeman's *History of the Norman*

Conquest (1867–76) traced a direct line from Teutonic tribes to the Victorians. J. A. Froude's *History of England* (1865–70) displayed an anti-Celtic bias. Luke Owen Pike's *The English and their Origin* (1866) criticized the contemporary fascination with Anglo-Saxonism.

21. From Thomas Warton's 1757 poem 'The Bard'.
22. Milton, Dryden and Wordsworth all contemplated writing an Arthurian epic.

CHAPTER TEN

Shuttling and soul making: tracing the links between Algeria and egalitarian feminism in the 1850s[1]

Deborah Cherry

If there has been a shift in recent accounts of Victorian feminism away from a metropolitan emphasis towards global readings and analyses of feminism's imperialism, isolationalist perspectives have not been wholly displaced. The first organized women's movement, based in the 1850s and 1860s at Langham Place (the central London address of their meeting rooms and offices) is well documented; its politics of equal rights and equal opportunities have been assessed in relation to other nineteenth-century feminisms. Yet there has been scant mention of the visits made by the Langham Place women to the French colony of Algeria, little discussion of the impact of Algeria on Western feminists and feminist discourse and even less consideration of the interventions of British feminists in this French colony.

In this short chapter I will provide some account of the shuttling between Algeria and Britain by Langham Place women, of their activities in this North African land and of the significance of Algeria as a stage for the development of feminist subjectivity and feminist discourse at the mid-nineteenth century. Although there is insufficient space to discuss in detail the wide range of images of and writings about Algeria produced by these travelling feminists, a rereading of Bodichon's *Women and Work*, written in Algeria in the winter of 1856–57, will draw attention to their preoccupations with women of the Arab world. My concern is to consider the ways in which, from the very moment of its emergence as an organized movement, feminism's discourses on women were tangled with discourses on race. If a discussion of Algerian connections brings to visibility what has been little noticed before, it also returns to issues central to feminist politics and history today: the relations between white women and women of colour. In focusing on the Langham Place circle I want to explore the issue of a feminism publically proclaiming equality *for* women which foreclosed equality *between* women.

Gayatri Chakravorty Spivak's (1985) analysis of the relations between feminism and imperialism is central to the arguments pursued here. In her article 'Three Women's Texts and a Critique of Imperialism' she takes up earlier work by Elizabeth Fox-Genovese (1982) to argue that the historical moment of feminism in the West was marked by claims for access to individualism. Spivak asserts that in writing the history of feminism it is important to identify and situate this historical phenomenon and to analyse its particular formation of subjectivity, not to canonize it as feminism as such. The project then is to move on from the celebration of individual endeavour to a reflection upon why and with what effect such narratives and subjectivities have been consti-tuted. She continues that the constitution of the female militant subject was founded on and steeped in imperialism, explaining,

> what is at stake, for feminist individualism in the age of imperial-ism, is precisely the making of human beings, the constitution and 'interpellation' of the subject not only as individual but as 'indi-vidualist'. This stake is represented on two registers: childbearing and soul making. The first is domestic-society-through-sexual-re-production cathected as 'companionate love'; the second is the imperialist project cathected as civil-society-through-social mission. (Spivak, 1985, p. 244)[2]

Rejecting and opposing prevailing notions of the selflessness of bour-geois femininity, nineteenth-century feminist discourses were concerned with the development of a female self as independent and autonomous. For Spivak it is the discourses of race which varyingly constituted the subject, forming the Western female as feminist militant, the agent of history, while subjecting the 'native female' to the relays of colonial and imperial power: 'As the female individualist, not-quite/not-male, articu-lates herself in shifting relationship to what is at stake, the "native female" as such (*within* discourse, *as* a signifier) is excluded from any share in this emerging norm' (Spivak, 1985, pp. 244–5).[3]

Spivak thus draws attention to the imperialism of nineteenth-century feminists. For Langham Place women, the female militant's sense of self was heightened by residence in a colonial society and shaped by preoc-cupations with and concerns to speak for women of the Arab world. In the passage cited above, Spivak identifies two distinct yet interrelated registers in the regulation of sexual and imperial relationships. In the first, Langham Place feminists were at the forefront of renegotiating matrimony in terms of companionate partnership and in campaigning for the rights of married women: Bodichon's *Women and Work*, for example, was as much concerned with marriage as with work – in Britain and in Algeria. In the second register, their stake and participa-tion in civil society were often framed in terms of 'women's mission'. Drawing on philanthropy, this mission was not infrequently framed in terms of what Spivak calls 'soul making': the conversion of the heathen, the rescue of the fallen, the improvement of the uneducated. All these were among the stated objectives of the Langham Place group, whether writing about Britain or Algeria, or about Australia or Canada, the colonial destinations to which women were dispatched by the Female Middle Class Emigration Society.[4]

A polarized division between (near) East and West, colonizer and colonized will be of little assistance in coming to terms with the connections between Algeria, then a French colony, and the women's movement in Britain. And, to anticipate a later argument, oppositional categorizations which seize upon the 'other' may oversimplify an analysis of race in nineteenth-century Algeria and Britain. One way of dealing with these issues may be through 'the logic of the supplement' proposed by Derrida (1972). Dispensing with the arguments that meaning is produced through binary opposition in which one term is pitted against an other, Derrida proposes that meaning is produced through difference/ *différance*, endlessly proliferating, continually deferred. Alluding to the double meaning in French of *supplément* as addition and replacement, Derrida writes in *La dissémination* that the supplement is dangerous precisely because its textual movement is instable and slippery, disrupting binary oppositions and securities of meaning: 'Pourquoi le supplément est-il dangereux? ... Son glissement le dérobe à l'alternative simple de la présence et de l'absence. Tel est le danger' (Derrida, 1972, p. 124).[5] Not only is the supplement dangerous, but it is also a movement of violence, and Derrida writes of 'ce supplément dangereux qui entre par effraction dans cela même qui voudrait avoir pu s'en passer et qui se laisse *à la fois* frayer, violenter, combler et remplacer, compléter par la trace même dont le présent s'augmente en y disparaissant' (Derrida, 1972, p. 126).[6] Not so much an oppositional here/there, present/absent, Algeria is everywhere in feminist discourse of the mid-nineteenth century, constantly spoken, referenced, drawn and drawn upon. To bring Algeria into conjunction with mid-century feminism, not as a polarized opposition, an other, an elsewhere, but in the terms of a dangerous and violent supplement, is to destabilize its foundations and to challenge the isolationist perspectives of its history, its concerns with the chronicling the advancement of the rights of women in the West. At the same time, to locate Victorian feminism in Algeria is to draw attention to what Spivak has identified as 'the general epistemic violence of imperialism' (Spivak, 1985, p. 251). External to North Africa, imported with French colonialism and yet not part of it, western feminism was a supplement to a supplement which dangerously and violently attempted to break into, usurp, replace existing frameworks of knowledge and culture. The 'logic of the supplement' proposed by Derrida indicates that neither Algeria nor Britain can be considered as separate areas in a 'divided life'.[7] Feminist subjectivities as much as feminist discourses and practices were constituted in and by shuttling north and south, by visits to, residence in, travelling from and to, writing about, and making images of Algeria.

Barbara Leigh Smith Bodichon first visited Algeria in the company of her family in the winter of 1856–57. Several reasons may have prompted this visit: the recent increase in tourism and publication of guidebooks in English and French, the promotion of Algeria as a winter health resort especially recommended for consumptives, and an interest among Radical politicians such as Barbara's father in the witnessing the effects of French colonization after the bloody genocidal war of the 1830s and 1840s.[8] Following her marriage in the summer of 1857 to Eugene Bodichon, a French colonial and physician, Barbara Bodichon bought a house in a smart suburb of Algiers, spending approximately eight months each year there and the summer months in Britain. Friends and feminists from the Langham Place circle, particularly Bessie Rayner Parkes, came to stay and new members were recruited. According to a recent account, Emily Davies and her friend Jane Crow first came in contact with this group in Algeria in 1858 when they encountered Barbara Bodichon and her sister Annie Leigh Smith sketching. Bodichon gave Davies reading matter and the four women discussed feminism and the women's movement (Bennett, 1990, p. 20).[9] Algeria quickly became a stage for western feminism, a space for meeting and planning, networking and strategizing, a storehouse of examples and ideas, a land of possibilities and experiments. Letters, publications, paintings and travellers shuttled north and south.

When in Algeria, British feminists kept in touch with friends and activists in Britain. Letters to and from Algeria were full of exchanges about campaigning, projects and new ideas: the progress of Elizabeth Blackwell's career, the conferences of the National Association for the Promotion of Social Science, activities at Langham Place and events in the wider movement were regular topics.[10] Providing an update for Bodichon in a long letter sent to Algeria, Parkes concluded, 'I know you will be eager after *all* news' (30 January 1859, V, 87). British visitors to Algeria often commented on their anticipation of news from the UK, the arrival or delay of the post; letters by Bodichon and Parkes were no exception. On her first visit to Algeria the latter wrote, 'one gets so hungry & *devours* all the little bits of home gossip'; she noted that an electric telegraph would soon carry news to London in the space of a half-hour (Parkes to Mary Merryweather, 26–28 January 1857, VI, 72). In addition, there were frequent discussions of crossings and boat journeys, of travelling through France, of sojourns anticipated and regretfully postponed because of feminist commitments in Britain.

Parcels of books, pamphlets, feminist publications, general interest magazines and newspapers were regularly dispatched to Algiers. Bodichon told one correspondent in 1862 of her delight when such packages arrived from Britain (Burton, 1949, p. 199). Newspapers were especially welcomed: as Bessie remarked, 'they constantly contain articles bearing on the Woman question' (Parkes to Merryweather, 26–28 January 1857, VI, 72). It would seem that by 1858 Bodichon had amassed enough of a library in Algiers to lend feminist reading matter to Emily Davies and Jane Crow. Several of Parkes' letters to Bodichon reassure her that the latest issue of *The English Woman's Journal* is in the post. Letters between the two friends often discussed the journal, its subscriptions, recent issues, potential contributions, Bodichon's loan of money to the journal and her articles. A drawing of Bessie Rayner Parkes at Bodichon's Algerian residence shows her surrounded by European books and papers including *The English Woman's Journal* (see Figure 10.1).

Correspondence by Bodichon and Parkes was as much concerned with North Africa. Although detailed analysis of their representations of Algeria are beyond the scope of this chapter, it can be noted that their letters were full of vignettes of the city of Algiers, accounts of their excursions, poetic descriptions of the landscape and graphic sketches of the population. Parkes and Bodichon by no means agreed on the situation in Algeria, and the latter wrote at length on her perceptions of French society and her doubts about colonization (B. R. Parkes to Elizabeth Parkes, 29 March 1859, II, 6; Parkes to Merryweather, 11 January 1857, VI, 71).

Feminist epistolary discourse thus constructed links between Britain and Algeria. What was happening in the women's movement in Britain was constituted as worthy of report, as the appropriate and desired substance of correspondence. In turn, letters from Algeria provided commentary on British news and gave accounts of schemes hatched in Algeria which could be put in place in the UK; reports were given on members of the circle in Algeria, their doings and acquaintances. With its relaying of news and views north and south this epistolary discourse, framed around western feminism and Algeria, centred a narrating subject at the same time as it provided focal points from which a cascade of sights, sensations and perceptions about Algeria could be observed.[11] It was in and by this discourse that the subject position of the female militant was constituted. Furthermore, not only did visits to Algeria cement feminist friendships and facilitate feminist strategizing, but these alliances and networks were also secured by the interchange, in conversation as much as in letters, of snippets of information about Algeria, news of friends there, descriptions of its society and scenery. Algeria became a token of exchange in the feminist community of Langham Place.

10.1 Barbara Bodichon, 'BRP at the Campagne du Pavillon'. Ink on paper,
170 × 115 mm. Beinecke Library, Yale University. (One of three drawings of Bessie Rayner Parkes on a visit to Bodichon in Algiers. Now in
the 'George Eliot and Henry Lewes Collection', the drawings may have
been sent to Mary Ann Evans (George Eliot) and referred to in a letter
from Eliot to Bodichon, 9 April 1861)

From the first Algeria was turned into texts for circulation by and between feminists: letters, accounts for magazines, guide books; into the visual texts of sketches in letters, exhibited paintings and drawings. Within a week of her arrival Bessie Parkes wrote to Mary Merryweather that she had 'already sent off papers to the *Illustrated Times*, the *Waverley Journal* and *Chambers*' and that she and Barbara had written to Jessie Boucherett (a member of the Langham Place circle) 'to commission her to arrange with Routledge, if she can, for the publication of a book on Algiers' (11 January 1857, VI, 71). Whereas some articles went to general interest magazines, and some, like Bodichon's article on Kabyle pottery were placed in the art press (Bodichon 1865), others were aimed at a feminist readership. *Algeria Considered as a Winter Residence for the English*, a guidebook compiled by Barbara Bodichon which drew on material by Eugene Bodichon and Annie Leigh Smith, was published at the offices of *The English Woman's Journal* in 1858. Between 1858 and 1864, the journal itself contained several articles about Algeria by Barbara Bodichon (1860, 1863), Bessie Rayner Parkes (1861b) and Eugene Bodichon (1860, 1861a, 1861b), as well as reviews of Bodichon's exhibitions of Algerian paintings and notices of publications about the French colony.

Wherever placed, published articles on Algeria generated income, as did the sale of watercolours and paintings, and this income assisted in keeping feminists and feminist projects afloat.[12] Parkes and Bodichon had embarked on careers as part of a feminist belief in the necessity of paid work for women and professional success was seen as important for the movement. Bodichon supported *The English Woman's Journal* under Parkes's editorship, providing funds and articles. Bessie acted as Barbara's agent, selling her pictures and arranging exhibitions in London galleries. Bodichon seems to have been a successful artist and to have sold her work regularly. Many of the watercolours of Algerian subjects brought by Parkes from Algeria to London for Bodichon's solo show at the French Gallery in the spring of 1861 found buyers on the day of the private view (Perry, 1991, p. 14); purchasers may well have included members of the women's movement. Openings were feminist occasions and according to Parkes, 'the whole of Langham Place ... went to the private view and exulted!' (Parkes to Bodichon, 19 April 1861, V, 104).

Algeria was turned into saleable goods which, in circulating for profit in an increasingly consumerist economy, funded the western women's movement. Feminist shopping was on the agenda in an unrealized project for a shop at Langham Place; its stock was to have included handkerchiefs made by Muslim pupils at Mme Luce's school in Algiers (admired by Parkes and Bodichon) as well as feminist pamphlets and books. This commercialization of feminism by the Langham Place group took place in the 1850s, the decade in which consumer spectacle was inaugurated (Richards, 1990) and global spectacle, the world on exhibition, inaugurated with the Great Exhibition of 1851 and the Exposition Universelle staged in Paris in 1855 (Mitchell, 1988). Displays of Algerian products at both exhibitions (Greenhalgh, 1988, pp. 56 ff.) contributed to the consumer packaging of colonial territories as did the development of tourism and travel, package tours, return tickets, guide books and couriers, all of which flourished in this decade and were available to and promoted by feminist travellers.[13]

It would seem that certain strategems central to the early organization of the women's movement were devised in Algeria. Although tracing conversations is an almost impossible and, perhaps, questionable task, the significance of conversational communities as well as the decided inscription of speech in these women's letters to maintain global connections is of interest. While Derrida has had much to say/write about the relations between speech and writing, his comments on the disappearance of speech on utterance and its grave(n) passageway to writing are particularly helpful (Derrida, 1965). Key to establishing an organized movement was a location in central London which would provide office space for various societies and a meeting place. Lynne Walker has noted, that from the 1850s onwards, the West End became 'the site of a women's community within the urban centre, based on the social networks, alliances and organisations of the women's movement' (Walker, 1995, p. 71). Already a place of residence for many including Bodichon, Parkes, Emily Davies and Millicent Garrett Fawcett, this area became the preferred location for numerous women's groups: 14a Princes Street and later 19 Langham Place were established as centres of feminist activity and exchange. Visiting Bodichon and her family in Algiers in January 1857, Parkes wrote to Mary Merryweather about their discussions for such a venue:

> Just the last few days we have been discussing a plan which I think we shall certainly put in execution, that of establishing a shop, for books, newspapers, stationery, drawings, etc. in London ... We should make it the place of sale for all our books & tracts, and advertise it well. (Parkes to Merryweather, 26–28 January 1857, VI, 72)

It seems likely that the friends also considered the best way of developing their connections with the *Waverley Journal*, a ladies' magazine based in Scotland. In the spring of 1857, Parkes was offered the editorship and on 19 May 1857 she expanded her ideas in a letter to Bodichon,

> If the Waverley can be ... brought to London ... we can have our own book shop, & the beginning of a Club; room for exhibiting pictures etc, etc. ... I shall try to have the shop in Oxford St. ... My

idea is to make the whole thing *respectable* & *practical*. (Parkes to Bodichon, 19 May 1857, V, 85)

The first issue under Parkes's editorship appeared in August 1857 and the magazine ran until January 1858; it was superseded by *The English Woman's Journal* published from March that year. Premises were taken and a Ladies Reading Room was founded. Works of art, notably Bodichon's watercolours of Algerian and American subjects, were displayed and on sale there.[14] Although a shop does not seem to have been established, there was considerable discussion of this scheme over the next few years and, as noted above, handkerchiefs made in Algiers were to be on sale (Parkes to Bodichon, 5 January [1859], V, 86).

Parkes's visit coincided with the period when Bodichon was completing *Women and Work*, first published in the *Waverley Journal* in 1857.[15] In the same letter to Mary Merryweather cited above Bessie wrote,

> I think it a grevious fact that women of all sorts of mind sh^d all be crowding into the arts, and that it only wants a start among ladies to make the setting up of businesses respectable & profitable. I can see openings in this way for so many poor idle girls, if only they were persuaded it could be done. (26–28 January 1857, VI, 72)

Parkes's letter speaks of facilitating women as capitalists, managers and traders while Bodichon's text deals with the possibilities of placing women in business (Bodichon, 1857, p. 43). As is well known, paid work for middle-class women became a major issue, the women's movement founded several businesses, notably *The English Woman's Journal*, a copying service for legal documents and the printing and publishing house, the Victoria Press, and women were increasingly employed in a limited number of professions and occupations. But the campaigns for women's work were as much structured by race as by gender; in her bid for employment and recognition, the Jamaican doctress Mary Seacole did not find support from the Langham Place women.

To locate feminist strategizing in Algeria by bringing together snippets of written letters, snatches of putative conversations and fragments of published articles is not so much to trace a source or initiator for these campaigns and organizations, if such an originary reading were possible. Rather it is to begin to reconstruct the global and in particular the North African context in which egalitarian feminist discourses and activities developed in the later 1850s and early 1860s, to draw attention to the supplementary pressures of Algeria.

The practices, lifestyles and textings of British feminists in and of Algeria can be located within Orientalism, analysed by Edward Said (1978) as an extensive network of political, scholarly and aesthetic discourses which turned a western gaze upon the Islamic world and in the accumulation of knowledges about a mythic domain constituted Western selfhood and identity.[16] According to Said, Europeans regarded the lands of the Arab Near East as a pleasure ground, a textual resource, a site of desire and fantasy, a space for personal fulfilment and freedom from social convention. In identifying Orientalism as 'an exclusively male province' (Said, 1978, p. 207) he emphasized masculine sexual gratifications including the eroticization of women of colour. Recent studies which have unsettled the totalizing tendencies and interpretations of Said's monumental work by inserting sexual difference into an analysis of Orientalism (Mills, 1991; Lewis, Chapter 12 in this volume) enable a reconsideration of the pleasures sought by feminist travellers and residents in Algeria. No different from tourist and literary writings in their perceptions of the Orient as distant from, yet comparable to, western Europe, feminist texts nevertheless identified a special pleasure for women – independent mobility, that freedom of movement so desired in the West. *Algeria Considered* stated that 'English ladies can walk alone in the town and environs of Algiers with as great comfort and safety as at home' (Bodichon, 1858, p. 32), while the review in *The English Woman's Journal* remarked that 'English ladies, as we ourselves have tested, may ride, walk, or sketch alone, with as much impunity as they might in the heart of old England' (anon., 1859, p. 66).[17] If Said is correct in his analysis of masculine sexuality, no less for feminists did living in the Orient engender feminine sexual pleasures, similarly perceived as outside current norms. The radical form of marriage developed by the Bodichons was viewed with misgivings by her father who protested that his daughter did not care for her husband (Burton, 1949, p. 96). In this partnership, in which the couple only occasionally lived and worked together, Barbara Bodichon had considerable autonomy to pursue her career, campaign for women and travel independently. Advocated by Barbara Bodichon as an 'equal union' (Bodichon, 1857, p. 41), this is the 'companionate love' which Spivak has identified as a first register for feminist individualism in the age of imperialism (Spivak, 1985, p. 244).

Not only did residence in Algeria facilitate the development of feminist subjectivities and the fantasizing about feminist projects, but it also had a profound impact on the development of feminist discourse and objectives. Not only did perceptions of Arab women as surrounded by a 'multitude of restrictions' (Bodichon, 1857, p. 47) assist representations of Western feminism as beyond as much as against social conventions, but the colonial context tended to intensify the racial structuring of desire in social disciplining and 'soul making' which were so much part of 'woman's mission'. Bodichon and Parkes initially went to Algeria as tourists, but for Radical families and feminists alike, tourism was more than seeing the sites; it involved philanthropic visiting (Pratt, 1992, pp. 155–64) and, in the case of Algeria, witnessing colonization. As a French citizen (by her marriage) Bodichon became increasingly interventionist, actively supporting colonizing ventures such as Mme Luce's school, the Sisters of St Vincent de Paul and the Orphanage.[18] More often regarded in terms of sexual and voyeuristic gratification (Kabbani, 1986), Arab women were viewed in egalitarian feminist discourse as targets for missionary 'soul making', women in need of 'moral superintendence', that special quality on which western middle-class women based their claims for access to the public world (Bodichon, 1857, p. 59; Parkes, 1860, p. 117).

Women and Work is a ragged, fragmented text, a compilation of quotations from contemporary newspapers, published articles and unpublished papers held together as much by its narratives of individual endeavour as by its campaigning theme. The account of Mme Luce's school in Algiers, in which the principal figures as a pioneer of female education, purports to be taken from, and to quote, a detailed report made by 'a lady who has recently visited' (Bodichon, 1857, p. 46). But why is this lengthy pamphlet advocating the necessity of work and professional employment for Western women so concerned with Algerian women? In part this may be because, as Spivak has indicated, feminist claims to individualism and citizenship rested on foreclosing the rights and claims of women of colour. It is certainly the case that neither the pupils nor the assistant teachers nor the women attendants, the 'negresses specially attached to the school' to escort the pupils to and from home (Bodichon, 1857, p. 51), are named in any of the feminist accounts of Mme Luce's school,[19] a strategy which is indicative of the exclusion of the 'native female' from feminist categorizations of the individual (Spivak, 1985, pp. 244–5).

In *Women and Work* the need for intervention, the stage of 'woman's mission', rests on allegations that Muslim women are illiterate, indolent and fat and characterized by their 'utter debased ignorance' and 'idle slovenly existence' (Bodichon, 1857, p. 47).[20] At Mme Luce's school, it is reported, pupils were 'taught the language, and somewhat of the civilization, of the conquering race' (Bodichon, 1857, p. 47); religious instruction in Islam was given by a westernized assistant teacher. In western feminism as in the imperialist mission 'soul making' is constituted as the betterment of women. The idle women of the Arab world and the West are to be put to work. If Western women are to be improved by paid work, Algerian women are to be ameliorated by westernization. Pupils at Mme Luce's school were trained in needlework, taught to 'appreciate the value of labour' (Bodichon, 1857, p. 51) and encouraged to earn a living. But feminist goals for Muslim and

Western women did not coincide; careers in needlework, for example, did not feature on any agenda for women in Britain.[21]

There was no uniformity however in feminist discourses about women, work and Algeria. A paper given to the National Association for the Promotion of Social Science by Bessie Rayner Parkes and later published in *The English Woman's Journal* doubted the benefits of putting female children from the orphanage of the Sisters of St Vincent de Paul to work in a silk factory set up outside Algiers by a leading French manufacturer:

> our modern civilization is in some respects a very singular thing when the kind hearts of a great nation can best show their kindness to orphan girls by shutting them up to spin silk at a machine for twelve hours a day from the age of thirteen to that of twenty-one. (Parkes, 1861a, p. 196)

In this text Muslim women are not represented perjoratively; colonization is viewed critically and the French do not appear as 'the conquering race'.[22]

There was also a divergence about the value of westernization and a disparity of views on Islamic culture. In *Women and Work* it is remarked with approval that the Muslim assistant at Mme Luce's school 'in all ways looks like a French woman' (Bodichon, 1857, p. 52), that is, attired in contemporary western fashion, not veiled. However in this same text fashionable wear is disparaged as a 'practical impediment' for working women, to be discarded in favour of shortened skirts, stout boots and waterproof capes (Bodichon, 1857, p. 63). Although Langham Place women tended to favour (and wear) reformed dress, feminists tended to promote conventional models of femininity for women of colour (Ware, 1992, p. 107). In *Women and Work* the veil is deemed to be 'far from conducive to true modesty of bearing', and the unveiling of the assistant in the presence of male officials of the French government is considered to be 'a great moral triumph' (Bodichon, 1857, p. 51). The veil, which may be understood as a form of attire and bodily presentation, thus becomes that sign of the physical and cultural transformation of colonization wrought on the body of woman. Yet elsewhere, as in a touristic account of a visit to Algeria written by Parkes for *The English Woman's Journal*, the veil is perceived as integral to Islamic codes of propriety and there is a recognition that western women transgressed these codes by providing a view of the female face which it was respectable neither to show nor to see (Parkes, 1861b, p. 174).

In *Women and Work* the imperial project for feminists is identified as a concern for the improvement of Muslim women: 'Such was the human material which Mme Luce dared to conceive of as capable of being raised to something approaching the condition of her European sister'

(Bodichon, 1857, p. 48). The appellation 'sister' is indeterminate in feminist discourse, slipping between registers of meaning. Sliding across from abolitionist and charitable texts, it offered an understanding of race founded on philanthropy and anti-slavery. If 'sister' projected kinship it simultaneously marked a gap. As it conjured a communality it denied differences and disavowed the violence of colonial conquest. In conjunction with the notion of raising upward and out of 'degradation', similarly in circulation in philanthropic and abolitionist texts, the term hinted at proximity while establishing a distance between the 'native female' – 'not quite/not white' – and the western feminist – 'not quite/ not male'. The term 'sister' was thus doubly inscribed. This double inscription which writes and rewrites, occurs as Derrida explains, 'quand une écriture marque et redouble la marque d'un trait indécidable' (Derrida, 1972, p. 220).[23] It is a textual movement which as it intervenes destabilizes and unsettles.

Feminist texts of the 1850s were saturated with references to Algeria; considerations of Western women were written through with reflections on Algerian women. But women of colour were not constructed in binary opposition to western women, nor positioned as an/the 'other'. Discourses on Western and Algerian women (Arab and African) collided, abutted, interrupted and supplemented each other, indispensible in their coexistence. Thus the thinking out of 'equal unions' in the 1850s took place alongside reflections on the current state of marriage in the West *and* a conviction that arranged marriages in Algeria were 'the crowning affliction and degradation of [women's] lives' (Bodichon, 1857, p. 48); opinions on arranged marriage and polygamy continued to permeate arguments for women's work, marital reform and companionate partnership.[24]

If this chapter has been unduly concerned with what Spivak has called 'the mesmerising focus of the subject-constitution of the female individualist' (Spivak, 1985, p. 245), it has at least drawn attention to this historic figuration and to the ways in which Victorian feminism was implicated in the violence of imperialism. At the moment of its emergence as an organized movement, egalitarian feminism's discourses on equal rights were shaped in and by the colonial context of Algeria and founded on the slippery discourses of race. Women of colour were construed neither as individuals, feminists nor militants but as targets for 'woman's mission', philanthropy and the imperial project. That Western feminism is beginning to come to terms with this legacy is undoubtedly due to the textings, revisions, displacements and departures of women of colour.

Notes

1. I am pleased to acknowledge the kindness of Kate Perry, archivist at Girtin College, Cambridge, in guiding me through the Bodichon and Parkes Papers; I am also indebted to Mary Poovey for her incisive comments on another version of this chapter.
2. Spivak has glossed 'cathect' as 'to occupy with desire' from the Freudian term *Besetzung* translated in the Standard edition as 'cathexis' (Spivak, 1990, p. 241).
3. With the phrase 'not quite/not male' Spivak (1985, p. 244) rewrites, as she acknowledges, Homi Bhabha's 'not quite/not white' elaborated in 'Of Mimicry and Man: The Ambiguity of Colonial Discourse', *October*, **28**, spring 1984, reprinted in Bhabha, 1994, pp. 85–92.
4. Founded in 1862 as part of a feminist demand for women's work, the Female Middle Class Emigration Society was closely associated with Langham Place; for Bessie Parkes (1860) and Maria Rye (1860) female emigration offered work opportunities. As Vron Ware indicates (1992, p. 127) the FMCES did not meet with wholehearted approval. In 1886 it was absorbed into the newly formed Colonial Emigration Society.
5. Translated by Barbara Johnson as 'Why is the supplement or surrogate dangerous? ... Its slidings slip it out of the simple alternative presence-absence. *That* is the danger'.
6. Translated by Barbara Johnson as 'that dangerous supplement that breaks into the very thing that would have liked to do without it yet lets itself *at once* be breached, roughed up, fulfilled, and replaced, completed by the very trace through which the present increases itself in the act of disappearing'.
7. Crabbe (1981) wrote of Bodichon as an 'artist divided'; Burton (1949) differentiated the 'artist' at work in Algeria from the 'pioneer' campaigning in Britain.
8. According to Burton the visit was prompted by concerns that Bella Leigh Smith (one of Barbara's sisters) was consumptive (1949, p. 81). Other Radical politicians to visit Algeria included John Bright in the winter of 1856–57 and Richard Cobden in 1860 (Hinde, 1987, pp. 300–1; Walling, 1971, pp. 207–11).
9. According to 'Family Chronicle' (Emily Davies' reminiscences written in 1905 and extracted in Stephen, 1927, pp. 28–9), Davies met Annie Leigh Smith who introduced her to the Langham Place circle. The manuscript is now in the Emily Davies papers at Girton College Cambridge, but sections relating to the years 1848–61 which were consulted by Stephen no longer survive. Davies was in Algeria accompanying a brother diagnosed as consumptive.
10. Correspondence of Bessie Rayner Parkes is held in the Parkes Papers in Girton College Library and is cited here by file number.
11. There is a marked tendency in the correspondence and published writings of Bodichon and Parkes to pictorialize, that is to turn into pictures, Algeria and its indigenous peoples. This discursive strategy, noted by Mary Louis Pratt as characteristic of travel and discovery literature of the period (Pratt, 1992, pp. 201–8) is discussed in detail in my forthcoming book *Feminism and Visual Culture in Britain before 1900* (Routledge).
12. Hester Burton (1949, p. 86) claimed that Bodichon's Algerian subjects

'were exhibited and sold in London, and provided her with money for the endowment of Girton and other charitable concerns'.

13. Bodichon (1858, p. 32) includes information on travel to Algeria, as does the review of this publication in *The English Woman's Journal*, 3, 1859, pp. 64–6.

14. Parkes to Bodichon, 30 January 1859, Parkes papers, V, 87 and 30 August [1859], V, 89. An advertisement for a display of Bodichon's art work and a leaflet advertising an English Boarding House in Algiers and providing tourist information bound with a copy of *Algeria Considered* is in the collection of Bodichon's library, Girton College. This conjunction indicates something of the proximities of tourism, travel and pictorializing.

15. Perry (1991, p. 3). The 1857 issues of the *Waverley Journal* have not survived. References in a letter from Joseph Parkes to Bessie Rayner Parkes, 12 February 1857, II, 57, suggest that *Women and Work* was first published in this magazine.

16. Chow (1993, p. 8) argues that Orientalism is not confined by the historical/geographical limits of colonialism and pervades western attitudes to East Asia.

17. Undecidable in feminist texts, 'alone' may signify at once solitary, unchaperoned, even accompanied by a servant, guide, person of colour.

18. Bodichon also purchased pottery for the Victoria and Albert Museum and with her husband organized the large-scale planting of eucalyptus (Burton, 1949, pp. 86, 89). For a feminist critique of eucalyptus as destructive to indigenous ecosystems see Shiva, 1988, pp. 80–7. Both Memmi (1957, 1972) and Prochaska (1990) have counselled against homogenizing *colons* or settlers.

19. Bodichon, 1858, pp. 72–3; *The English Woman's Journal*, 1859, p. 65; Parkes, 1861b, p. 177.

20. This representation, which coincides with the imperialist myth of the 'lazy native', can be compared to Lucy Snowe's assessment in Charlotte Brontë's *Villette* of a woman of colour depicted in a painting of *Cleopatra* (Cherry, 1993, pp. 113–19; Lewis, Chapter 12 in this volume).

21. Like Harriet Martineau (1859), Bodichon was convinced that 'there is no way of aiding governesses or needlewomen but by opening more ways of gaining livelihoods for women' (1857, p. 44).

22. A western presence is however inserted and the report is given from the subject position of the female militant, the individual 'I' who witnesses and comments upon what she has seen.

23. Translated by Barbara Johnson as 'whenever any writing both marks and goes back over its mark with an undecidable stroke'.

24. For example, Rhoda Garrett (1872) advocated work for women on the grounds that 'a great many women are, willing or unwilling, compelled, by the law of this land that a man shall have only one wife at a time, to remain in single blessedness'.

CHAPTER ELEVEN

Other women and new women: writing race and gender in *The Story of an African Farm*

Anita Levy

Olive Schreiner's *The Story of an African Farm* (1982, first published in 1883) is often read critically according to a just-so story casting novelist and female character alike as 'new women' tragically shackled by the bonds of Victorian womanhood. Scholarly articles and studies abound detailing Schreiner's lifelong personal and artistic struggle against the exhausting demands of Victorian 'patriarchy', and her heroic efforts to excel as a writer and an intellectual in a cultural climate hostile to women. Recounted are tales of her unconventional marriage to and long separations from South African businessman Samuel Cron Cronwright, her neurotic illnesses, or her intellectual and romantic entanglements with Havelock Ellis, Karl Pearson and his Men and Women's Club in late-Victorian London (First and Scott, 1980; McClintock, 1995; Walkowitz, 1992). 'Some feminists in the United States,' concludes Carol Barash, 'have reclaimed Schreiner's as a lost feminist voice or discussed her life as that of a tragic heroine' (Barash, 1989, p. 269).[1]

So too, Schreiner's most famous literary creation, Lyndall, heroine of *African Farm*, is celebrated for her efforts to resist Victorian conventions of marriage and motherhood, a resistance often translated into something more closely resembling Schreiner's own advocacy for poor and working women. To this effect, professional readers sometimes cite the remembrances of a Lancashire working woman, who said, after reading *African Farm* when it was first published: 'I think there is hundreds of women what feels like that but can't speak, but *she* could speak what we feel' (Barash, 1987, p. 2). At the same time, Lyndall's desperate flight from the stifling intellectual and social confines of the impoverished Boer farm and the pathological family that inhabits it – Tant' Sannie and her corrupt overseer cum husband, Bonaparte Blenkins, the aged caretaker Otto and his misfit son Waldo – takes on a resemblance to Schreiner's own journey from colonial periphery to imperial metropolis.[2]

When the category of race or ethnicity is factored into analyses founded upon gender, it is to admit, if somewhat reluctantly, that embedded within both life and novel are embarrassingly irreconcilable ideological and narrative contradictions. Schreiner's progressive feminism suffers from the taint of bad Victorian science, becoming, as Barash (1987, p. 19) argues, 'fundamentally and unmistakably racist'. Those readings that deploy 'race' as an interpretative tool, moreover, often do so in isolation from the category of gender. Hence, one such study counts the number of times 'natives' appear in *African Farm* and concludes, rightly I think, that the novel is indifferent to the 'kaffirs', 'Hottentots', and 'Bushmen' who dot the landscape. They matter only inasmuch as they facilitate, explain or mimic the actions of the Europeans (McClintock, 1995, p. 271; Vivan, 1991, p. 96). Others, like Schreiner biographers Ruth First and Ann Scott, turn bare necessity into abundant virtue. Maintaining that the absence or the invisibility of Africans makes 'a statement about the violence of colonialism', they argue, '[the novel] has been criticized for not being the "race relations novel" that people expect, in that blacks are merely "extras". But that was the point about the colonial condition: Africans were kept so far outside white society that that in itself was a statement about it' (First and Scott, 1980, p. 97).

If I have oversimplified somewhat this spectrum of recent critical responses, it is to suggest that those who write about the construction of gender in *African Farm* either neglect the role of race or subordinate one category to another. By the same token, those cataloguing the representation of race have difficulty factoring gender into their analyses. In so acceding to critical models presupposing a distinction between gender and race, many readings reproduce unwittingly the logic of nineteenth-century terminologies of the human sciences and fiction. This, despite evidence to suggest that they collaborated discursively and practically to produce a single set of differences between self and other.

This chapter begins, instead, from a recent critical tradition maintaining the indivisibility of the racial and the sexual subjects.[3] To read Schreiner's novel in the interstices of categories of race and gender, it will demonstrate that the discursive strategies with which the novel constructs the 'other' woman, as represented by the critically neglected figure of the Boer-woman, Tant' Sannie, are inseparable from those imagining the 'new woman', Lyndall. I want to establish three points simultaneously. First, Schreiner's novel implicitly produces a notion of colonial Englishness in opposition to 'Boer-ness'. It does so by organizing these national categories according to a hierarchy of gendered features as embodied in and through the strategic juxtaposition of Lyndall, Em and the Boer-women, Tant' Sannie.[4] Secondly, and by extension, when the novel pathologizes the domestic domain making it the place suitable only for comic, grotesque or absurd Boer-women, it cancels out an older historical model of gender. This earlier model identified the woman with the signs and symbols of domesticity as imagined in novels of the 1830s and 1840s, *Mary Barton*, *Oliver Twist* and *Jane Eyre*, among them. Finally, this discursive strategy permits the novel to rethink the category of gender, or what makes a female a woman. Hence, 'gender' is reconfigured as a highly interiorized, psychological feature of female mind or consciousness.

Let us now observe the Boer-woman as she tosses restlessly about in bed:

> In the farm-house, on her great wooden bedstead, Tant' Sannie, the Boer-woman, rolled heavily in her sleep. She had gone to bed, as she always did, in her clothes; ... and dreamed bad dreams. Not of the ghosts and devils that so haunted her waking thoughts; nor of her second husband, the consumptive Englishman ... ; nor of her first, the young Boer; but only of the sheep's trotters she had eaten for supper that night. She dreamed that one stuck fast in her throat, and she rolled her huge form from side to side, and snorted horribly. (Schreiner, 1982, pp. 35–6)

Woman so represented in terms of grotesque bodily and material excess, violates boundaries of space, time and desire. While Tant' Sannie's waking hours are filled with superstitious thoughts of 'ghosts and devils', her dreams are consumed by appetite. Like the so-called primitive females anatomized by nineteenth-century anthropologists and medical men, her sexuality is in excess and overwhelms her gender.[5] Hence, the voracious hunger for sheep's trotters merges seamlessly with the sexual desire for men. Bakhtinian logic, moreover, connects her to the lower regions of the body, to earth, to dung, to food and to flesh. Hers is a body out of control; it is overly large, excessively desirous, and too noisy, while her speech similarly violates social and verbal boundaries. As Graham Pechey notes, it 'is filled with "low images" of bodily provenance and typically takes the form of cursing or swearing, angry imperatives, exclamations ambivalently mingling praise with abuse' (Pechey, 1983, p. 72). More importantly, the Boer aunt's monstrous body and demeanour foregrounds her deformation of domestic authority that in her hands is excessive, violent, and out of control. Abusive and ill tempered, Tant' Sannie then is the figure of domestic authority gone awry.[6]

Simply put, she is represented as an improperly gendered female. In this she grotesquely embodies the other woman of 'race', her lack of self-control linking her rhetorically to the figure of the native, as imagined in texts such as H. Rider Haggard's *King Solomon's Mines* (first published in 1885) and *She* (first published in 1887). Certainly the 'wizened, monkey-like figure' Gagool, evil witch of *King Solomon's Mines*, is far more horrific than Schreiner's Boer aunt. Described as a 'sun-dried corpse' the size of a 'year-old child' with a scalp that 'moved and contracted like the hood of a cobra', she befits a creature dreamed up in Piccadilly or the Strand (Haggard, 1957, pp. 121–2). There, as Schreiner chided writers of 'wild adventure' like Haggard, 'the gifts of the creative imagination untrammelled by contact with any fact, may spread their wings' (Schreiner, 1982, p. 28). Despite Schreiner's claim to write, unlike Haggard, the truth of Africa, Tant' Sannie shares certain common features with Gagool. Figures of illicit combination, they violate, to differing degrees, categories of animal/human, genders and generations all combined in one figure of undecidability. Both, finally, are represented as harsh and capricious female rulers who govern 'societies' in need of rule because lacking in good self-government.

If the Boer-woman is a figure more suitable for parody, her stepdaughter Em resembles a female from an earlier moment in the history of fiction. Like the Boer-woman, Em's body exceeds proper boundaries, until '[s]he was grown into a premature little old woman of sixteen, ridiculously fat' (Schreiner, 1982, p. 155). Her domestic aspirations, along with her 'white linen', and 'embroidery', once so crucial to establishing a household as depicted in earlier domestic fiction, become the source of shame and ridicule, subject of Lyndall's scorn (Schreiner, 1982, p. 184).

Taken together, Tant' Sannie's grotesque body and Em's outmoded domesticity suggest what it means to be female in a narrative where the domestic domain will no longer materialize gender. The important point is neither woman is the heroine of this novel, nor can they be. For what these figures signal is precisely the impossibility that a novel like *African Farm* could be headed either by heroine as domineering mother or devoted wife. In becoming ridiculous, the good mother or the dutiful wife who domesticates the man in the end is becoming outmoded. Her central role in the cultural imaginary to be superseded by a new model of what makes a female a woman.[7]

If the woman at home is rendered a grotesque parody of heroines we remember from our most beloved early Victorian novels – Catherine Morland, Mary Barton, Jane Eyre – the farm household becomes the stuff of the comic or the absurd, especially as literalized in the antics of Bonaparte Blenkins or the oddities of Waldo. When the household is linked to the representation of quaint or comic Boer customs, it is marginalized even further. One instance must suffice here to sketch the shape of this pattern. During the ritual courtship night, called the 'upsitting', between Tant' Sannie and young Piet Vander Walt, the following conversation takes place. Praising his dead wife, Piet declares:

'She was such a good wife, aunt: I've known her break a churn-stick over a maid's head for only letting dust come on a milk–cloth.'

Tant' Sannie felt a twinge of jealousy. She had never broken a churn-stick on a maid's head. (Schreiner, 1982, p. 203)

Notice that the exercise of female authority and domestic governance becomes ridiculous, downright laughable. Both the dead and the pro-spective wives become absurd figures of household regulation out of control who govern by force rather than by the moral suasion so necessary to earlier Victorian housekeepers, as represented in countless novels, household manuals, educational treatises, and the like. Here, as elsewhere, *African Farm* calls into question an older, culturally power-ful model of domestic governance by revising the domestic scene through its association with arcane rituals of the Boer community. Given this, it is no wonder that the Englishman's daughter, Lyndall, must go else-where.

In so propelling Lyndall off the farm, Schreiner makes a dialectical move that opens up the category of the intellectual woman for the heroine to occupy. That is, *African Farm* demonstrates what happens when the household becomes an untenable site. Specifically, the female is forced to construct a new being outside of the home. To remain within the farm household with its grotesque 'family' is never a think-able option for the intellectual woman as represented by Lyndall. To look for gratification in the outside world, however successfully, be-comes the only viable alternative in the logic of the novel.[8] This is because it cancels out historical choices available to the respectable young colonial Englishwoman. *African Farm* relegates them to the gro-tesque, the absurd, the comic or the foreign.

The world of the mining towns to which Lyndall flees is hardly more satisfactory than the one she abandons. Interestingly, Schreiner does not represent her experiences there directly. Rather, the narrative takes up Lyndall's story after her return from a four-year absence apparently spent, in part, attending a girl's finishing school. So described, this educational institution closely resembles an English school of the 1840s and 1850s, as characterized by Martha Vicinus (1985), among others. It is fair to say that such schools probably survived largely unchanged in the colonies long after their reform in England. In 'unreformed' schools at mid-century, credentialled teachers, standardized subjects and exams, familiar to educational institutions of a later period, were largely un-known. Both girls' and boys' schools often resembled large houses inhabited by an institutional family governed benevolently by parent figures. Their tutelary programme, according to Elaine Showalter, relied upon a mode of governance that took the domestic sphere as its example and female domestic authority as its desired form (Foucault, 1967; Showalter, 1985; Vicinus, 1985).[9]

When Schreiner subjects the boarding-school to sustained scrutiny, she finds it woefully lacking. Indeed, seen through Lyndall's eyes, it becomes little better than a glorified prison, designed to 'crush the soul'. 'I have discovered that of all the cursed places under the sun,' Lyndall tells Waldo in a passage worth quoting at length:

> a girl's boarding school is the worst. They are called finishing schools, and the name tells accurately what they are. They finish everything but imbecility and weakness, and that they cultivate ... Can you form an idea, Waldo, of what it must be like to be shut up with cackling old women ... ? It is suffocation only to breathe the air they breath ... I did not learn music, because I had no talent; and when the drove made cushions, and hideous flowers ... and a footstool in six weeks that a machine would have made better in five minutes, I went to my room. (Schreiner, 1982, pp. 185–6)

What is crucial here is that the abilities of the good mother and the good wife – to practise domestic economy and to cultivate one's innate qualities – become forms of punishment cruelly inflicted upon the young by 'cackling old women'. In so invoking this moment in the history of education simply to ridicule it, Schreiner clears a rhetorical and historical space for a new female figure to emerge out of the ruins. This figure must make her place in the world outside domestic institutions and the home upon which they are modelled. In so imagining this new female figure, however flawed, the novel, I suggest, updates gender itself.

It is significant that *African Farm* does not provide an institutional or a cultural place for this female, as will be the case in 'new woman' fiction. George Gissing's *The Odd Women* and Dorothy Richardson's *Pilgrimage* come to mind here. Instead, Schreiner endows Lyndall with new internal dimensions that mark a significant departure from femaleness so represented in terms of Tant' Sannie and Em. Hence, with spirit and toughness in abundance, the young Lyndall seems perfectly suited to her role as quintessential 'new woman'. Her physical delicacy and 'elfin-like beauty' form an extreme contrast to the gross physicality of Tant' Sannie and Em. Whereas their bodies increase in bulk as time passes on the farm, Lyndall's gradually fades away virtually into thin air. Hers is the late nineteenth-century 'salon body' of élite females. So identified by Nancy Armstrong (1990), this body graced the walls of London art galleries, lay on 'tea tables in open photo albums' and 'animated fashion-sheets' like the one pasted up at the foot of Tant' Sannie's bed. This body is no more in evidence than upon Lyndall's return to the farm, when she is captured in the following pose: 'She leaned back in the little armchair; she wore a grey dressing-gown, and her long hair was combed out and hung to the ground' (Schreiner, 1982, p. 183). Dressed in subdued colours, her hair coiling about her, the figure of Lyndall is aestheticized; she becomes a figure for art itself. In this, she resembles not simply the drowning Ophelias of Pre-Raphaelite painting, but the languid, pale females photographed by Julia Margaret Cameron and Lewis Carroll.[10]

Most importantly, even as Lyndall is defined by the lack of bodily materiality, 'she' is materialized simultaneously as a metaphysical body. In so revising the aesthetics for representing the female, Schreiner relocates 'gender' to the place of mind or consciousness, and thus contributes to the rhetorical construction of a new domain of gendered information. Victorian psychology, in turn, will extract this information from the female individual and endow it with sense. In contrast to the sociological mode of earlier domestic novels emphasizing the structure of the household and the skills of the woman within, this psychological mode focuses on the internal structure of female mind and desire.

As illness further deprives Lyndall of her body, she is aestheticized more completely. Nursed by Gregory, the rejected suitor who dons women's clothes to be near her, Lyndall becomes: 'A little white, white face, transparent as an angel's, with a cloth bound round the forehead, and with soft shorn hair tossed about on the pillow' (Schreiner, 1982, p. 272). Notice how Schreiner 'replaces' her heroine, earlier the strident, confident intellectual, with a more saintly and recognizably late Victorian figure. As she is beatified before our eyes, the spirit subsumes all traces of the material Lyndall. The passage creates a new self to which it then attributes superior beauty. The following passage shows her thus doubled and split by the look in the mirror: 'She looked into the glass ... Such a queenly little figure in its pink and white. Such a transparent little face, refined by suffering into an almost angel-like beauty. The face looked at her; she looked back, laughing softly' (Schreiner, 1982, p. 281). Several features of this passage warrant particular attention. First, the fully transformed Lyndall is literally and figuratively unrecognizable from the impetuous figure who ran wild on the veld, challenged Tant' Sannie's rule, and escaped the farm to find her place in the outside world. Secondly, notice how this description incorporates many of the characteristic features of Victorian 'femininity' that exist today in the form of powerful clichés and stereotypes. In place of a spirited, desiring subject, there is now a dreamy, soft, melancholic, damaged female deprived of material reality. Thirdly, the splitting of the self – the woman and the woman in the mirror – permits the production of the notion that there exists an essential woman apart from and other than her body. The making of the aestheticized body, then, also signifies the

hollowing out of the material body, which is then filled with the language of the metaphysical self.

It is fair to say that when Tant' Sannie and Em are coded as grotesquely female because possessed of highly physical, sexualized or
domesticated bodies, an older notion of the Englishwoman is displaced
onto the ethnic body; in becoming 'other' women, they become un-
thinkable. Thus emerges the figure for female mind, so materialized by
Lyndall, who comes to life, becomes most 'herself', paradoxically, in the
absence of body, sex and household. As a prototypical figure for the
modernist preoccupation with the writing of female consciousness,
Lyndall must take her place with Virginia Woolf's Clarissa Dalloway,
Dorothy Richardson's Miriam Henderson, James Joyce's Molly Bloom.
For nothing will demonstrate the professional abilities of the modernist
writer, bring about the moments of highest aesthetic value in modernist
fiction, more than such figures – artfully crafted abstractions of female
mind. Ultimately, *The Story of an African Farm* can only bring this 'new
woman' into being once it has dismantled the discursive materials com-
posing the British female in an earlier historical moment, relegating
them to the far outposts of empire.

Notes

1. Sandra Gilbert and Susan Gubar's (1988, p. 82) treatment of Schreiner is
    a classic example of this approach. *The Story of an African Farm*, they
    argue, 'meditates on the inexorability of female victimization in patriar-
    chal culture, more explicitly identifying femininity with martyrdom'.
2. Graham Pechey (1983, p. 76), however, argues that *African Farm* prioritizes
    the colonial otherness of the farm rather than the imperial metropole. As
    Itala Vivan (1991, p. 95) notes, the inhabitants of the farm represent the
    components of the Euro-white population transplanted to the Cape Colony:
    the Dutch, the English, the Anglo-Irish and the Germans.
3. See, for instance, Gilman (1985a), Levy (1991a), Sharpe (1993), and
    Spivak (1986).
4. In a similar fashion, Rudyard Kipling organizes an imperial erotic hierar-
    chy based upon the related categories of national, ethnic and racial differ-
    ence in 'The Ladies' (Kipling, 1940, pp. 442–3).
5. See, for example, Flower and Murie (1867) and Lombroso and Ferrero
    (1898).
6. On the centrality of the domestic model of governance to Victorian
    culture, see Armstrong (1987) and Showalter (1985).
7. In this respect, Schreiner's colonial heroine is remarkably similar to those
    imagined in metropolitan fiction at this historical moment. There is evi-
    dence to suggest that late Victorian fiction contributes significantly to the
    new figure of the properly public woman who comes into being during
    the second half of the nineteenth century. This figure mediates between
    the extremities of the intensely private woman at home and the overtly

public woman of the streets, the prostitute. 'She' and her activities constitute a new domain of social and philanthropic engagement, called 'the
social' by Denise Riley (1990, p.49). See also, Koven and Michel (1993),
Prochaska (1974), Ryan (1990) and Summers (1979).

8. This strategy is similar to one deployed by Dorothy Richardson in *Pilgrimage* to map the progress of her protagonist, Miriam Henderson, from the household to the public world. See Levy (1991a).

9. During the first half of the nineteenth century, according to Foucault (1967), this tutelary programme not only infused schools with a new type of authority, but prisons, asylums, hospitals and workhouses as well.

10. On the relationship between British Aestheticism and gender, see Psomiades (1992).

CHAPTER TWELVE

Women and Orientalism: gendering the racialized gaze[1]

Reina Lewis

This chapter is concerned with a variety of female Orientalist gazes. It explores the contribution of European women artists and writers to an area of representation that was hugely popular throughout the nineteenth century; an area that, as Edward W. Said argued powerfully in 1978, was never neutral but was inextricably bound up with European domination over large parts of the globe (Said, 1978).[2] Using a Foucauldian model of discourse, Said and many others working in the area of imperialism and culture have demonstrated that knowledge about the Orient was linked to power over it; a power relation which applied equally, but differently, to fiction and painting as it did to government reports (Lowe, 1991; Mills, 1991; Young, 1990).

This study attends to the gendering of the racialized gaze that Europe directed at its Oriental other. In general, work on Orientalism tends either to emphasize Orientalist images *of* women or to analyse a classificatory and voyeuristic gaze that is inevitably understood as male, or as paradigmatically male. Here, I look at selected works by European women artists who inserted themselves into an Orientalist visual tradition, and read literary representations by women which, like Charlotte Brontë's *Villette* (1853), draw on an Orientalist mode of representation to create an independent female subjectivity. It is clear that in its flattering vision of the superiority of Western civilization over the despotic, heathen and primitive Orient, Orientalist discourse obscured the reality of class, gender and race tensions at home, as much as it misrepresented any such thing as the 'real' Orient. However, what is also clear is that a racialized discourse like Orientalism did offer European women artists and writers a route to professional success and, crucially, a way of articulating alternative femininities. But rather than simply delineate good anti-imperialist feminists versus bad racists, I want here to explore how women created or reconceptualized spaces in which could be articulated a series of imperial positionings for both artists and writers and their readers. The balance of payments this produces for European women is then briefly counterposed to the problems of and opportunities for textual self-presentation faced by Oriental women who wrote about segregated Muslim life in English for European readers.

In my research into women's contribution to Orientalist culture in the nineteenth century, I found a number of European women artists who represented the Orient and was able to formulate an argument about the gender- and class-specific restraints on the production and reception of their work (Lewis, 1996). On the whole, I found that women representing the harem in both visual and literary forms tended to challenge the Orientalist myth of the harem as an isolated sexual prison by depicting it as a social and familial realm, analogous to the European bourgeois domestic. Henriette Browne's painting *A Visit (Harem Interior; Constantinople, 1860* (1861, see Figure 12.1), typifies this strand in visual art and I would also reference Billie Melman's work on women travellers and writers (Melman, 1992).

It is clear from contemporary responses to women's Orientalist art that the existence of women's accounts of the Islamic world was well known and that their gendered point of production was important. It was uniformly understood that when it came to the harem, women could see what was denied to western men and that, therefore, their accounts had a privileged access to truth. With a few notable exceptions, this 'alternative' discourse was generally subordinate to hegemonic Orientalism, surfacing only when one of its exponents reached new levels of notoriety or when a specifically feminine knowledge was required (e.g. Edward William Lane – author of *Manners and Customs of the Modern Egyptians*, 1837 – asking his sister Sophia Poole to write about the segregated lives of Muslim women, in Poole, 1844). But the clearest evidence of contemporary familiarity with women's accounts is revealed in critics' responses to women's work. Rather than position every woman Orientalist artist as a rare exception, critics frequently refer to other women in their reviews. This serves both to keep women in a marginal and self-referential field, and to pit women against each other as a way of invalidating accounts which challenge key masculinist fantasies and the visions of established male Orientalist artists and writers.

Browne's painting differs from the generic codes of Orientalism. Typically in visual art the Orient is represented in lush colours on canvases crammed with detailed exotica, featuring strangely costumed people and their 'primitive' customs. In the work of artists such as J.-L. Gérôme, J. A. D. Ingres and J. F. Lewis, there is an emphasis on the (often depraved) sexuality of the Oriental, with numerous representations of the harem and the bath, each providing an opportunity to paint languorous nudes incarcerated in ossified spaces of sumptuous luxury in which they await the sultan's pleasure.[3] The ideological significance of

12.1   Henriette Browne, *The Visit (Harem Interior; Constantinople, 1860), Une visite (intérieur de harem, Constantinople, 1860)*, 1861. Oil on canvas, 86 × 114 cm

the high gloss Orientalist technique, typified by Gérôme, is discussed by Linda Nochlin (1983). Browne disrupts these conventions by painting fully clothed women in relatively plain spaces and, significantly, by inserting gazes *between* women into a situation which paradigmatically relies on inactive female figures suspended in static space. Like narrative film, the myth of the harem is activated by the male hero who alone has the power to move the narrative; to be, as Teresa de Lauretis puts it, the agent of transformation (de Lauretis, 1988). Browne, as the only other possible witness/viewer of the harem symbolically replaces the husband as the transforming agent but, rather than simply climb into his meta-phorical shoes and parody a typical harem painting, she sidesteps the myth and socializes rather than sexualizes the harem's petrified space. Here I am thinking of Laura Mulvey's initial formulation of the female gaze in narrative cinema, where the assumption of an active female gaze requires the adoption of a transvestite position; since to identify with a female on screen is to assume a passive position in a genre where male characters alone have the ability to drive filmic action (Mulvey, 1975, 1981). Browne paints from a position that *had to be female*, according to the prevailing ideas of artistic production, femininity and the harem, and that *had to be active*, according to the construction of her as the author of a text predicated on a direct viewing of an unremittingly gendered space (and she did have a reputation for always working scrupulously from observation). She thus intervenes in the dynamic of active/male and passive/female by being, and being understood to be, a female painting subject who actively looks at and represents the harem, and can facilitate a pleasurable viewing position for the women in her audience.[4]

But although this allows the western female viewer to stand in the artist's shoes, the distance between the artist/viewer and the subject of the picture is retained. Unlike the pathos of the 'woman's' film where weeping – a sign of overidentification with filmic characters – is a sign of the film's success, the *Interiors* cannot risk collapsing the distance between the western observers and the eastern observed. In the final analysis the points of similarity and empathy must not override the points of difference. Browne's status as westerner and artist requires the construction of difference at the same time as her gender allows the construction of an affinity between herself and the woman's space.

The possibility of a female spectator's pleasure in Browne's images take me to a passage in *Villette* that has long fascinated me because it is concerned precisely with the visual pleasure of the female Orientalist spectator; what bell hooks would call the pleasure of the 'interrogative' gaze (hooks, 1992). Lucy Snowe is in an art gallery in Belgium looking at a painting that has all the tropes of an Orientalist odalisque:

It represented a woman, considerably larger, I thought, than the life. I calculated that this lady, put into a scale of magnitude suitable for the reception of a commodity of bulk would infallibly turn from fourteen to sixteen stone. She was, indeed, extremely well fed: very much butcher's meat – to say nothing of bread, vegetables, and liquids – must she have consumed to attain that breadth and height, that wealth of muscle, that affluence of flesh. She lay half-reclined on a couch: why, it would be difficult to say; broad daylight blazed round her: she appeared in hearty health, strong enough to do the work of two plain cooks; she could not plead a weak spine; she ought to have been standing or at least sitting bolt upright. She had no business to lounge away the noon on a sofa. She ought likewise to have worn decent garments; a gown covering her properly, which was not the case: out of abundance of material – seven-and-twenty yards, I should say, of drapery – she manages to make inefficient raiment. Then, for the wretched untidiness surrounding her, there could be no excuse. Pots and pans – perhaps I ought to say vases and goblets – were rolled here and there on the foreground; a perfect rubbish of flowers was mixed amongst them, and an absurd and disorderly mass of curtain upholstery smothered the couch and cumbered the floor. On referring to the catalogue, I found that this notable production bore name [*sic*] 'Cleopatra'. (Brontë, 1994, p. 275)

I think it perfectly clear that Lucy and, by implication, her readers are quite familiar with the iconography of visual Orientalism. Jane Miller, one of the many critics who has analysed this passage, argues that Lucy must undertake a male impersonation in order to adopt the position of white superiority that so judges the *Cleopatra*; an image which Miller sees as a male fantasy of female sexuality and male pleasure (Miller, 1990).

While I agree that the text projects onto the *Cleopatra* the negative aspects of an active female sexuality with which Lucy cannot be associated, I do not think that Lucy critiques the *Cleopatra* as a man. The dynamics of imperialism give Lucy the ability to criticize social norms not because she displaces them and her implications in them (onto the picture or a masculine alter ego), but because they provide a series of positional superiorities in which Lucy can claim for herself *as a woman* the authority to judge and represent that the codes of femininity and class normally deny her. The terms of Lucy's analysis are intrinsically female: evaluating the figure's stature in relation to the domestic labour (shopping and cooking) that its maintenance would require; casting a housewifely eye over the jumble of accoutrements in the Oriental interior that to other (male) eyes might constitute the essential elements of an Orientalist fantasy of sexual fulfilment; recasting the Oriental drapes in terms of the yardage required to make clothes; asserting the Protestant work ethic over the lassitude of Oriental sexuality. To Lucy, this is not a room of inviting sexual relaxation and pleasure but an untidied (i.e. waiting to be tidied) domestic space. This is a judgement encoded in the terms of a feminine positionality that is structurally dependent on, at the same time as it is productive of, a concept of femininity that is white and western. What Jane Miller misses out from her analysis of Lucy's judgement is that the chapter sets it from the very beginning into a context of public viewing and contested meanings which mobilizes not just gender but the other shifting relational terms of class, nation and race that structure the social. It is in this light that Protestant Lucy disputes the curatorial advice of M. Paul – who directs her away from the *Cleopatra* towards the worthy but dull series *Vie d'une femme* – and sarcastically discusses the whole incident with the English Dr Bretton:

> 'Pooh!' said he, 'My mother is a better-looking woman. I heard some French fops, yonder, designating her as "le voluptueux" is little to my liking. Compare that mulatto with Ginevre!' (Brontë, 1994, p. 282)

Although Lucy uses the opportunity of viewing the *Cleopatra* to pass judgement on people normally considered to be above her, she does not do this by pretending to be male. While it is clear that in order to differentiate herself from the orientalized femininity on display,[5] Lucy must refuse the erotic voyeurism of the *Cleopatra*, the alliance with Graham reframes the gendered gaze of her white femininity with the signifiers of nation and class.[6]

So far, so good: Browne paints respectable interiors; Lucy Snowe tries to evacuate sexuality from the Oriental interior. Respectability, it seems, will out, as women artists and writers struggle to maintain professional identities that will not overtly contaminate their classed femininity.

But I also found images by women artists that appeared to reproduce precisely the masculinist myth of the harem and the orientalized woman that it had at first seemed was subverted by a female gaze. Into this camp I would place *An Odalisque* (n.d.; see Figure 12.2) by the Danish/Polish woman artist Elisabeth Jerichau-Baumann. This, with all its sexualized nudity and detail has far more in common with the high Orientalist sexual fantasies of Ingres or Gérôme than the domestic, understated elegance of Brown. Given that women's accounts of the harem, visual or written, were understood to offer the truth about a realm from which men were forbidden, how do we approach these images? If work by an artist like Henrietta Browne can be seen to have challenged treasured Orientalist stereotypes – thus fitting neatly into an analysis in which her classed and gendered conditions of production led her to enunciate an alternative version of the harem – what do we make of Jerichau-Baumann's *An Odalisque* and *Vandbaerersker/The Water*

12.2   Elisabeth Jerichau-Baumann, *An Odalisque*, n.d. Oil on canvas, 99 × 74.2 cm

Carriers (1875; see Figure 12.3) or Margaret Murray Cookesley's *Nubian Girl* (1886; see Figure 12.4)? Were these women artists hounded out of polite society for representing things about which no decent woman was meant to know? Or, did the discourse of Orientalism provide a space for both the counterhegemonic desexualizing representations of

12.3 Elisabeth Jerichau-Baumann, *Vandbaerersker (The Water Carriers)*, 1875.
Engraving

Browne and an opportunity for women to enter into what had previously been seen as the male preserve of the sexualized nude?

It seems to me that the way to understand the space in which these
paintings were situated is to look at the intersection between discourses
of art, gender and ethnography. As well as the usual art critical concerns (of subject choice, technique and morality) women's Orientalist
images, in particular those that were more overtly sexualized, were also
discussed in relation to ethnography. This relationship functions in

12.4 Margaret Murray Cookesley, *Nubian Girl*, 1886. Oil on canvas, 41.7 ×
31.2 cm. Photograph courtesy of the Mathaf Gallery, London

contradictory ways; ethnography works both as a rationale for wom-
en's venture into sexualized images (thus Cookesley's *Nubian Girl* can
be positioned as a pseudo-scientific ethnographic type) and as a device
by which the critic can introduce an overtly sexualized tone into the
discussion of apparently blameless images by women (as was the case
with Browne's *Rhodian Girl*, 1867, not illustrated, which I have discussed elsewhere, see Lewis, 1995).

Jerichau-Baumann was an artist with a successful portrait practice among élite circles in Europe and the Middle East, yet who also produced these potentially risqué pseudo-classical nudes. One way in which these potentially transgressive pictures were legitimated was in terms of prevailing discourses of ethnography. A space is opened up for women to paint the nude if such images could be favourably received because, like Jerichau-Baumann's use of Oriental settings and accoutrements, they could be coded as authentic (pseudo) scientific enquiry. But as the tortured effort of this review from the *Art Journal* shows, reviewers had to work hard to read Jerichau-Baumann's work as both ethnographic and feminine:

> The paintings of this lady command attention as they are marked by characteristics which are by no means common to woman's work ... This lady is impelled upwards into the epic vein by her tastes and feelings, and, at the same time, is more pronouncedly ethnographical than perhaps any artist of the day. There is, however, one tie which her woman's heart acknowledges, and that is a love of children [an emotive description of the pictures of children follows] ... *The Favourite of the Hareem*, an oil-picture, declares itself at once a veritable study from Oriental life. All attempts at the improvisation of Hareem beauty by painters and poets have been very wide of the truth, as we learn from this and all other genuine representations of so-called eastern beauty ... what is most valuable in [her work] is their indisputable nationality, which is brought forward without any modification or dalliance with conventional prettiness of feature. (*Art Journal*, 1871, p. 165)

In this case, the rigours of objective ethnographic reality sit uneasily with the definition of feminine art. The review cannot but admire Jerichau-Baumann's depiction of 'nationality', but would far rather see the conventional prettiness that the artist eschews. Similarly, while it is forced to applaud the assertiveness of her independent thought, the review does its best to give her *oeuvre* a feminine complexion by affirming her womanly love for children. What interests me here is that her *oeuvre was* mixed and did include paintings which could be received as unproblematically womanly, but that despite this there is something about her Orientalist subjects that creates a problem big enough to destabilize the overall classification of the artist and her work, something that other women Orientalists generally manage to avoid.

While *Vandbaerersker* has at least the rationale of a geographical location (Memphis) and a potentially pseudo-classical subject, Jerichau-Baumann's *Odalisque* stands on her own. Of course all images of the harem were instantly located within an ongoing dialogue about the harem, but there is little in this painting that sets up a particular narrative. The lone figure is placed very close to the picture plane,

12.5   Sophie Anderson, *In the Harem, Tunis*, n.d. Oil on canvas, 77.5 × 63 cm

filling the space as she gazes rapt at her own image. As we have seen the female point of origin of images of the harem was always significant, so perhaps in this instance it works to save the image from being considered unrespectable. When one compares this image to Sophie Anderson's *In the Harem, Tunis* (n.d.; see Figure 12.5), one begins to see how interventionist was Jerichau-Baumann's work. The number of similarities between Jerichau-Baumann's and Anderson's odalisques (both single figures wearing similar headresses and much jewellery, reclining in an interior with a small table at their side) make their different treatment of this typically Orientalist ensemble more pronounced. Anderson's lovely young woman is certainly available to the voyeuristic gaze, but her demeanour of passive langour or even ennui (since unhappiness was never hard to attribute to harem women) differently inflects the viewing experience. Where Jerichau-Baumann's odalisque is assertively naked and engaged in self-appreciation as she smiles at her own reflection, Anderson's figure gazes off-screen and presents her body obliquely; she is set further back in the picture space and, though fully clothed, reveals a shapely arm in a seemingly accidental way. Although the suggestion that a sleeve just 'happens' to have fallen from her arm might fool no one, this time-honoured artistic convention provides an alibi for the artist that excuses her from charges of salaciously painting female flesh. Jerichau-Baumann, in contrast, paints a self-conscious (semi-) nude with no excuse at all. Hardly surprising that critics mobilize discourses of ethnography to make sense of her work.

Yet women were not usually understood to have access to the neutral, scientific gaze of the ethnographer. As Melman has shown, when women did provide ethnographic information it was coded as empathetic and emotional, rather than disinterested and scientifically detached. It does not appear that Jerichau-Baumann's female ethnographic gaze offers a critical commentary on the life of the Oriental woman; certainly her paintings do not fit into Joyce Zonana's description of feminist Orientalism as a discourse that analogized the oppression of Islamic woman as a way to talk about the oppression of white women in Europe (Zonana, 1993).

So women cultural producers are faced with the problem of trying to claim a gendered authenticity against attempts to devalue their specific knowledge, while at the same time not tainting themselves with the potentially immoral scenes they represent and, for western women, continually balancing that gendered empathy against the need to differentiate themselves in terms of race. That most women artists tend to paint desexualized versions of the harem, could be either because (for those that actually travelled) they really never did see anything immoral, or that they edited it out of their accounts lest it impinge on them as witnesses of the scene. In literary representation, although women writers did have to fend off charges that they were only as moral as their last novel, the conjunction of literary-critical practice and the increasing number of women writers gave them more opportunity to establish a morally essential distance. Despite their position as the gendered other at home, Western women writers, like Emmeline Lott

(1866, 1867), are able to appropriate an imperial and disapproving distance with which to disassociate themselves from any immoral acts they might depict. Additionally, the woman writer, unlike the woman artist, can phrase risqué parts of her story as recounted, rather than first person observation. But, none the less, the representation of even mundane subjects is complicated for the western woman writer, since scenes of the women's quarters or of children can be both the familiar terrain of femininity and the immutable other of the Orient. Sophia Poole, for example, challenges the sexualization of the harem by emphasizing how the shared female interest in children is a great ice-breaker on visits to new harems, but then feels compelled to assert a western distance and superiority, in this case by dismissing as superstitious some of the child-rearing practices of the Oriental mothers.

For 'Oriental' women writing in Europe, where they clearly had to contend with racist assumptions about their own morality, the textual encoding of a gendered and racialized authorial self is even harder. Emily Said-Ruete, originally from Zanzibar, writes scathingly of the vagaries of Christian marriage ('Is it not bitter irony and delusion to talk of only "one" wife?'), offering the moderated (remember she is now dependent of European goodwill) voice of the orientalized other answering back (Said-Ruete, 1981). Her book self-consciously tries to challenge European stereotypes about Islamic women while also distancing its author from their negative associations. That Said-Ruete and the Georgian/Turkish writer Melek-Hanum found a market in Europe suggests the potential take-up for this other alternative Orientalist discourse (Melek-Hanum, 1872). But, rather than see their accounts as the transparent inscription of an observable 'reality', we must deal with them as representations that adopt and alter Western narrative conventions through the insertion of a gendered orientalized interrogative gaze. The reverse-shot of the orientalized woman writing back to Europe in Europe's own languages illustrates what Lisa Lowe calls the multivalency of Orientalist discourse: Victorian Orientalism was indeed fractured from within and challenged from without.

Notes

1. Sections of this article have previously appeared in versions elsewhere. I am grateful to Routledge for permission to reproduce from Reina Lewis, *Gendering Orientalism: Race, Representation, Femininity* (1996) and to Oxford University Press, for permission to reproduce from 'Women Orientalist Artists: Diversity, Ethnography, Interpretation', *Women: A Cultural Review*, 6(1), summer 1995.
2. In the imaginary geography of Orientalism, different parts of the globe are

categorized as the Orient depending on the different spheres of Western influence and activity concerned (India for the British more than for the French, for example). While there may be at times a precise relationship to recognizable geopolitical entities, it would be a mistake to try to tie it down: it is precisely the fantasy nature of the Orient that accounts for its longevity in Western discourse. Places can be both generically 'other' and specifically different within a play of interconnecting stereotypes, knowledges and experiences.

3. It is impossible in this article to include enough illustrations to indicate properly the characteristics and range of the mainstream Orientalist painting in relation to which I am discussing Browne and the other women artists. Readers not familiar with the genre are directed to the following sources for access to reproductions (Thornton, 1983, 1985).

4. See Lorraine Gammon on the importance of relationships and looks between women on screen for the visual pleasure of the female viewer (Gammon, 1988) and see Wendy Leeks for an alternative formulation of the female viewer of Orientalist art (Leeks, 1986).

5. Although, it must be noted, the scope of this transgression is limited. The derisive tone of Lucy's rejection of the *Cleopatra* and the judgement of those who admire it suggest the tension involved in denying an image (however patriarchal) of an active female sexuality. In a novel without a 'happy ending' the attempt to represent or enact an active female sexuality is problematized and unresolved. Neither the insupportable choice of images in the gallery nor the deathly Vashti in the theatre provide a sexuality to which Lucy can be reconciled.

6. See Judith Newton on how the strategic disadvantaging of Paul places him in a suitably equitable position to Lucy to be her help-meet and lover. With the superior Graham the only possible female positionality is the child-like dependence of Paulina (Newton, 1985).

CHAPTER THIRTEEN

'Tracing the route to England': nineteenth-century Caribbean interventions into English debates on race and slavery

Helen M. Cooper

In 1857 Mary Seacole wrote: 'As I grew into womanhood ... I was never weary of tracing upon an old map the route to England; and never followed with my gaze the stately ships homeward bound without longing to be in them, and see the blue hills of Jamaica fade into the distance' (Seacole, 1988, p. 4). A free-born Jamaican woman with a black mother and a white father, Seacole published in London this passage about her adolescence in Jamaica in *Wonderful Adventures of Mrs Seacole in Many Lands.* Paul Gilroy draws attention to the significance of 'ships in motion across the spaces between Europe, America, Africa, and the Caribbean' (Gilroy, 1993, p. 4) as a central image of 'the difficult journey from slaveship to citizenship' (Gilroy, 1993, p. 31) for people of the Black Atlantic. Seacole elides herself with those stately ships, identifying England as her home. She thereby allows for an extension of Benedict Anderson's (1991) argument about imagined communities to a consideration of how the colonized who sailed to England imagined themselves as participating in England as a nation.

The Anti-Slavery Reporter represented one point of view: 'we ... solemnly pledge ... to exert ourselves ... in vindicating the indefeasible claims of these unfriended and outcast children of humanity to the rights of British subjects; to equal laws; to justice; to freedom; and to all the blessings of the gospel' (Anon., 1829, p. 468). Certainly after the abolition of slavery 'black Jamaicans were encouraged to consider themselves to be as British as any citizen born in Yorkshire or Midlothian ... [through] economic and political dependence so pervasive that few areas of life in the English-speaking Caribbean were unaffected' (Alexander and Dewjee, 1984, pp. 12–13). Conversely during slavery, as Gilroy claims, both 'the moral and political problem of slavery ... was once recognised as *internal* to the structure of western civilisation and appeared as a central political and philosophical concept in the emergent discourse of modern cultural English uniqueness'; the history of slavery constitutes not just the history of black people but 'a part of the ethical and intellectual heritage of the West as a whole' (Gilroy, 1993, pp. 9, 49).

This chapter contextualizes the work of two ship travellers, who traced the route from the Caribbean to England and who negotiated their positions as British slave and British subject respectively. Mary Prince (c.1788–1830s) a slave, sailed from Bermuda, to the salt fields of Turks Island, Antigua, and finally to England where, in hope of gaining her freedom, she related *The History of Mary Prince, a West Indian Slave* to Susanna Strickland.[1] Thomas Pringle (Secretary of the Anti-Slavery Society) edited her *History*, including a long supplement, for publication in London in 1831. *The Times* reported the legal controversies it produced through 1833. Secondly, Mary Seacole (1805–81) sailed from Jamaica to Cuba, Haiti, Panama, New Granada, the Crimea and England. In 1857, lauded (along with Florence Nightingale) as a Crimean heroine for her service to English soldiers there in her capacity as both hotel-keeper and Jamaican 'doctress', she published her *Wonderful Adventures*.

Prince's *History* and Seacole's *Wonderful Adventures* document how their authors negotiated their positions as women of African and 'hybrid' African-European descent in relation to English ideas of national and racial identity, and thereby contributed to 'the emergent discourse of modern cultural English uniqueness' (Gilroy, 1993, p. 9). These texts reveal the tension between and interdependence of Caribbean and English identities that allow for an engagement with the history of black women's participation in England as a nation. Citizens of what Gilroy terms the 'black Atlantic', or in Carole Boyce Davies's (1992) words positioned as 'migrating subjects', they both represented Caribbean nations and were also constitutive of England's 'imagined community'.

Prince and Seacole occupied very different positions in that community. Prince in England in the early 1830s was black, a slave, yet because slavery was abolished earlier in England than in its colonies, she was a free woman in England in working-class occupations – laundress and domestic servant. Seacole in England in the 1850s was of mixed race, free-born, and celebrated as a Crimean War heroine. She imagined herself as middle class, yet her documentation of her professional life resists the identification of middle-class English women with the domestic sphere. However, she maternalizes her business and medical work, identifying herself as 'Mother Seacole' to England's soldier sons.

I want to draw attention to two facts that marked the abolitionist movement in England from the 1780s until the 1860s. First, the anti-slavery movement in England, especially during its focus on West Indian slavery in the late eighteenth and early nineteenth centuries, was primarily a print movement. Benedict Anderson has shown how print capitalism contributed to the idea of nation in late eighteenth-century Europe. He argues that one of the factors that bound otherwise disconnected and anonymous people together into what he designates an 'imagined community' was newspapers. James Walvin records how the Anti-Slavery Society published 3,000,000 copies of tracts between 1823 and 1831. David Turley adds how 'other tracts, printed speeches and sermons and local publications by antislavery bodies' as well as the 'reciprocal relationship between pamphlet and newspaper insertion' contributed to the anti-slavery movement understood as a national print culture (Turley, 1991, p. 48). Turley lists four developments in print capitalism available to and deployed by the anti-slavery movement: technical developments; geographical expansion in printing; specialization in publishing; national distribution network for books and pamphlets. He argues that conditions were ripe for 'the cheap and rapid production of vast quantities of anti-slavery material and for the expansion and relative cheapness – and consequent probable expansion in readership – of newspapers' (Turley, 1991, p. 50), and concludes that print propoganda aimed both to agitate people to help shape anti-slavery public policies through the sustained force of public opinion and also to influence those who exercised power and authority. Thus, the fact of slavery was intimately associated with the formation of the imagined community of the English nation, even if the practice within England's geographical borders was limited.

Secondly, the anti-slavery movement was marked by the widespread participation of women, who often represented their own legal bondage to men as a kind of slavery, and who found in the abolition movement a valid way to engage in the nation's public life. Indeed, anti-slavery activity probably represented the first mass movement of women in political life. Vron Ware documents four themes that characterized women's abolitionist writing: an imagined audience of women; women's moral responsibility to emancipate the slaves; the need for white women to understand both the brutality of slavery through empathy with black women and also that black and white were part of the same human [English] family; emphasis on the hypocrisy of British claims to civilization in the light of British slavery (Ware, 1992, pp. 60–3). White women's participation in abolitionism was a complex strategic alliance rather than natural and essentialist; slave owners' wives (for equally complex reasons) in the West Indies could be as brutal as their husbands towards women slaves, as Prince records.[2]

As part of this historical phenomenon of abolitionism Susanna Strickland transcribed two slave narratives – Prince's *History* and that of *Ashton Warner A Native of St Vincent* – in January 1831. The first was then edited and published by Thomas Pringle, secretary of the Anti-Slavery Society,[3] thereby contributing to the outpouring of tracts and pamphlets that consolidated an English national Protestant identity of moral superiority (especially in relation to Catholic France's reinstitution of slavery following the rebellion in San Domingue). The Anti-Slavery Society was, however, problematically positioned in relation to a nationally imagined English identity because of its 'avowed and implacable hostility to the Colonies, and … general treachery to the interests of the empire' (Anon., 1830, p. 376).

Readers of anti-slavery tracts could contextualize Prince's *History* in relation to the celebrated case 'respecting the slavery of the mongrel woman Grace' from Antigua. Grace Jones had accompanied her owner, Mrs Allan, to England in 1822 and returned to Antigua with her in 1823. In 1825 Grace was seized 'as forfeited to the king, on suggestion of having been illegally imported in 1823' (Haggard, 1827, p. 4). Grace's case rested on the central paradox that 'the law of England discourages slavery' while that same law 'gives an almost unbounded protection' to slavery in its colonies (Haggard, 1827, p. 43). Lord Mansfield in 1771 had ruled that a slave who escaped in England could not be sent back to his owner in the West Indies. In 1806 the slave trade was abolished. Thus Grace's case rested both on the notion that transporting her back to Antigua violated the ban on the slave trade, and also on the philosophical question as to whether a slave in England could have that freedom reversed in the colonies. The final judgement against Grace's case hinged on the appropriate definition of freedom: 'the arguments of Counsel, in that decisive case of Sommersett [Lord Mansfield's decision, 1771], do not go further than to the extinction of slavery in England, as unsuitable to the genius of the country and to the modes of enforcement. They look no further than to the peculiar nature, as it were, of our own soil: the air of our island is too pure for slavery to breathe in' (Haggard, 1827, p. 21). Grace's freedom was defined by the purity of English air rather than by her legal manumission. Lord Stowe ruled that she remained in a state of slavery in spite of her time in England where she was technically but not legally free.

Prince, free to leave her owners in England, wanted to return to Antigua as a free woman to live there with her husband. She could not argue her case, based on her status in England, for legal precedent in Grace's case ruled against her. Her appeal, therefore, was for manumission on the basis of the cruelty visited on her as a slave.

The situations of other female slaves had also been recorded in *The Anti-Slavery Reporter* such as: 'Cruelties Perpetrated by Henry and Helen Moss, on a Female Negro Slave [Kate] in the Bahamas'; and 'The

Rev. G. W. Bridges, and his Slave Kitty Hilton'. The extreme cruelty inflicted on both women resulted in the death of Kate. Elements of these earlier records also mark Prince's *History*. First, the torture visited on her naked body informs the Revd Bridges's punishment of Kitty Hilton when he ordered her 'stripped of every article of dress, tied up by the hands, her toes barely touching the ground, and flogged until the back part of her, from the shoulders down to the calves of her legs, was one mass of lacerated flesh and gore' (Anon., 1830, p. 374). Secondly, Kate's punishment was justified as resulting from 'a persevering obstinate disposition on the part of the slave, Kate, and an equal determination on the part of her owners to carry their authority into effect'. This battle between the slave woman's disposition and her owners' authority is at the heart of the debate in Pringle's 'Supplement' over the validity of Prince's testimony. Barbara Bush (1990) asserts that Europeans in the West Indies often found women slaves more troublesome than men; their resistance to their slave status took the form of verbal abuse, pretending illness, working slowly, stealing, lying, practising obeah and myalism, and concocting poisons. Slave-owners, accustomed to English women's subordinate position were particularly incensed at female slaves' insolence and defiance, indicating as it did that they could not ultimately control their women slaves by whip, sex, or tortures and degradations. Thirdly, Kate's death as a result of Moss's punishment was contextualized with testimony pointing to 'the respectability of Mr and Mrs Moss, and of their general kindness to their slaves, and ... to the high estimation in which they are held by "all who have visited Mr Moss and partaken of his hospitality"' (Anon., 1829, p. 467). Prince's detractors, supporters of the plantocracy, also offered character references for the Woods to invalidate her claims against them.

If, as Ware claims, women abolitionists assumed a female readership, then Strickland's introduction to Warner's narrative provides a context for reading her transcription of Prince's *History*. She assumes readers who are well educated but of an 'apathetical and deluded class' such as she had been: believing the 'prejudices and misinformation' of the West Indian plantocracy as expressed in 'literary periodicals on the side of the planters, such as the *Quarterly Review, Blackwood's Magazine*' (Strickland, 1831, p. 6); participating in 'criminal ignorance' about slavery (Strickland, 1831, pp. 5–6), sharing in the 'great national crime'; dismissing 'statements of the cruelty and oppression which prevail in our colonies' as 'absolutely fabricated for political purposes', 'far too shocking to be true' (Strickland, 1831, p. 7). Strickland credits her commitment to abolitionism to the power of personal testimony, that is, she responds not to reasoned argument but emotionally to 'conversing with several negroes, both male and female, who had been British colonial slaves' whose bodies were marked with 'the brand and the whip'. Recognizing that 'the voice of truth and nature prevailed over my former prejudices' (Strickland, 1831, p. 11), Strickland came to assume Africans into English domestic ideology:

> Does the African mother feel less love to her offspring than the white woman? – or the African husband regard with less tenderness the wife of his bosom? Is his heart dead to the ties of kindred – his nature so brutalised that the sacred associations of home and country awaken no emotions in his breast? (Strickland, 1831, p. 10)

She embraces slaves as fellow human beings who, she assumes, subscribe to the same domestic and patriotic sentiments as English people. She supported the successful slave rebellion in San Domingue on the grounds that it represented how 'the abrogated rights of humanity were there re-conquered by the African race' (Strickland, 1831, p. 10). English people tended to be fearful not supportive of this rebellion, but Strickland exemplifies Ware's claim that women abolitionists encouraged white women readers' empathy with brutalized black women through an appeal to a common domestic humanity.

While Strickland offers readers access to slave stories so they will share her conversion to the slaves' cause, her comments on her transcriptions point to the vexed issue of authorship and authenticity they raise; namely: how much did Prince and Warner censor what they told? How much did Strickland consciously and unconsciously edit or change what they said? What opportunities for revision were they given by Strickland or Pringle?[4] Strickland claims she adhered to 'the voice of truth and nature ... wherever it could conveniently be done' in reproducing Warner's language (Strickland, 1831, p. 15); of 'black Mary's Life' she adhered 'to her own simple story and language without deviating to the pathos of flourish or romance. It is a pathetic little history' (Ballstadt, Hopkins and Peterman, 1985, p. 57). Strickland undermines the expectations of women, accustomed to novel reading, that Prince's story will reflect generic English forms. Yet, her description of the 'pathetic little history' is dismissive but also a promise that the work still employs the appeal of pathos.

Strickland's own position as transcriber of Prince's history is of necessity intriguing and complex: we can unravel little of it, except to note that Warner's story was published with Strickland as named author. However, she wrote to friends about the printing of Prince's *History*: 'Of course my name does not appear. Mr. Pringle has added a very interesting appendix' (Ballstadt, Hopkins and Peterman, 1985, p. 57). Later, she describes Prince's presence in her wedding party: 'Mr. Pringle "gave me" away, and Black Mary, who had treated herself with a complete new suit upon the occasion, went on the coach box, to see her dear Missie and Biographer wed' (Strickland, 1831, p. 60). There is a regret in the fact that, as an aspiring writer, her name does not appear on Prince's work, and also a significance that she describes Pringle as Prince's biographer, rather than acknowledging Prince's own authorship. Strickland presents the *History* as Pringle's product not Prince's story, and acknowledges the temptation to rewrite the story, spicing it up as an English romance. Certainly, we know that the story fits a certain formula to engage its English readers with its emphasis on family, marriage, religion, on the indecent cruelty visited on women's naked bodies, and with the repression of all overt references to one of the most central facts of West Indian slavery – sexual relations between woman slave and master. Prince's *History* also retains, however, an opposition which speaks to Prince's material and textual resistance, to her self-determination and self-esteem, and to her strategic but not committed engagement with Christianity.

Strickland and Pringle may claim to have produced Prince, but in the *History* she claims her own specific narrative authority: 'I have been a slave – I have felt what a slave feels, and I know what a slave knows' (Strickland, 1831, p. 64). She contrasts her knowledge with English ignorance, assuming that 'few people in England know what slavery is'. Prince defines her purpose as education, so 'all the good people in England ... know it too, that they may break our chains, and set us free' (Strickland, 1831, p. 64). Prince positions slavery as integral to English national knowledge, while revealing how fragile English goodness is: 'Since I have been here I have often wondered how English people can go out into the West Indies and act in such a beastly manner. But when they go to the West Indies, they forget God and all feeling of shame' (Strickland, 1831, p. 83), so that Captain I — could 'abuse me with every ill name he could think of, (too, too bad to speak in England)' (Strickland, 1831, p. 58). Prince both participates in a national narrative of English purity, while also reversing the English ethnographic gaze to focus on English bestiality.

If bestiality haunted the narrative of English goodness so also did English desire: 'the debates about theories of race in the nineteenth century, by settling on the possibility or impossibility of hybridity, focused explicitly on the issue of sexuality and the issue of sexual unions between whites and blacks. Theories of race were also covert theories of desire' (Young, 1995, p. 9). Young foregrounds the black/white sexual relationships at the heart of English slavery, but Prince's focus on brutal beatings – which also characterized *The Anti-Slavery Reporter*'s presentation of the cases of Kitty Hilton and of Kate – speak to another formation of 'colonial desire', to what Mary Favret describes as the 'British Antislavery Movement Writing Pornography'.[5] Prince documented her treatment by two of her owners: for Captain I —, 'to strip me naked – to hang me up by the wrists and lay my flesh open with the cow-skin, was an ordinary punishment for even a slight offence' (Strickland, 1831, p. 56), while 'Mr. D — has often stripped me naked, hung me up by the wrists, and beat me with the cow-skin, with his own hand, till my body was raw with gashes' (Strickland, 1831, pp. 62–3). The fascination that English people showed for the buttocks and genitalia of black woman as exemplified by their attention to Saartje Baartman, popularly known as 'the Hottentot Venus', has been documented by Sander Gilman (1985c). While black men were also stripped naked and brutally beaten, the material act and literary representation of clothed white men beating naked black women suggests sexual desire displaced into a discourse of punishment. Foucault argues that the eighteenth-century European practice of making 'the body ... the major target of penal repression' and 'torture ... a public spectacle' gave way around the turn into the nineteenth century to an idea of 'punishment [as] ... the most hidden part of the penal process' (Foucault, 1979, pp. 7–9). However, slave-masters and the narratives about them perpetuate the older public spectacles of torture. Slave-owners indulged in this violent display in an attempt to exert control over constantly rebellious slaves. Prince, however, refocuses attention away from the rebellious slave and onto the slave owners' brutality, a holdover from an earlier age and an exemplar of a cruel sexuality.

Prince is silent about overt sexual relations with her owners, although she implies that Mr D — assumed his rights to her, acknowledged only as his 'ugly fashion of stripping himself quite naked and ordering me then to wash him in a tub of water' (Strickland, 1831, p. 68). Prince refused at times because 'my eyes were so full of shame'. She reports how he would beat her for this refusal: her juxtaposition of Mr D's nudity, his beatings, and her shame engage a sexual discourse without directly speaking it. Claiming her own agency Prince manipulates a sense of English national virtue to her advantage: 'I then told him I would not live longer with him, for he was a very indecent man.'

Prince both participates in an English discourse of shame and decency, but she also reverses the national assumptions about English civilization and African primitiveness. Prince speaks to Mr D, in a way that would resonate to women readers whose own bodies were subject to the legal ownership of their husbands or fathers. Yet where abolitionists saw themselves as offering a common humanity to slaves, Prince claims a moral superiority to the practices legally condoned by the mother country. Her decision to live no longer with Mr D, and her subsequent ability to persuade him to sell her to the Woods exemplifies an agency which escapes English delineation of Africans as primitive or as victim, but incorporates slave-owners' fears and knowledge of how impossible it was to control by brute force the African majority in the West Indies. Prince claims a subjectivity which both allows her to participate in the code of decency claimed as an English national characteristic to justify imperial activities, and also permits her to question the limits of that decency. Prince addresses the problematic issues of where England's boundaries lay, and who was designated English. Certainly she speaks to a distinction between the good people of England and the bestial English in the West Indies, yet English laws protected those West Indians. She includes herself, a black slave, in an imagined community of readers who understand her sense of shame and decency, while redrawing its boundaries to exclude the white English in the West Indies.

Pringle's Supplement included testimony for and against the veracity of Prince's *History*, and the rhetoric of decency lay at the heart of the Woods's written response justifying their refusal to legally manumit Prince. Both her conversion by the Moravians and her marriage to Daniel James, a free black man, without permission from her owners, were causes of contention between Prince and the Woods in Antigua and in the controversies surrounding the publication of her *History*. However, both marriage and conversion to Christianity were increasingly part of the abolitionists' programme for slaves in the 1820s and 1830s and spoke to the domestic ideology which Strickland had invoked to convert readers to the abolitionist cause. While Prince emphasized her conversion and marriage, Wood charged Prince with laziness and indecency.

The facts upon which Wood based his charge of indecency were omitted from the *History*; Pringle in his Supplement represented the facts by ellipses and a footnote: 'I omit the circumstance here mentioned, because it is too indecent to appear in a publication likely to be perused by females' (Strickland, 1831, p. 91). Pringle, however, included in the Supplement as support for Prince's veracity a letter from Joseph Phillips, a white resident of Antigua and an active abolitionist married to a black woman, who described Prince's relationship with a white Captain Abbott before she married. Phillips speaks to the double narrative that makes such an act 'immoral conduct' in England and 'almost universal' in the West Indies, where legal marriage was denied to slaves. He asserts that Wood, therefore, was accusing Prince of 'immorality' '*for effect in England*, a tale ... not intended for Antigua so much as for Stoke Newington, and Peckham, and Aldermanbury' (Strickland, 1831, p. 101). In cross-examination in the final legal battle between Wood and Pringle for libel, as reported in *The Times* in March 1833, Prince admitted: 'she did not live in the house with [Captain Abbott], but slept with him sometimes in another hut which she had'; she also admitted to beating up a woman whom she found sleeping in her hut with Captain Abbott. *The Times* reported, 'She told all this to Miss Strickland when that lady took down her narrative. These statements were not in the narrative published by the defendant' (1 March 1833, pp. 6–7). Wood assumes a sympathetic hearing when he reveals Prince's sexual relationship with Captain Abbot. However, while a slave woman's desire might be designated as indecent in England, Harriet Jacobs in *Incidents in the Life of a Slave Girl* offers a different reading when she delineates how relationships with white men who were not their owners served to help slave women gain power and protection. When women were officially forbidden to marry, they learned to use their bodies strategically for power in a way not possible for unmarried, middle-class, white English women readers. Thus descriptions of the torture of naked slave women were deemed appropriate reading material for Aldermanbury and English females, but knowledge of how unmarried women could wield power even under the brutal restrictions of slavery was not.

What Strickland deemed 'a pathetic little history' participated in the rhetoric of England as an imagined community of goodness and decency, yet Prince's self-determination, her ability to earn market money, to decide her own sexual relationships, and to manipulate her environment even under the devastating conditions of slavery violated the rhetoric of English middle-class domesticity and the subordination of English women in the early nineteenth century. Yet the same energy that brought thousands of English women into the abolitionist movement as a way of addressing their own dissatisfaction with limited roles, resonates to Prince's oppositional narrative. Even Pringle described her as having the faults of 'a somewhat violent and hasty temper, and a considerable share of natural pride and self-importance'; while he delineated 'her religious knowledge [as] still but very limited ... and her views of christianity indistinct' (Strickland, 1831, pp. 105–6). Pringle participated in certain English assumptions about the appropriate behaviour of black women; but these attributes in fact represent an oppositional narrative of strength and determination, and of a refusal to accept slavery and religious platitudes from a culture that violated its stated religious precepts.

Prince's *History* is a product of an English abolitionism whose cohering commitment was to emancipate slaves to be educated and converted into a malleable work force to fulfill English economic goals. Her *History* certainly participates in an imagined division between good English and contaminated West Indians, the narrative of English national superiority forged during the years of abolitionism. However, her

History and its subsequent legal fallout also speak to a Caribbean identity, to a slave resistance which gave rise after abolition to post-emancipation evidence that black West Indians had quite different ideas about their own freedom from the destiny imagined for them by their colonial government as compliant wage labourers on white plantations.

How then do we view Mary Seacole's *Wonderful Adventures* published 26 years later with its depiction of Jamaican Seacole labouring on England's Crimean battlefields? Seacole wrote her book as an entrepreneurial project to raise money after declaring bankruptcy when the large inventory of the British Hotel she ran in the Crimea lost all market value when the war ended suddenly. Seacole was an experienced businesswoman and medical practitioner; only in England with its restricted understanding of middle-class women's roles was she unable to deploy her professional skills. In a complex move, therefore, she both appeals to the imperial patriotism of her readers upon whom she depended for money, while managing to construct a narrator who does not fully participate in that English narrative, as she negotiates the colonial desire to produce a 'mimic man [*sic*] ... in which to be Anglicized, is *emphatically* not to be English' (Bhabha, 1984, p. 128). Seacole complicates the imperial narrative by appropriating the trope of England as Mother Country to tell a narrative of herself as England's 'Mother Seacole'. She ironizes her identification with English values in a critique of their racism while depicting her own racial roots.

Readers today often respond to Seacole's *Wonderful Adventures* in terms similar to those Pringle used to describe Prince's 'faults': namely as exhibiting 'a considerable share of natural pride and self-importance'. Critics note the tensions between Seacole's origins and connections with her African ancestry and her admiration for English endeavours and her use of English racial stereotyping: 'Unintentionally her narrative yields a valuable insight into the divided loyalties of colonial people of mixed blood and heritage' (Edwards and Dabydeen, 1991, p. 169); contrasting Prince's 'peasant rootedness' with Seacole's 'colonial psychology', Sandra Pouchet Paquet claims that Prince's *History* 'reflects an embryonic nationalism formed in resistance to slavery' whereas Seacole's *Wonderful Adventures* 'reflects an enthusiastic acceptance of colonialism in the aftermath of slavery' (Pouchet Paquet, 1992b, p. 651). She concludes, however, that 'even while she surrenders to the "superior" values and judgement of British culture, she exerts a powerful, muscular energy that forces new perimeters on the imperial center as a site of self-definition' (Pouchet Paquet, 1992b, p. 662).

The 'aftermath of slavery' had seen: the economy of the West Indian plantations in decline; large numbers of indentured workers brought in from India to replace black workers especially in Trinidad and Guyana;

Carlyle and Mill debating in the pages of *Fraser's Magazine* Carlyle's indictment of 'lazy Quashee's' refusal to work on the plantations after emancipation and also his praise of the heroism of 'the great white enchanter' who saved the West Indies from swamps and jungle; England's attention turned to defending her eastern trade routes from Russian incursion in the Crimean campaign. In the same year as Seacole published *Wonderful Adventures*, England transformed its paternalistic attitude towards India into a more violent and repressive control as a result of the 'Indian Mutiny'. In 1854 women began to demand changes in laws and institutions and to establish communication networks: in 1854 Barbara Bodichon published *A Brief Summary in Plain Language of the Most Important Laws Concerning Women*; in 1855 a petition circulated which had 60,000 signatures by 1857 to reform laws concerning married women; and in 1857 Barbara Bodichon published *Women and Work*. Scientific racial thinking introduced polygenesism (the theory of races as different species) alongside the more humanitarian yet paternalistic monogenesist thought.

While not a narrative of Seacole's own enslavement, *Wonderful Adventures* is firmly rooted in the history of slavery both as part of the ethical and intellectual history of nineteenth-century England and also as a text published during ongoing abolitionist activity in England directed against slavery in America. Both English and American abolitionists toured England. The latter included escaped or freed slaves: Frederick Douglass, for example, was well known on the lecture circuit. *Uncle Tom's Cabin*, published in 1852, continued as a bestseller.

Seacole's 'full history of my struggles to become a Crimean heroine' (Seacole, 1988, p. 76) was in dialogue therefore both with abolitionists' struggles which pitted good England against bad America and also with heated scientific debates around and literary representations of the nature of racial difference, especially in relation to the place of the hybrid.

Race was a fluid word in nineteenth-century England, used to denote the human race, different ethnic Europeans, differences between Europeans and Africans, tribal peoples in the Americas and different species. Victorian attitudes to race were as varied as the meaning of the word. Nancy Stepan hypothesizes a conjunction of events that produced a science of human racial differences at the end of the eighteenth century in Europe, the most important being black slavery in European colonies in the Americas and the emergence of the modern, biological and human sciences. The complex origins of racial thinking precede racial slavery but the 'association between blackness and inferiority produced by racial slavery was grafted onto an earlier, primarily literary tradition, in which blackness and whiteness comprised the terms of a binary opposition ... By the sixteenth century this aesthetic device was being transformed into a theory of nature' (Stepan, 1982, p. xii). Douglas Lorimer (1978) argues that by mid-century racial thinking was also imposed on existing class categories and hierarchies.

When Strickland assumed that Africans enjoyed the same maternal and uxorial feelings as English people she was consistent in her thinking with late eighteenth- and early nineteenth-century monogenesists who claimed that Europeans and Africans were of the same race and species, if differently developed. Paradoxically, the belief that all people were brothers in God's eyes, which motivated abolitionists, also positioned them as initiating cultural colonization through their belief that England's role was to civilize black people through conversion to Christianity, English marriage forms and English education. Thus those who worked for abolition also worked to negate the slaves' cultural subjectivity. For complex social, political and scientific reasons, after the abolition of slavery in the English colonies eliminated an obvious distinction between black and white people, polygenesis gained greater credibility as the kind of race thinking exhibited by Robert Knox in *The Races of Men*: 'Men are of various Races; call them Species, if you will; call them permanent Varieties; it matters not ... in human history race is everything ... literature, science, art, in a word, civilization, depend on it' (Knox, 1850, p. 9).

The intense nineteenth-century interest in and anxiety about hybridity 'reflected the desire to keep races separate, which meant that attention was immediately focused on the mixed race offspring that resulted from interracial sexual intercourse, the proliferating, embodied, living legacies that abrupt, casual, often coerced, unions had left behind' (Young, 1995, p. 25). Knox, however, dismissed the 'wild, visionary, and pitiable theories' about hybridity: 'the black man ... is no more a white man than an ass is a horse or a zebra' (Knox, 1850, pp. 162–3). Where the Anglo-Saxon 'race still hopes ultimately to be masters of the world' (Knox, 1850, p. 42), destiny 'seems to have marked [the dark races] for destruction' (Knox, 1850, p. 147); 'No one can believe them to be of the same race with ourselves; ... They are shrewd, and show powers of mimicry – acquire language readily, but can never be civilized' (Knox, 1850, p. 158). Repudiating racial intermixing, Knox asserts that the 'Saxon race will never tolerate them – never amalgamate – never be at peace' (Knox, 1850, p. 158). Where humanitarian monogenesist thinking had acknowledged mixed race offspring, polygenesists dismissed them as degenerate and sterile.

Seacole was the hybrid product of mixed race sexuality. She opens *Wonderful Adventures* by identifying herself as:

> a Creole ... [with] good Scotch blood coursing in my veins. My
> father was a soldier, of an old Scotch family ... My mother kept a
> boarding-house in Kingston, and was, like many of the Creole
> women, an admirable doctress; in high repute with the officers of
> both services, and their wives, who were from time to time sta-
> tioned at Kingston. (Seacole, 1988, p. 56)

Seacole makes no other mention of her father. Edward Brathwaite
found records of 'mixed marriages' in some parishes in Jamaica during
the eighteenth and nineteenth centuries, but 'although Kingston contained the largest number of coloreds, no mixed marriages are reported
from that municipality' in the Kingston Register of Marriages (1713–
1814) (Brathwaite, 1971, p. 189). Seacole's parents' relationship presumably fell into the 'custom of the country', establishing Seacole within
a specific socio-economic culture in early nineteenth-century Jamaica –
that of the free-born people of colour. As slave rebellions and resistance
increased after the successful slave rebellion in San Domingue in 1794
resulting in Haitian independence in 1804, white planters and colonial
administrators strategized to cultivate the allegiance of the free-born
population of colour to pre-empt any union with slaves that would
strengthen slave resistance, while at the same time limiting the political
and civil rights of the free-born people of colour so as not to be
outnumbered by this growing population. This became especially crucial as the Anti-Slavery Society grew more active in England and missionaries more active in working with slaves in Jamaica. The coloured
population absorbed the hierarchical assumptions of white people to
the extent that mid-nineteenth-century commentators record the gulf
between the people of colour and the black population. However, Stephen
Small cautions against overgeneralizing about this group. He claims
that although a powerful minority dissociated itself from black people,
the majority defined themselves as culturally black and engaged in
reistance and solidarity: 'The most fundamental issue in all of this will
be to systematically distinguish the experiences of the various groups by
gender so that we can examine how the circumstances and attitudes of
women varied from those of men, especially because of the power
relations involved' (Small, 1994, p. 31).

Seacole, proud of her 'good Scotch blood', pays equal attention to
her mother's work that had inculcated in her 'from my early youth a
yearning for medical knowledge and practice'. Through her mother
Seacole positions herself as connected both to slavery and an African
past:

> I think, if I have a little prejudice against our cousins across the
> Atlantic ... it is not unreasonable. I have a few shades of deeper
> brown upon my skin which shows me related – and I am proud of

the relationship – to those poor mortals whom you once held
enslaved, and whose bodies America still owns. And having this
bond, and knowing what slavery is; having seen with my eyes and
heard with my ears proof positive enough of its horrors – let others
affect to doubt them if they will – is it surprising that I should be
somewhat impatient of the airs of superiority which many Americans have endeavoured to assume over me? (Seacole, 1988, p. 14)

Employing the same firsthand testimony which marked Prince's work,
Seacole's condemnation of American slavery carries with it, by implication, an 'impatience' with English assumptions of superiority. Seacole,
while free-born, lived for 30 years alongside the 'poor mortals whom
[England] once held enslaved', including the turmoil caused by the slave
rebellion that swept through Jamaica in 1831–32.

Recording her work during 1853 in Kingston when 'the yellow fever
never made a more determined effort to exterminate the English in
Jamaica' (Seacole, 1988, p. 59), Seacole distinguishes 'the English' from
'my people' to comment on 'the vain contest with a climate that refused
to adopt them' and 'how the mother country pays a dear price for the
possession of her colonies'. In a claim of some ambiguity, Seacole
writes: 'Nature has ... instill[ed] into the hearts of the Creoles an
affection for English people and an anxiety for their welfare, which
shows itself warmest when they are sick and suffering' (Seacole, 1988,
p. 60). Seacole records an imperial lament for the price paid and suffering endured by 'young people in the youth and bloom of life', while her
emphasis on Creole affection being at its strongest when the English are
'sick and suffering' suggests also a pleasure in an imperial fall from
grace.

Although Seacole's fame rested on her Crimean war service to sick,
suffering, and dying Englishmen, she laid out the terms on which the
narrative of that fame should be read in the first third of her book,
where she records events prior to her war work in the Crimea. Seacole's
'adventures' in Kingston, Panama, Granada and England provide interest in a crowded field of Crimean War memoirs; they also testify to her
medical expertise prior to the Crimea.

Constructed as a hybrid colonial subject Seacole describes how, 'she
was never weary of tracing upon an old map the route to England'
(Seacole, 1988, p. 57). She realized this dream when as a young woman
she accompanied relatives to England for a year's visit. Although she
refuses to 'bore the reader with her first impressions of London' (Seacole,
1988, p. 58), she does, in fact, linger on one memory:

Strangely enough, some of the most vivid recollections are the
efforts of the London street-boys to poke fun at my and my companion's complexion. I am only a little brown – a few shades

duskier than the brunettes whom you all admire so much; but my companion was very dark, and a fair (if I can apply the term to her) subject for their rude wit. (Seacole, 1988, p. 58)

Through humour Seacole contests this English narrative of Africans, and lauds the industry and leadership of the African population in New Granada – formed by runaway slaves; to her they contrast strikingly with the crude Americans who pass through prospecting for gold. Seacole refutes the privileged narrative of 'whitening' and substitutes for it a narrative figuring the 'uncivilized' American. When she was leaving Panama, 'a thin, sallow-looking American' proposed a toast to 'Aunty Seacole' because of her courageous work ridding the town of cholera: he laments Seacole's colour, and assumes all in the audience wish they could bleach her. Seacole responds: 'If [my complexion] had been as dark as any nigger's, I should have been just as happy and as useful, and as much respected by those whose respect I value; and as to his offer of bleaching me, I should, even if it were practicable, decline it without any thanks' (Seacole, 1988, pp. 97–8). Rejecting any society which would not give her admittance she toasts 'the general reformation of American manners' (Seacole, 1988, p. 98).

Seacole's criticisms of prejudiced Americans allows her to record racist attitudes that clearly informed English opinion also, as a result of its own past slave trade and its current imperial incursions, as exemplified by the London boys, and also by those at the War Office whom she unsuccessfully tried to 'persuade ... that an unknown Creole woman would be useful to their army before Sebastopol' (Seacole, 1988, p. 121). She contrasts the English rejection of 'a motherly yellow woman' to nurse her 'sons', with the Jamaican recognition of the medical skill of 'doctresses'. Her claim that 'here it was natural enough – although I had references, and other voices spoke for me – that they should laugh, goodnaturedly enough, at my offer' (Seacole, 1988, pp. 124–5) ironically questions assumptions about 'nature'. Florence Nightingale's recruiter also rejected Seacole: 'I read in her face the fact, that had there been a vacancy, I should not have been chosen to fill it' (Seacole, 1988, p. 125). Evoking abolitionist sentiment Seacole asks rhetorically: 'Was it possible that American prejudices against colour had some root here?' (Seacole, 1988, p. 206).

Seacole eventually paid her own way to the Crimea, where she both set up the British Hotel as a mess for officers, and also resumed her medical work on the battlefield. She delights, while demurring, in including, as part of 'Mrs Seacole's' story, titled officers' letters, excerpts from *The Times*, verses from a tribute to her in *Punch*. As her narrative proceeds she progresses from being Mother Seacole with her 'sons', to an identification with the Madonna (Seacole, 1988, p. 212), and finally she took pleasure in a jest: 'My companions were young and full of fun, and tried hard to persuade the Russians that I was Queen Victoria' (Seacole, 1988, pp. 224–5). While her adulation for war and the brave English officers locates Seacole at the heart of empire, such adulation serves not only as praise, but also as strategy. Seacole finds a way to validate her knowledge and learning, gained not from English 'civilization' but from her industrious doctressing black mother.[6] Seacole legitimated such knowledge by reversing the trope that justified European imperialism: where English racial thinking viewed other races as primitive and childlike in comparison with the 'civilized' Mother Country, Seacole negotiates this English imperial narrative as Mother Seacole to the sick and dying Englishmen she names 'her sons'. She negates the image both of the lazy Negro who needs to be educated/christianized/civilized and of the degenerate hybrid. She claims her own slave heritage, acknowledges the 'colonial desire' between her white father and her black mother and the formative influence of both on her, and condemns by association with Americans, England's slave owning past and its ongoing racial thinking.

I conclude this discussion of Prince's and Seacole's interventions into English debates on race and slavery by focusing briefly on some passages from the work of Anthony Trollope. A year after Seacole published *Wonderful Adventures* Trollope sailed to the West Indies with the task of reorganizing the dysfunctional Postal Service in the English Caribbean colonies. In 1859 he published his account of that experience, *The West Indies and the Spanish Main*. He writes of his stay in Kingston, Jamaica: 'the landlady in whose custody I had placed myself was a sister of good Mrs. Seacole' (Trollope, 1985, p. 16). Trollope assumes his readers know who Seacole is and share his view of her. In a later chapter Trollope engages in the debate on hybridity in his discussion of the 'coloured' population of Kingston. He 'can hardly think that anything so natural [as despising 'coloured people' and 'negroes'] can be very wrong' (Trollope, 1985, p. 57), yet he theorizes that hybridity is a Divine plan, 'Providence has sent white men and black men to these regions in order that from them may spring a race so fitted by intellect for civilization; and fitted also by organization for tropical labour' (Trollope, 1985, p. 57). He doesn't deny that 'as a race [hybrids] have deteriorated both in mind and body', nor that 'the mulatto race partakes largely of the intelligence and ambition of their white forefathers' (Trollope, 1985, p. 59). Nevertheless, Trollope argues that the 'semi-African' people should assume responsibility in the West Indies, even though he knows such a position may be deemed 'unpatriotic ... unworthy of an Englishman, who should foster the ascendancy of his own race and his own country' (Trollope, 1985, p. 63). He concludes, however, that 'when civilization, commerce, and education shall have been spread; when sufficient of our blood shall have been infused into the veins of those children of the sun' the English can 'bid farewell' to the West Indies (Trollope, 1985, p. 64). Trollope adopts the position of the paternalistic monogenesist in his acknowledgement of the divine plan for the hybrid population, exemplified in his praise of Seacole. He recognizes, however, that the infusion of English blood into African veins does not only have a divine future but also a particular and violent material history. Trollope answers white women who shrink from contact with Creole women like Seacole for fear their daughters will be contaminated by contact with those whose mothers and grand-mothers did not marry:

> Their mothers and grandmothers ... had but little opportunity of thinking of [matrimony] ... These very people ... would they not be your cousins but for the lack of matrimony? Your uncle, your father, your cousins, your grandfather, nay, your very brother, are they not the true criminals in this matter – they who have lived in this unhallowed state with women of a lower race? (Trollope, 1985, p. 66)

Trollope, the quintessential middle-class entrepreneurial nineteenth-century English novelist, embodies the racial thinking that binds together the imagined community of white English people. Yet he also gives voice to the positions that both Prince and Seacole embodied as they engaged those racial assumptions. His knowledge of 'good Mrs Seacole' connects him with his landlady in Kingston, and must contribute to his determination that hybridity is not doomed to sterility but rather to regeneration. And even while he participates in English thinking that African women are of a lower race, he certainly concurs with Prince's position that criminal indecency belongs to white English men not to the black women slaves. Ships allowed Prince and Seacole to trace the route to England; once there the two women in their work engaged in the racial debates that defined English modernity, placing black people as subjects, not objects, of the 'ethical and intellectual heritage of the West' (Gilroy, 1993, p. 49).

Notes

1. Susanna Strickland was an aspiring writer in Thomas Pringle's circle. Pringle was secretary of the Anti-Slavery Society, through which Strickland gained exposure to slaves and their stories. She married and emigrated to Canada where as Susanna Moodie she published numerous books.
2. For discussion of white women's involvement in anti-slavery activities see Ferguson (1992) and Midgley (1992); for discussion of relations between

black women slaves and their white male and female owners in America see Carby (1987).

3. However, Pringle emphasizes that Prince's *History* was not an official publication of the Society, suggesting it did not fully adhere to the necessary model.

4. The literature on 'testimonio' in relation to *I, Rigoberta Manchu* and Carole Boyce Davies's (1992) work on collaboration is relevant here in thinking of the means of production of this *History*.

5. Mary Favret (1994), 'Flogging: The British Antislavery Movement Writes Pornography', paper delivered at the Modern Language Association conference, San Diego.

6. Seacole's knowledge and experience were certainly at variance with Nightingale's childhood and adolescence spent reclining in middle-class leisure, as she reveals in 'Cassandra'.

Bibliography

Aijazuddin, F. S. (1979), *Sikh Portraits by European Artists*, London and New York: Sotheby Parke Bernet.

Akenson, D. H. (1988), *Small Differences: Irish Catholics and Irish Protestants, 1815–1922*, Dublin: Gill and Macmillan.

Alexander, M. and Anand, S. (1980), *Queen Victoria's Maharajah*, London: Weidenfeld and Nicolson.

Alexander, Z. and Dewjee, A. (eds) (1984), *The Wonderful Adventures of Mrs. Seacole in Many Lands*, Bristol: Falling Wall Press.

Alford, H. (1835), *The School of the Heart and Other Poems*, 2 vols, London: Longman.

Allen, C. (1975), *Plain Tales from the Raj: Images of British India in the Twentieth Century*, Aylesbury: Hazell Watson and Viney.

Allen, G. (1979), 'Are We Englishmen?', in M. Biddiss (ed.), *Images of Race*, Victorian Library Leicester: Leicester University Press, pp. 238–56.

Altick, R. (1978), *The Shows of London*, Cambridge, Mass.: Belknap Harvard.

Anderson, B. (1991), *Imagined Communities*, 2nd edn, London and New York: Verso.

Anderson, P. (1991), *The Printed Image and the Transformation of Popular Culture*, Oxford: Clarendon Press.

Anon. (1815), *The Loyal Orangeman's Song Book: Being a Collection of the Most Approved Songs now in Use by that Institution*, North Shields: Stanhope Press.

Anon. (1829), 'Cruelties Perpetrated by Henry and Helen Moss, on a Female Negro Slave in the Bahamas', *The Anti-Slavery Reporter*, 2, (47).

Anon. (1830), 'The Rev. G.W. Bridges, and his Slave Kitty Hilton', *The Anti-Slavery Reporter*, 3, (18).

Anon. (1859), 'Algeria Considered as a Winter Residence for the English', *The English Women's Journal*, 3, 64–6.

Anthias, F. and Yuval-Davis, N. (1994), 'Women and the Nation-State', in J. Hutchinson and A. D. Smith (eds), *Nationalism*, Oxford and New York: Oxford University Press.

Appleby, J., Hunt, L. and Jacob, M. (1994), *Telling the Truth about History*, New York: W. W. Norton.

APS [British and Foreign Aborigines Protection Society] (1837), *Regulations of the Society and Address*, London.

APS [British and Foreign Aborigines Protection Society] (1900a), 'The Claims of Uncivilised Races', *The Aborigines' Friend*, new series, 5, December, appendix.

APS [British and Foreign Aborigines Protection Society] (1900b), *The Native Question in South Africa*, London: P. S. King.

APS [British and Foreign Aborigines Protection Society] (1908), 'Annual Report, 1908', *The Aborigines' Friend*, new series, 8, 1–15.

Arata, S. D. (1990), 'The Occidental Tourist: Dracula and the Anxiety of Reverse Colonization', *Victorian Studies*, 33, (4), Summer, 621–45.

Arbousset, T., and Daumas, F. (1846), *Narrative of an Exploratory Tour to the North-East of the Colony of the Cape of Good Hope*, trans. J. Croumbie Brown, Cape Town: A. S. Robertson.

Archer, W. (1910), *Through Afro-America: An English Reading of the Race Problem*, London: Chapman Hall.

Armstrong, N. (1987), *Desire and Domestic Fiction: A Political History of the Novel*, Oxford: Oxford University Press.

Armstrong, N. (1990), 'The Occidental Alice', *Differences*, 2, (2), Summer, 3–40.

Arnold, T. (1842), *Inaugural Lecture on the Study of Modern History*, Oxford: Parker.

Arnstein, W. L. (1975), 'The Murphy Riots: A Victorian Dilemma', *Victorian Studies*, 19, (1).

Arnstein, W. L. (1982), *Protestant Versus Catholic in Mid-Victorian England*, Columbia: University of Missouri Press.

ASL [Anthropological Society of London] (1869), 'Report of the Committee of Investigation', *Journal of the Anthropological Society of London*, 7, i–xxi.

Aylmer, F. (1964), *The Drood Case*, London: Rupert Hart-Davis.

Bakshi, S. R. (1981), *Bhagat Singh and his Ideology*, Delhi: Capital Publishers.

Ballstadt, C., Hopkins, E. and Peterman, M. (1985), *Susanna Moodie: Letters of a Lifetime*, Toronto, Buffalo and London: University of Toronto Press.

Banton, M. (1977), *The Idea of Race*, London: Tavistock.

Barash, C. (1987), 'Introduction', in C. Barash (ed.), *An Olive Schreiner Reader*, London: Pandora Press.

Barash, C. (1989), 'Virile Womanhood: Olive Schreiner's Narratives of a Master Race', in E. Showalter (ed.), *Speaking of Gender*, New York and London: Routledge.

Barkan, E. (1992), *The Retreat of Scientific Racism: Changing Concepts of Race in Britain and the United States between the World Wars*, Cambridge: Cambridge University Press.

Barksdale, R. K. (1958), 'Thomas Arnold's Attitude Toward Race', *Phylon*, 18, 174–80.

Barrell, J. (1991), *The Infection of Thomas de Quincey: A Psychopathology of Imperialism*, New Haven: Yale University Press.

Barringer, T. (1994), 'Representations of Labour in British Visual Culture 1850–1875', PhD, University of Sussex.

Barringer, T. (1996), 'Fabricating Africa: Livingstone and the Visual Image, 1850–1874', in J. McKenzie (ed.), *Livingstone and the Victorian Encounter with Africa*, London: National Portrait Gallery.

Bayly, C. A. (ed.) (1990), *The Raj*, exhibition catalogue, London: National Portrait Gallery.

Baynes, J. (1988), *Soldiers of Scotland*, London: Brassey's Defence Publishers.

Beall, K. F. (1975), *Kaufrufe und Strassenhandler: Cries and Itinerant Trades: A Bibliography*, Hamburg: E. Hanswedell.

Beer, G. (1983), *Darwin's Plots: Evolutionary Narrative in Darwin, George Eliot, and Nineteenth-Century Fiction*, London: Routledge and Kegan Paul.

Bennett, D. (1990), *Emily Davies and the Liberation of Women, 1830–1921*, London: André Deutsch.

Best, G. F. A. (1967), 'Popular Protestantism in Victorian Britain', in R. Robson, *Ideas and Institutions of Victorian Britain*, London: G. Bell and Son.

Bhabha, H. (1984), 'Of Mimicry and Man: The Ambivalence of Colonial Discourse', *October*, 28, 125–33.

Bhabha, H. (1986), 'The Other Question: Difference, Discrimination and the Discourse of Colonialism', in F. Barker, P. Hulme, M. Iversen and D. Loxley (eds), *Literature, Politics and Theory: Papers from the Essex Conferences, 1976–84*, London and New York: Methuen.

Bhabha, H. (ed.) (1990), *Nation and Narration*, London: Routledge.

Bhabha, H. (1994), *The Location of Culture*, London and New York: Routledge.

Biddiss, M. (1976), 'The Politics of Anatomy: Dr. Robert Knox and Victorian Racism', *Proceedings of the Royal Society of Medicine*, 69, 245–50.

Biddiss, M. (ed.) (1979), *Images of Race*, Victorian Library, Leicester: Leicester University Press.

Blackett, R. J. M. (1983), *Building the Anti-Slavery Wall: Black Americans in the Atlantic Abolitionist Movement, 1830–1860*, Baton Rouge: Louisiana State University Press.

Bodichon, B. (1854), *A Brief Summary in Plain Language of the Most Important Laws Concerning Women*, London: J. Chapman.

Bodichon, B. (1857), *Women and Work*, London: Bosworth and Harrison; reprinted in Lacey, C. (1987) *Barbara Leigh Smith Bodichon and the Langham Place Group*, London and New York: Routledge.

Bodichon, B. (1858), *Algeria Considered as a Winter Residence for the English*, London: printed at the offices of *The English Woman's Journal*.

Bodichon, B. (1860), 'Algiers, First Impressions', *The English Woman's Journal*, 6, September, pp. 21–32.

Bodichon, B. (1863), 'Cleopatra's Daughter, St Marciana, Mama Marabout, and Other Algerian Women', *The English Woman's Journal*, 10, February, 404–16.

Bodichon, B. (1865), 'Kabyle Pottery', *Art Journal*, February, 45–6.

Bodichon, E. (1860), 'Society in Algiers', *The English Woman's Journal*, 6, 95–106.

Bodichon, E. (1861a), 'Algerine Notes, part 1: Algerine Animals', *The English Woman's Journal*, 8, September, 31–7.

Bodichon, E. (1861b), 'Algerine Notes, part 2: Algerine Animals', *The English Woman's Journal*, 8, October, 90–6.

Bolt, C. (1971), *Victorian Attitudes to Race*, London: Routledge and Kegan Paul.

Boucherett, J. (1862), 'On the Choice of a Business', *The English Woman's Journal*, 9, November, reprinted in Lacey, C. (1987), *Barbara Leigh Smith Bodichon and the Langham Place Group*, London and New York: Routledge.

Bourne, H. R. Fox (1899), *The Aborigines Protection Society: Chapters in its History*, London: P. S. King.

Bourne, H. R. Fox (1900), *Blacks and Whites in South Africa: An Account of the Past Treatment and Present Conditions of South African Natives under British and Boer Control*, London: P. S. King.

Boyce, D. G. (1986), '"Marginal Britons": The Irish', in R. Colls and P. Dodd (eds), *Englishness: Politics and Culture, 1880–1920*, London: Croom Helm.

Boyce Davies, C. (1992), 'Collaboration and the Ordering Imperative in Life Story Production', in S. Smith and J. Watson (eds), *De/Colonizing the Subject: The Politics of Gender in Women's Autobiography*, Minneapolis: University of Minnesota Press.

Boyce Davies, C. (1994), *Black Women, Writing and Identity: Migrations of the Subject*, London and New York: Routledge.

Brantlinger, P. (1977), *The Spirit of Reform: British Literature and Politics, 1832–1867*, Cambridge, Mass.: Harvard University Press.

Brantlinger, P. (1986), 'Victorians and Africans: The Genealogy of the Myth of the Dark Continent', in H. L. Gates, *'Race', Writing and Difference*, Chicago: University of Chicago Press.

Brantlinger, P. (1988), *Rule of Darkness: British Literature and Imperialism, 1830–1914*, Ithaca: Cornell University Press.

Brathwaite, E. (1971), *The Development of Creole Society in Jamaica 1770–1820*, Oxford: Clarendon Press.

Bridges, R. C. (1994), 'James Augustus Grant's Visual Record of East Africa', *Annual Report of the Hakluyt Society*, London: British Museum.

Broca, P. (1864), *On the Phenomena of Hybridity in the Genus Homo*, ed. C. Carter Blake, London: Longman.

Brontë, C. (1994), *Villette*, Harmondsworth: Penguin.

Bruce, H. (1913), *The Eurasian*, London: John Long.

Bryce, J. (1979), *The Relations of the Advanced and the Backward Races of Mankind*, Oxford: Clarendon Press; facsimile Ann Arbor: University Microfilms International.

Bulwer-Lytton, E. (1853), *Poetical and Dramatic Works*, 5 vols, London: Chapman and Hall.

Burrow, J. W. (1970), *Evolution and Society: A Study in Victorian Social Theory*, Cambridge: Cambridge University Press.

Burton, H. (1949), *Barbara Bodichon*, London: Constable.

Bush, B. (1990), *Slave Women in Caribbean Society, 1650–1838*, London: James Currey; Bloomington and Indianapolis: Indiana University Press; Kingston: Henemann.

Butler, W. F. (1881), *Far Out: Rovings Retold*, London: Isbister.

Butler, W. F. (1887), *The Campaign of the Cataracts*, London: Sampson Low.

Cairns, H. A. C. (1965), *Prelude to Imperialism: British Reactions to Central African Society, 1840–1890*, London: Routledge.

Calder, J. (1987), *The Story of the Scottish Soldier*, Edinburgh: National Museums of Scotland.

Camden, W. (1586), *Britannia*, London: R. Newbery.

Campbell, A. B. (1979), *The Lanarkshire Miners: A Social History of their Trade Unions, 1775–1874*, Edinburgh: John Donald.

Carby, H. V. (1987), *Reconstructing Womanhood: The Emergence of the Afro-American Woman Novelist*, Oxford and New York: Oxford University Press.

Carlyle, T. (1841), *On Heroes, Hero-Worship, and the Heroic in History*, London: James Fraser.

Carlyle, T. (1849), 'Occasional Discourse on the Negro Question', *Fraser's Magazine*, December, 670–9.

Carlyle, T. (1888), *Sartor Resartus: Lectures on Heroes, Chartism, Past and Present*, London: Chapman and Hall.

Carlyle, T. (1967), *On Heroes, Hero-Worship, and the Heroic in History*, London: Dent.

Carlyle, T. (1969a), *Past and Present*, in *The Works of Thomas Carlyle*, Centenary Edition, vol. X, New York: AMS Press.

Carlyle, T. (1969b), *Chartism*, in *The Works of Thomas Carlyle: Critical and Miscellaneous Essays*, Centenary Edition, vol. IV, New York: AMS Press.

Cassius Dio, *Roman History*.

Casteras, S. P. (1988), *Virtue Rewarded*, exhibition catalogue, Louisville: Speed Art Museum.

Cell, J. W. (1982), *The Highest Stage of White Supremacy: The Origins of Segregation in South Africa and the American South*, Cambridge: Cambridge University Press.

Chadwick, E. (1965), *Report on the Sanitary Conditions of the Labouring Population of Great Britain*, Edinburgh: Edinburgh University Press.

Cherry, D. (1993), *Painting Women: Victorian Women Artists*, London and New York: Routledge.

Childers, J. W. (1994), 'Observation and Representation: Mr. Chadwick Writes the Poor', *Victorian Studies*, 37, 405–32.

Chow, R. (1993), *Writing Diaspora: Tactics of Intervention in Contemporary Cultural Politics*. Bloomington: Indiana University Press.

Coetzee, J. M. (1988), *White Writing: On the Culture of Letters in South Africa*, New Haven: Yale University Press.

Collins, P. (1964), *Dickens and Education*, London: Macmillan.

Collins, P. (1971), *Dickens: The Critical Heritage*, London: Routledge and Kegan Paul.

Colls, R. (1986), 'Englishness and Political Culture', in R. Colls and P. Dodd (eds), *Englishness: Politics and Culture, 1880–1920*, London: Croom Helm.

Coombes, A. E. (1994), *Reinventing Africa: Museums, Material Culture and Popular Imagination in Late Victorian and Edwardian England*, New Haven: Yale University Press.

Corfield, P. J. (1991), *Language, History and Class*, Oxford: Basil Blackwell.

Cowling, M. (1989), *The Artist as Anthropologist*, Cambridge: Cambridge University Press.

Crabbe, J. (1981), 'An Artist Divided: The Forgotten Talent of Barbara Bodichon', *Apollo*, May, 311–13.

Cunningham, H. (1981), 'The Language of Patriotism 1750–1914', *History Workshop Journal*, 12, Autumn, 8–33.

Cunningham, J. D. (1915), *History of the Sikhs*, reprint, Delhi: Low Price Publications.

Curtin, P. (1964), *The Image of Africa: British Ideas and Action, 1780–1850*, Madison: University of Wisconsin Press; London: Macmillan.

Curtis, L. P. (1968), *Anglo-Saxons and Celts: A Study of Anti-Irish Prejudice in Victorian England*, New York: New York University Press.

Curtis, L. P. Jr (1971) *Apes and Angels: The Irishman in Victorian Caricature*, Newton Abbot: David and Charles.

D'Ancona, M. (1957), *The Iconography of the Immaculate Conception in the Middle Ages and Early Renaissance*, New York: Archaeological Institute of America and College Art Association of America.

Davis, D. B. (1984), *Slavery and Human Progress*, Oxford: Oxford University Press.

de Lauretis, T. (1988), 'Aesthetic and Feminist Theory: Rethinking Women's Cinema', in E. D. Pribham (ed.), *Female Spectators: Looking at Film and Television*, London: Verso.

Dempster, C. (1875), *Iseulte*, 2 vols, London: Smith Elder.

De Quincey, T. (1971), *The Confessions of an English Opium Eater*, Harmondsworth: Penguin.

Derrida, J. (1965), *L'écriture et la différence*, Paris: Editions du Seuil. Trans. A. Bass as *Writing and Difference*, Chicago: University of Chicago Press (1978).

Derrida, J. (1972), *La dissémination*, Paris: Editions du Seuil. Trans. B. Johnson as *Dissemination,* Chicago: Chicago University Press (1981).

Dickens, C. (1853), 'The Noble Savage', *Household Words*, vii, 337–9.

Dickens, C. (1982), *Oliver Twist*, Oxford: Oxford University Press World's Classics.

Dickens, C. (1985), *The Mystery of Edwin Drood*, London: Penguin.

Dilke, C. (1869), *Greater Britain: A Record of Travel in English-Speaking Countries during 1866 and 1867*, New York: Harper.

Dilke, C. (1901), 'Remarks of Sir Charles Dilke to the Annual Meeting of the Aborigines Protection Society', *The Aborigines' Friend*, April, 3–5.

Dilke, C. (1985), *Greater Britain: Charles Dilke Visits Her New Lands, 1866 and 1867*, ed. G. Blainey, Sydney: Methuen Haynes.

Disraeli, B. (1852), *Lord George Bentinck: A Political Biography*, London: Colburn.

Disraeli, B. (1970), *Tancred or the New Crusade* (first published in 1847), Westport: Greenwood.

Diver, M. (1942), *Royal India*, London: Hodder and Stoughton.

Donald, J. (1992), *Sentimental Education: Schooling, Popular Culture and the Regulation of Liberty*, London: Verso.

Dowling, L. (1986), *Language and Decadence in the Victorian Fin de Siècle*, Princeton: Princeton University Press.

Doyle, A. C. (1929), 'The Green Flag', in *The Conan Doyle Stories*, London: Murray.

only 5 i wrong, whatever

Drescher, S. (1992), 'The Ending of the Slave Trade and the Evolution of European Scientific Racism', in J. E. Inikori and S. L. Engerman (eds), *The Atlantic Slave Trade: Effects on Economies, Societies, and Peoples in Africa, the Americas, and Europe*, Durham, N.C.: Duke University Press, pp. 361–95.

Dunae, P. (1989), 'New Grub Street for Boys', in J. Richards (ed.), *Imperialism and Juvenile Literature*, Manchester: Manchester University Press, pp.12–33.

Earle, J. (1865), *Two of the Anglo-Saxon Chronicles Parallel*, Oxford: Clarendon Press.

Edwards, E. (ed.) (1992), *Anthropology and Photography 1860–1920*, New Haven and London: Yale University Press.

Edwards, P. and Dabydeen, D. (eds) (1991), *Black Writers in Britain 1760–1890*, Edinburgh: Edinburgh University Press.

Engen, R. (1985), *Dictionary of Victorian Wood Engravers*, Cambridge: Chadwyck-Healey.

Fabian, J. (1983), *Time and the Other: How Anthropology Makes its Object*, New York: Columbia University Press.

Faverty, F. E. (1968), *Matthew Arnold the Ethnologist*, New York: AMS.

Ferguson, M. (1992), *Subject to Others: British Women Writers and Colonial Slavery, 1670–1834*, London and New York: Routledge.

Fielding, S. (1993), *Class and Ethnicity: Irish Catholics in England, 1880–1939*, Buckingham: Open University Press.

Fildes, L. V. (1968), *Luke Fildes, R.A.: A Victorian Painter*, London: Michael Joseph.

First, R. and Scott, A. (1980), *Olive Schreiner*, New York: Schocken Books.

Flower, W. H. (1881), 'Opening Address, Section D, Report of the British Association', *Nature*, 24, (8 September).

Flower, W. and Murie, J. (1867), 'Account of the Dissection of a Bushwoman', *Journal of Anatomy and Physiology*, 1, 189–208.

Foner, E. (1983), *Nothing but Freedom: Emancipation and its Legacy*, Baton Rouge: Louisiana State University Press.

Forrest, D. W. (1974), *Francis Galton: The Life and Work of a Victorian Genius*, London: Paul Elek.

Forster, J. (1928), *The Life of Charles Dickens*, ed. J. W. T. Ley, London: Cecil Palmer.

Foucault, M. (1967), *Madness and Civilization: A History of Insanity in the Age of Reason*, trans. R. Howard, New York: Random House.

Foucault, M. (1979), *Discipline and Punish: The Birth of the Prison*, New York: Vintage.

Fox, C. (1988), *Graphic Journalism in England during the 1830s and 1840s*, New York: Garland.

Fox, R. (1985), *Lions of the Punjab: Culture in the Making*, Berkeley: University of California Press.

Fox-Genovese, E. (1982), 'Placing Women's History in History', *New Left Review*, 133, 5–29.

Frederickson, G. M. (1981), *White Supremacy: A Comparative Study in American and South African History*, Oxford: Oxford University Press.

Freeman, E. A. (1867–76), *History of the Norman Conquest*, 6 vols, Oxford: Clarendon Press.

Freeman, E. A. (1979), 'Race and Language', in M. Biddiss, *Images of Race*, Victorian Library, Leicester: Leicester University Press, pp. 205–35.

Froude, J. A. (1865–70), *History of England*, New York: C. Scribner's and Sons.

Fussell, P. (1975), *The Great War and Modern Memory*, New York: Oxford University Press.

Gallagher, C. (1986), 'The Body Versus the Social Body in the Works of Thomas Malthus and Henry Mayhew', *Representations*, Spring.

Gallagher, T. (1985), '"A Tale of Two Cities": Communal Strife in Glasgow and Liverpool', in R. Swift and S. Gilley (eds), *The Irish in the Victorian City*, London: Croom Helm.

Gallagher, T. (1987), *Glasgow: The Uneasy Peace: Religious Tensions in Modern Scotland*, Manchester: Manchester University Press.

Galton, F. (1892), *Hereditary Genius: An Inquiry into its Laws and Consequences*, London: Macmillan.

Galton, F. (1908), *Memories of My Life*, London: Methuen.

Gamman, L. (1988), 'Watching the Detectives: The Enigma of the Female Gaze', in L. Gamman and M. Marshmant (eds), *The Female Gaze: Women as Viewers of Popular Culture*, London: The Women's Press.

Garrard, M. (1993), *Artemisia Gentileschi: The Image of the Female Hero in Italian Baroque Art*, Princeton: Princeton University Press.

Garrett, R. (1872), 'The Electoral Disabilities of Women', *A Lecture Delivered at the Corn Exchange*, Cheltenham, 3 April.

Gates, H. L. (1986), *'Race', Writing and Difference*, Chicago: University of Chicago Press.

Gell, S. M. S. (forthcoming), 'Dalip Singh and the Origins of the Sikh "Look"', *History and Anthropology*.

Gellner, E. (1983), *Nations and Nationalism*, Oxford: Blackwell.

Gerdts, W. (1966), 'Egyptian Motifs in Nineteenth-Century American Painting and Sculpture', *Art Bulletin*, October, 445–50.

Gilbert, E. L. (1989), 'The Female King: Tennyson's Arthurian Apoca-
lypse', in E. Showalter (ed.), *Speaking of Gender*, London and New
York: Routledge, pp. 163–86.

Gilbert, S. and Gubar, S. (1988), *No Man's Land: The Place of the
Woman Writer in the Twentieth Century*, vol.1, New Haven and
London: Yale University Press.

Gilbert, W. M. (1897), 'Robert Gibb', *The Art Journal*, 25–8.

Giles, J. A. (1847), *The History of the Ancient Britons from the Earliest
Period to the Invasion of the Saxons*, 2 vols, London: Bell.

Gilman, S. (1985a), 'Black Bodies, White Bodies: Towards an Iconography of Female Sexuality in Late Nineteenth-Century Art, Medicine
and Literature', *Critical Inquiry*, 12, 204–42.

Gilman, S. L. (1985b), *Difference and Pathology: Stereotypes of Sexuality, Race, and Madness*, Ithaca: Cornell University Press.

Gilman, S. L. (1985c), 'The Hottentot and the Prostitute', in S. L.
Gilman, *Difference and Pathology: Stereotypes of Sexuality and Race*,
Ithaca: Cornell University Press, pp. 76–108.

Gilmour, R. (1993), *The Victorian Period: The Intellectual and Cultural
Context of English Literature 1830–1890*, London and New York:
Longman.

Gilroy, P. (1993), *The Black Atlantic: Modernity and Double Consciousness*, Cambridge, Mass.: Harvard University Press.

Girouard, M. (1981), *The Return to Camelot: Chivalry and the English
Gentleman*, New Haven and London: Yale University Press.

Godwin, W. (1965), *The Enquirer: Reflections on Education, Manners
and Literature in a Series of Essays*, New York: Augustus M. Kelley.

Green, D. (1984), 'Photography and Anthropology: The Technology of
Power', *Ten.8*, 14, 30–7.

Greenhalgh, P. (1988), *Ephemeral Vistas: The Expositions Universelles,
Great Exhibitions and World Fairs, 1851–1914*, Manchester: Manchester University Press.

Groom, C. O. Napier [later, Groom Napier] (1868), 'Notes on Mulattoes and Negroes', *Anthropological Review*, 6, (2), April.

Gwynn, S. and Tuckwell, G. M. (1917), *Life of Sir Charles Dilke*, 2
vols, London: John Murray.

Haggard, H. Rider (1957), *King Solomon's Mines*, New York: Random
House.

Haggard, J. (1827), 'The Judgement of the Right Hon. Lord Stowell,
Respecting the Slavery of the Mongrel Woman, Grace, on an Appeal
from the Vice-Admiralty Court of Antigua', London: W. Benning and
Thomas Wilson.

Hall, C. (1992), *White, Male and Middle-Class: Explorations in Feminism and History*, New York: Routledge.

Hall, C. (1993), '"From Greenland's Icy Mountains ... to Afric's Golden Sand": Ethnicity, Race, and Nation in Mid-Nineteenth-Century England', *Gender and History*, 5, (2), Summer, 202–30.

Hamer, M. (1993), *Signs of Cleopatra: History, Politics, Representation*, New York: Routledge.

Hanham, H. J. (1967), 'Mid-Century Scottish Nationalism: Romantic and Radical', in R. Robson (ed.) *Ideas and Institutions of Victorian Britain*, London: G. Bell and Son.

Hanham, H. J. (1978), *Elections and Party Management: Politics in the Age of Disraeli and Gladstone*, Hassocks, Sussex: Harvester.

Harrington, P. (1898), 'The Man Who Painted *The Thin Red Line*', *The Scots Magazine*, 130, (March), 587–95.

Harvey, P. (1937), *The Oxford Companion to Classical Literature*, Oxford: Clarendon Press.

Haskell, F. and Penny, N. (1981), *Taste and the Antique*, New Haven and London: Yale University Press.

Hasler, A. B. (1981), *How the Pope Became Infallible: Pius IX and the Politics of Persuasion*, New York: Doubleday.

Hawker, R. S. (1864), *The Quest of the Sangraal*, Exeter: privately published.

Hawthorne, J. (1903), *Hawthorne and his Circle*, New York: Harper Brothers.

Hawthorne, N. (1968), *The Marble Faun: or the Romance of Monte Beni*, Centenary Edition, Columbus: Ohio State University Press.

Heleniak, K. M. (1980), *William Mulready*, Paul Mellon Centre for Studies in British Art, New Haven: Yale University Press.

Helly, D. O. (1987), *Livingstone's Legacy: Horace Waller and Victorian Mythmaking*, Athens, Ohio: Ohio University Press.

Herbert, A. (1836), *Britannia after the Romans: Neo-Druidic Heresy*, London: Henry Bohn.

Herbert, C. (1974), 'De Quincey and Dickens', *Victorian Studies*, 17, 247–63.

Herstein, S. (1985), *A Mid-Victorian Feminist: Barbara Bodichon*, New Haven: Yale University Press.

Hichberger, J. (1988), *Images of the Army*, Manchester: Manchester University Press.

Hichberger, J. (1989), 'Old Soldiers', in R. Samuel (ed.), *Patriotism*, vol. III, London: Routledge, pp. 50–63.

Higginbotham, E. B. (1992), 'African-American Women's History and the Metalanguage of Race', *Signs*, 17, 251–74.

Himmelfarb, G. (1984), *The Idea of Poverty: England in the Early Industrial Age*, London: Faber and Faber.

Hinde, W. (1987), *Richard Cobden: A Victorian Outsider*, London and New Haven: Yale University Press.

Honour, H. (1989), 'Black Models and White Myths', in *The Image of the Black in Western Art: From the American Revolution to World War I*, part 2, Cambridge, Mass. and London: Harvard University Press.

hooks, b. (1992), *Black Looks: Race and Representation*, London: Turnaround.

Houston, C. J. and W. J. Smyth (1984), 'Transferred Loyalties: Orangeism in the United States and Ontario', *American Review of Canadian Studies*, 14, (2), 193–211.

Hugel, C. (1844), *Travels in Kashmir and the Punjab*, 2nd reprint, Delhi: Nirmal.

Humpherys, A. (1977), *Travels into the Poor Man's Country: The Work of Henry Mayhew*, Athens, Georgia: University of Georgia Press.

Hunt, J. (1863), *The Negro's Place in Nature*, London: Trubner.

Huttenback, R. A. (1976), *Racism and Empire: White Settlers and Colored Immigrants in the British Self-Governing Colonies, 1830–1910*, Ithaca: Cornell University Press.

Hutton, J. (1795), *Theory of the Earth*, Edinburgh: Messrs Cadell junior and Davies.

Huxley, T. H. (1901), 'Anniversary Address of the President of the ESL, May 24, 1870', in M. Foster and E. R. Lankester (eds), *Scientific Memoirs of T. H. Huxley*, vol. 3, London: Macmillan, pp. 554–63.

Huxley, T. H. (1979), 'The Forefathers and Forerunners of the English People' (1870), in M. Biddiss, *Images of Race*, Victorian Library, Leicester: Leicester University Press, pp. 159–69.

Hyam, R. (1990), *Empire and Sexuality: The British Experience*, Manchester: Manchester University Press.

Impey, C. (1888), *The Anti-Caste*, 1, March.

Irigaray, L. (1993), *Je, Tu, Nous: Towards a Culture of Difference*, New York and London: Routledge.

Jackson, J. W. (1979), 'Race and Legislation and Political Economy', in M. Biddiss, *Images of Race*, Victorian Library, Leicester: Leicester University Press, pp. 115–40.

Jacobs, H. (1987), *Incidents in the Life of a Slave Girl*, ed. Jean Yellin, Fagan, Cambridge: Harvard University Press.

Jacobson, W. S. (1986), *The Companion to 'The Mystery of Edwin Drood'*, London: Allen and Unwin.

James, H. (1903), *William Wetmore Story and his Friends*, Boston: Houghton Mifflin.

JanMohamed, A. R. (1983), *Manichean Aesthetics: The Politics of Literature in Colonial Africa*, Amherst: University of Massachusetts Press.

JanMohamed, A. (1986), 'The Economy of Manichean Allegory: The Function of Racial Difference in Colonialist Literature', in H. L. Gates, *'Race', Writing and Difference*, Chicago: University of Chicago Press.

Jarves, J. J. (1960), *The Art Idea*, Cambridge: Belknap Press of Harvard University Press.

Jeal, T. (1973), *Livingstone*, London: Heinemann.

Jenkyns, R. (1980), *The Victorians and Ancient Greece*, Oxford: Blackwell.

Johnson, D. H. (1982), 'The Death of Gordon: A Victorian Myth', *Journal of Imperial and Commonwealth History*, 10 (May), 285–310.

Johnson, E. (1952), *Charles Dickens: His Tragedy and Triumph*, Boston: Little, Brown and Co.

Jones, G. (1980), *Social Darwinism and English Thought: The Interaction between Biological and Social Theory*, Brighton: Harvester.

Jones, G. S. (1983), *Languages of Class: Studies in English Working Class History, 1832–1982*, Cambridge: Cambridge University Press.

Jordanova, L. (1989), *Sexual Visions: Images of Gender in Science and Medicine between the Eighteenth and the Twentieth Centuries*, Brighton: Harvester Wheatsheaf.

Joyce, P. (1980), *Work, Society and Politics: The Culture of the Factory in Later Victorian England*, Brighton: Harvester.

Joyce, P. (1991), *Visions of the People: Industrial England and the Question of Class, 1848–1914*, Cambridge: Cambridge University Press.

Kabbani, R. (1986), *Europe's Myths of the Orient: Devise and Rule*, London: Macmillan.

Kasson, J. S. (1990), *Marble Queens and Captives: Women in Nineteenth Century American Sculpture*, New Haven: Yale University Press.

Kay-Shuttleworth, J. (1973), *Four Periods of Public Education as Reviewed in 1832, 1839, 1846, 1862*, Brighton: Harvester Press.

Keane, A. H. (1894), 'China', *Cassell's Storehouse of General Information (1890–1894)*, London: Cassell, pp. 97–8.

Keane, A. H. (1899), *Man, Past and Present*, Cambridge: Cambridge University Press.

Keane, A. H. (1908), *The World's Peoples*, London: Hutchinson.

Keane, A. H., Richard Lydekker, et al. (1905), *The Living Races of Man*, London: Hutchinson.

Kennedy, J. (1861), *Essays Ethnological and Linguistic*, London: Williams and Norgate.

Kestner, J. A. (1995), *Masculinities in Victorian Painting*, Aldershot: Scolar.

Kingsley, C. (1866), *Hereward the Wake, 'Last of the English'*, London: Macmillan and Co.

Kingsley, C. (1881), *The Roman and the Teuton* (first edn 1864), London: Macmillan.

Kingsley, C. (1883), *Charles Kingsley: His Letters and Memories of his Life, Edited by his Wife*, vol II, London: Kegan Paul, Trench and Co.

Kipling, R. (1888a), *Plain Tales from the Hills*, Calcutta: Wheeler.

Kipling, R. (1888b), *Soldiers Three*, Calcutta: Wheeler.

Kipling, R. (1891a), *Life's Handicap*, London: Macmillan.

Kipling, R. (1891b), *The Light That Failed*, London and Philadelphia: Ward, Lock and Co.

Kipling, R. (1940), *Rudyard Kipling's Verse*, London: Hodder and Stoughton.

Kirk, N. (1980), 'Ethnicity, Class and Popular Toryism', in K. Lunn (ed.), *Hosts, Immigrants and Minorities: Historical Responses to Newcomers, 1870–1914*, Folkestone: Dawson.

Kliger, S. (1952), *The Goths in England: A Study in Seventeenth and Eighteenth-Century Thought*, Cambridge, Mass.: Harvard University Press.

Knox, R. (1850), *The Races of Man: A Fragment*, Philadelphia: Lea and Blanchard.

Knox, R. (1862), *The Races of Man: A Philosophical Enquiry into the Influence of Race over the Destinies of Nations*, 2nd edn, London: Henry Renshaw.

Knox, R. (1969), *The Races of Man, a Fragment*, first published 1850, reprint, Miami: Mnemosyne.

Koebner, R. and Schmidt, H. (1964), *Imperialism: The Story and Significance of a Political Word, 1840–1960*, Cambridge: Cambridge University Press.

Koven, S. and Michel, S. (eds) (1993), *Mothers of a New World: Maternalist Politics and the Origins of the Welfare State*, New York and London: Routledge.

Kuklick, H. (1991), *The Savage Within: The Social History of British Anthropology, 1885–1945*, Cambridge: Cambridge University Press.

Lacan, J. (1978), *The Four Fundamental Concepts of Psycho-Analysis*, New York: Norton.

Lacey, C. (ed.) (1987), *Barbara Leigh Smith Bodichon and the Langham Place Group*, London and New York: Routledge.

Leclaire, S. (1979), 'Sexuality: A Fact of Discourse', in G. Stambolian (ed.), *Homosexualities and French Literature*, Ithaca: Cornell University Press.

Lee, F. (1988), *Fabianism and Colonialism: The Life and Political Thought of Lord Sydney Olivier*, London: Defiant.

Leeks, W. (1986), 'Ingres Other-Wise', *Oxford Art Journal*, 9, (1), 29–37.

Le Normand-Romain, A. (1994), 'Sculpture et ethnographie', in A. Le Normand Rollin, A. Roquebert, J. Durand-Revillon and D. Serena (eds), *La sculpture ethnographique: de la Vénus Hottentote a la Tehura de Gauguin*, editions de la Réunion des musées nationaux, Les Dossiers du Musée d'Orsay, Paris: Orsay.

Lévi-Strauss, C. (1985), *The View from Afar*, Oxford: Basil Blackwell.

Levine, P. (1987) *Victorian Feminism, 1850–1900*, London: Hutchinson.

Levy, A. (1991a), 'Gendered Labor, the Woman Writer and Dorothy Richardson', *Novel*, Fall, 50–70.

Levy, A. (1991b), *Other Women: The Writing of Class, Race, and Gender, 1832–1898*, Princeton and London: Princeton University Press.

Lewis, R. (1995), 'Women Orientalist Artists: Diversity, Ethnography, Interpretation', *Women: A Cultural Review*, 6, (1), 91–106.

Lewis, R. (1996), *Gendering Orientalism: Race, Femininity, Representation*, London: Routledge.

Lightman, B. (ed.) (1996), *Contexts of Victorian Science*, Chicago: University of Chicago Press.

Livingstone, D. (1857), *Missionary Travels and Researches in South Africa; including a Sketch of Sixteen Years' Residence in the Interior of Africa, and a Journey from the Cape of Good Hope to Loanda, on the West Coast: Thence Across the Continent, Down the River Zambesi, to the Eastern Ocean ...*, London: John Murray.

Livingstone, D. (1968), *Dr. Livingstone's Cambridge Lectures*, Farnborough, Hants: Gregg International.

Livingstone, D. N. (1992), 'A "Sternly Practical Pursuit": Geography, Race and Empire', in D. Livingstone (ed.), *The Geographical Tradition*, Oxford: Blackwell, pp. 216–59.

Livingstone, D. and Livingstone, C. (1865), *Narrative of an Expedition to the Zambesi and its Tributaries; and of the Discovery of the Lakes Shirwa and Nyassa, 1858–1864*, London: John Murray.

Lloyd, C. (ed.) (1991), *The Queen's Pictures*, London: National Gallery.

Lombroso, C. and Ferrero, W. (1898), *The Female Offender*, London: T. Fisher Unwin.

Lorimer, D. A. (1978), *Colour, Class and the Victorians: English Attitudes to the Negro in the Mid-Nineteenth Century*, Leicester: Leicester University Press.

Lorimer, D. A. (1988), 'Theoretical Racism in Late Victorian Anthropology, 1870–1900', *Victorian Studies*, 31, 405–30.

Lorimer, D. A. (1990), '*Nature*, Racism and Late Victorian Science', *Canadian Journal of History*, 25, 369–85.

Lorimer, D. A. (1996), 'Science and the Secularization of Victorian Images of Race', in B. Lightman (ed.), *Contexts of Victorian Science*, Chicago: University of Chicago Press.

Lott, E. (1866), *The English Governess in Egypt: Harem Life in Egypt and Constantinople*, London: Richard Bentley.

Lott, E. (1867), *The Mohaddetyn in the Palace: Or Nights in the Harem*, London: Chapman and Hall.

Lowe, L. (1991), *Critical Terrains: French and British Orientalism*, Ithaca: Cornell University Press.

Lowe, W. J. (1990), *The Irish in Mid-Victorian Lancashire: The Shaping of a Working-Class Community*, New York: Peter Lang.

Lubbock, J. (Lord Avebury) (1870), *The Origin of Civilisation and the Primitive Condition of Man*, New York: D. Appleton and Co.

Lucas, C. P. (1908), C.O.886/1 Dominions No. 1. Confidential. The Self-Governing Dominions and Coloured Immigration, July.

Lucas, C. P. (1912), 'Class, Colour and Race', ch. 7 of *Greater Rome and Greater Britain*, Oxford: Clarendon.

Lucas, J. (1991), *England and Englishness*, London: Hogarth Press.

Lyell, C. (1830–33), *Principles of Geology*, 3 vols, London: J. Murray.

Macaulay, T. B. (1952), 'Minute on Indian Education', *Macaulay: Prose and Poetry*, London: Rupert Hart-Davis.

McBratney, J. (1990), 'Lovers Beyond the Pale: Images of Indian Women in Kipling's Tales of Miscegenation', *Works and Days*, 8, (1), Spring.

McBratney, J. (1992), 'Imperial Subjects, Imperial Space in Kipling's *Jungle Book*', *Victorian Studies*, 35, (3), Spring, 277–93.

McClintock, A. (1995), *Imperial Leather: Race, Gender and Sexuality in the Colonial Contest*, New York and London: Routledge.

McCully, B. T. (1966), *English Education and the Origins of Indian Nationalism*, Gloucester, Mass.: Peter Smith.

MacDougall, H. (1982), *Racial Myth in English History: Trojans, Teutons, and Anglo-Saxons*, Montreal: Harvest House.

McFarland, E. (1990), *Protestants First: Orangeism in Nineteenth-Century Scotland*, Edinburgh: Edinburgh University Press.

McFarland, E. (1994), '"A mere Irish faction": The Orange Institution in Nineteenth Century Scotland', in T. M. Devine (ed.), *Scotland and Ulster*, Edinburgh: Edinburgh University Press.

McIntire, C. T. (1983), *England Against the Papacy, 1858–61*, Cambridge: Cambridge University Press.

Mackenzie, J. (1995), *Orientalism: History, Theory and the Arts*, Manchester: Manchester University Press.

MacLeod, R. (1977), 'Changing Perspectives in the Social History of Science', in I. Spiegel-Rosing and D. J. de Solla (eds), *Science, Tech-*

nology and Society: A Cross-Disciplinary Perspective, London: Sage, pp. 149–95.

MacMunn, G. (1933), *The Martial Races of India*, London: Sampson Low, Marston and Co.

MacRaild, Donald M. (1993), 'William Murphy, The Orange Order and Communal Violence: The Irish in West Cumberland, 1871–1884', in P. Panayi (ed.), *Racial Violence in Britain, 1840–1950*, Leicester: Leicester University Press.

Malchow, H. L. (1993), 'Frankenstein's Monster and Images of Race in Nineteenth-Century Britain', *Past and Present*, **139**, May.

Malleson, G. B. (1889), *Sir John Login and Duleep Singh*, reprint, New Delhi: Lal.

Mantell, G. (1838), *Wonders of Geology: Or, A Familiar Exposition of Geological Phenomena*, 2 vols, London: Relfe and Fletcher.

Marshall, J. and J. K. Walton (1981), *The Lake Counties from 1830 to the Mid-Twentieth Century*, Manchester: Manchester University Press.

Martineau, H. (1859), 'Female Industry', *Edinburgh Magazine*.

Matthews, J. (1983), 'Barbara Bodichon: Integrity in Diversity', in D. Spender (ed.), *Feminist Theorists*, London: Women's Press.

Mayhew, H. (1968), *London Labour and the London Poor: A Cyclopaedia of the Condition and Earnings of Those that Will Work, Those that Cannot Work and Those that Will Not Work*, 4 vols, New York: Dover.

Mayhew, H. (1980), *The Morning Chronicle Survey of Labour and the Poor: The Metropolitan Districts*, Firle, Sussex: Caliban Books.

Melek-Hanum (1872), *Thirty Years in the Harem: or the Autobiography of Melek-Hanum, Wife of H.H. Kibrizli-Mehemet-Pasha*, London: Chapman Hall.

Melman, B. (1992), *Women's Orients: English Women and the Middle East, 1718–1918*, Basingstoke: Macmillan.

Memmi, A. (1957, 1972), *The Colonizer and the Colonized*, Boston: Beacon Press.

Midgley, C. (1992), *Women Against Slavery: The British Campaigns 1780–1870*, London and New York: Routledge.

Mill, J. S. (1850), 'The Negro Question', *Fraser's Magazine*, January, 25–31.

Miller, D. W. (1983), 'The Armagh Troubles, 1784–85', in S. Clark and J. S. Donnelly (eds), *Irish Peasants: Violence and Political Unrest, 1780–1914*, Manchester: Manchester University Press.

Miller, J. (1990), *Seductions: Studies in Reading and Culture*, London: Virago.

Milligan, B. (1995), *Pleasures and Pains: Opium and the Orient in*

Nineteenth-Century British Culture, Charlottesville and London: University Press of Virginia.

Mills, S. (1991), *Discourses of Difference: An Analysis of Women's Travel Writing and Colonialism*, London and New York: Routledge.

Mitchell, T. (1988), *Colonising Egypt*, Cambridge: Cambridge University Press.

Morris, J. (1968), *Pax Britannica: The Climax of an Empire*, Harmondsworth: Penguin.

Mulvey, L. (1975), 'Visual Pleasure and Narrative Cinema', *Screen*, **16**, (3).

Mulvey, L. (1981), 'On *Duel in the Sun*: Some Afterthoughts on Visual Pleasure and Narrative Cinema', *Framework* (issues 15–17).

Murray, F. H. (1916), *Emancipation and the Freed in American Sculpture*, Washington DC: published by the author.

Murray, G. (1900), 'The Exploitation of Inferior Races in Ancient and Modern Times', in F. W. Hirst, G. Murray and J. L. Hammond (eds), *Liberalism and Empire*, London: R. B. Johnson.

Nayder, L. (1992), 'Class Consciousness and the Indian Mutiny in Dickens's "The Perils of Certain English Prisoners"', *Studies in English Literature*, **32**, 689–705.

Neal, F. (1988), *Sectarian Violence: The Liverpool Experience, 1819–1914*, Manchester: Manchester University Press.

Newton, J. (1985), '*Villette*', in J. Newton and D. Rosenfelt (eds), *Feminist Criticism and Social Change: Sex, Class and Race in Literature and Culture*, London: Methuen.

Nochlin, L. (1983), 'The Imaginary Orient', *Art in America*, May, 119–31, 186–91.

Norman, E. R. (1968), *Anti-Catholicism in Victorian England*, London: George Allen and Unwin.

O'Connor, E. (ed.) (1958), *The Dogma of the Immaculate Conception*, Notre Dame: Notre Dame University Press.

O'Day, A. (1993), 'Anti-Irish Behaviour in Britain, 1846–1922', in P. Panayi (ed.), *Racial Violence in Britain, 1840–1950*, Leicester: Leicester University Press.

Odeh, L. A. (1993), 'Feminism and the Veil: Thinking the Difference', *Feminist Review*, (43), 26–37.

Olivier, S. (1970), *White Capital and Coloured Labour*, Westport: Negro Universities Press.

Ord, J. W. (1834–35), *England: A Historical Poem*, 2 vols, London: Simpkin and Marshall.

Panayi, P. (ed.) (1993), *Racial Violence in Britain, 1840–1950*, Leicester: Leicester University Press.

Parker, J. (1831), *The Passengers: Containing, The Celtic Annals*, London: Macmillan.

Parkes, B. R. (1860), 'A Year's Experience in Woman's Work', *The English Woman's Journal*, 6, October, reprinted in C. Lacey (ed.), *Barbara Leigh Smith Bodichon and the Langham Place Group*, London and New York: Routledge.

Parkes, B. R. (1861a) 'The Condition of Working Women in England and France', *The English Woman's Journal*, 8, September, reprinted in C. Lacey (ed.), *Barbara Leigh Smith Bodichon and the Langham Place Group*, London and New York: Routledge.

Parkes, B. R. (1861b), 'Moustapha's House', *The English Woman's Journal*, 8, October, 173–9.

Parry, G. (1989), *The Seventeenth Century: The Intellectual and Cultural Context of English Literature 1603–1700*, London and New York: Longman.

Partridge, L. and Stern, R. (1980), *A Renaissance Likeness: Art and Culture in Raphael's Julius II*, Berkeley, London and Los Angeles: University of California Press.

Paz, D. G. (1992), *Popular Anti-Catholicism in Mid-Victorian Britain*, Stanford: Stanford University Press.

Pechey, G. (1983), '*The Story of An African Farm*: Colonial History and the Discontinuous Text', *Critical Arts: A Journal for Media Studies*, 3, (1), 65–78.

Pelling, H. (1967), *A Social Geography of British Elections, 1885–1910*, London: Macmillan.

Pellizzi, F. (1995), 'Remains', *Res*, 27, Spring.

Perera, S. (1990), *Reaches of Empire: The English Novel from Edgeworth to Dickens*, New York: Columbia University Press.

Perry, K. (1991), *Barbara Leigh Smith Bodichon 1821–91*, Cambridge: Girton College.

Phillips, M. E. (1897), *Reminiscences of William Wetmore Story*, Chicago and New York: Rand McNally.

Pike, L. O. (1866), *The English and their Origin*, London: Longmans, Green.

Pointon, M. (1986), *Mulready*, exhibition catalogue, London: Victoria and Albert Museum.

Poliakov, L. (1971), *The Aryan Myth*, New York: Basic Books.

Poole, S. (1844), *The Englishwoman in Egypt*, London: Charles Knight.

Porter, B. (1968), *Critics of Empire: British Radical Attitudes to Colonialism in Africa, 1895–1914*, London: Macmillan.

Pouchet Paquet, S. (1992a), 'The Heartbeat of a West Indian Slave: *The History of Mary Prince*', *African American Review*, 26, (1), 131–46.

Pouchet Paquet, S. (1992b), 'The Enigma of Arrival: *The Wonderful Adventures of Mrs. Seacole in Many Lands*', *African American Review*, 26, (4), 651–63.

Pratt, M. L. (1992), *Imperial Eyes: Travel Writing and Transculturation*, London: Routledge.

Prichard, J. C. (1848), *The Natural History of Man comprising Inquiries into the Modifying Influence of Physical and Moral Agencies on the Different Tribes of the Human Family*, London: H. Ballière.

Prichard, J. C. (1855), *The Natural History of Man*, 4th edn, London: Ballière.

Prince, M. (1992), *The History of Mary Prince, a West Indian Slave, Related by Herself*, ed. M. Ferguson, Ann Arbor: University of Michigan Press.

Prochaska, D. (1990), *Making Algeria French: Colonialism in Bone, 1870–1920*, Cambridge: Cambridge University Press.

Prochaska, F. K. (1974), 'Women in English Philanthropy 1790–1830', *International Review of Social History*, 19, (3), 426–45.

Psomiades, K. (1992), 'Beauty's Body: Gender Ideology and British Aestheticism', *Victorian Studies*, 36, (1), Fall, 31–52.

Punter, D. (1980), *The Literature of Terror: A History of Gothic Fictions from 1765 to the Present Day*, London: Longman.

Quatrefages, M. de (1869), 'The Formation of the Mixed Human Races', *Anthropological Review*, 7, (24), January.

RAI [Royal Anthropological Institute] (1900), Memorial of the Anthropological Institute and of the Folklore Society to the Right Hon. Joseph Chamberlain, Secretary of State for the Colonies on the native races of South Africa, RAI Archives, Anthropological Institute Council Minutes A10 (3), 12 June.

RAI [Royal Anthropological Institute] (1907), 'Anthropological Institute: Augmentation of Title', *Man*, 7, no. 70, p. 112.

RAI [Royal Anthropological Institute] (1909), 'Anthropology and the Empire: Deputation to Mr. Asquith', *Man*, 9, pp. 85–7.

RAI [Royal Anthropological Institute] (1911), 'Memorial on Imperial Bureau of Anthropology', printed copy, no date, Royal Anthropological Institute Archive A56.

RAI [Royal Anthropological Institute] (1912), 'Report of the Council for 1911', *Journal of the Anthropological Institute*, 42, 5.

Rainger, R. (1978), 'Race, Politics and Science: The Anthropological Society of London in the 1860s', *Victorian Studies*, 22, 51–70.

Ramirez, S. J. (1985), 'A Critical Reappraisal of the Career of William Wetmore Story (1819–1895): American Sculptor and Man of Letters', PhD, 4 vols, Boston University.

Reader, W. J. (1988), 'At Duty's Call': A Study in Obsolete Patriotism, Manchester: Manchester University Press.

Reid, M. (1856), The Quadroon, New York: R. M. deWitt.

Reid, M. (1859), Oçeola, London: Hurst and Blackett.

Reid, M. (1861), The Wild Huntress, London: Bentley.

Rendall, J. (1987) '"A moral engine"?: Feminism, Liberalism and The English Woman's Journal', in J. Rendall (ed.), Equal or Different: Women's Politics 1800–1914, Oxford: Blackwell.

Rendall, J. (1989), 'Friendship and Politics: Barbara Leigh Smith Bodichon (1827–91) and Bessie Rayner Parkes (1829–1925)', in S. Mendus and J. Rendall (eds), Sexuality and Subordination, London and New York: Routledge.

Report of Proceedings Connected with the East Indians' Petition to Parliament (1831), Calcutta: Baptist Mission Press.

Richards, E. (1989a), 'Huxley and the Woman's Place in Science: The "Woman's Question" and the Control of Victorian Anthropology', in J. R. Moore (ed.), History, Humanity and Evolution: Essays for John C. Green, Cambridge: Cambridge University Press.

Richards, E. (1989b), 'The "Moral Anatomy" of Robert Knox: The Inter-Play between Biological and Social Thought in Victorian Scientific Naturalism', Journal of the History of Biology, 22, 373–436.

Richards, T. (1990), The Commodity Culture of Victorian England, London: Verso.

Ricks, C. (ed.) (1987), The Poems of Tennyson, 3 vols, Harlow: Longman.

Riley, D. (1990), 'Am I That Name?': Feminism and the Category of 'Women' in History, Minneapolis: University of Minnesota Press.

Ripley, C. P. (ed.) (1985), The Black Abolitionist Papers, vol. 1: The British Isles, 1830–1865, London and Chapel Hill: University of North Carolina Press.

Robson, R. (ed.) (1967), Ideas and Institutions of Victorian Britain, London: G. Bell and Son.

Rose, M. (1981), The Curator of the Dead: Thomas Hodgkin (1778–1866), London: Peter Owen.

Ryan, M. P. (1990), Women in Public: Between Banners and Ballots, 1825–1880, Baltimore and London: Johns Hopkins University Press.

Rye, M. S. (1860), 'On Assisted Emigration', The English Woman's Journal, 5, June, reprinted in C. Lacey (ed.), Barbara Leigh Smith Bodichon and the Langham Place Group, London and New York: Routledge.

Said, E. (1978), Orientalism: Western Conceptions of the Orient, Harmondsworth: Penguin.

Said, E. (1994), Culture and Imperialism, New York: Alfred A. Knopf.

Said-Ruete, E. (1981), *Memoirs of an Arabian Princess: Princess Salme bint Said ibn Sultan al-Bu Saidi of Oman and Zanzibar*, London: East West Publications.

Sanyal, J. N. (1931), *Sardar Bhagat Singh: A Short Life-sketch*, India Office Library PIB.8.11.

Schapera, I. (ed.) (1960), *Livingstone's Private Journals 1851–1853*, London: Chatto and Windus.

Schreiner, O. (1982), *The Story of an African Farm*, New York and London: Penguin Books.

Scott, J. W. (1988), *Gender and the Politics of History*, New York: Columbia University Press.

Seacole, M. (1988), *Wonderful Adventures of Mrs. Seacole in Many Lands*, Oxford and New York: Oxford University Press.

Sedgwick, E. K. (1985), *Between Men: English Literature and Male Homosocial Desire*, New York: Columbia University Press.

Semmel, B. (1962), *The Governor Eyre Controversy*, London: Macgibbon and Kee.

Sharpe, J. (1993), *Allegories of Empire: The Figure of Woman in the Colonial Text*, Minneapolis: University of Minnesota Press.

Shiva, V. (1988), *Staying Alive: Women, Ecology and Development*, London: Zed.

Showalter, E. (1985), *The Female Malady: Women Madness, and English Culture, 1830–1980*, New York and London: Penguin.

Showalter, E. (1990), *Sexual Anarchy: Gender and Culture at the Fin de Siècle*, New York: Viking.

Silverman, K. (1992), *Male Subjectivity at the Margins*, New York: Routledge.

Simpson, G. C. (ed.) (1992), *The Scottish Soldier Abroad, 1247–1967*, Edinburgh: John Donald.

Simpson, R. (1990), *Camelot Regained: The Arthurian Revival and Tennyson 1800–1849*, Cambridge: Brewer.

Singh, K. (1977), *A History of the Sikhs*, 2 vols, Delhi: Oxford University Press.

Skelley, A. R. (1977), *The Victorian Army at Home*, Montreal: Queen's University Press.

Smailes, H. (ed.) (1987), *The Queen's Image*, exhibition catalogue, Edinburgh: Scottish National Portrait Gallery.

Small, S. (1994), 'Racial Group Boundaries and Identities: People of "Mixed Race" in Slavery across the Americas', *Slavery and Abolition*, 15, (3), 17–37.

Smith, R. T. (1982), 'Race and Class in the Post-emancipation Caribbean', in R. Ross (ed.), *Racism and Colonialism*, The Hague: Martinus Nijhoff, pp. 93–119.

Snowden, F. (1970), *Blacks in Antiquity*, Cambridge, Mass.: Belknap Press.

Somerville, S. (1994), 'Scientific Racism and the Emergence of the Homosexual Body', *Journal of the History of Sexuality*, 5, (2), October.

Speke, J. H. (1863), *Journal of the Discovery of the Source of the Nile, with Maps, Portraits and Numerous Illustrations*, London: William Blackwood.

Spencer, H. (1876), 'The Comparative Psychology of Man', *Popular Science Monthly*, 8, 257–69.

Spiers, E. M. (1980), *The Army and Society 1815–1914*, London: Longman.

Spiers, F. (1992), 'Black Americans in Britain and the Struggle for Black Freedom in the United States', in J. S. Gundara and I. Duffield (eds), *Essays on the History of Blacks in Britain*, Aldershot: Avebury, pp. 81–98.

Spivak, G. C. (1985), 'Three Women's Texts and a Critique of Imperialism', *Critical Inquiry*, 12, 243–61.

Spivak, G. C. (1986), 'Three Women's Texts and a Critique of Imperialism', in H. L. Gates *'Race', Writing and Difference*, Chicago: Chicago University Press.

Spivak, G. C. (1990), 'Poststructuralism, Marginality, Postcoloniality and Value', in P. Collier and H. Geyer-Ryan (eds), *Literary Theory Today*, Cambridge: Polity.

Spivak, G. C. (1994), 'Can the Subaltern Speak?', in P. Williams and L. Chrisman (eds), *Colonial Discourse and Post-Colonial Theory: A Reader*, New York and London: Harvester Wheatsheaf.

Stanley, B. (1983), '"Commerce and Christianity": Providence Theory, the Missionary Movement, and the Imperialism of Free Trade, 1842–1860', *Historical Journal*, 26, (1), 71–94.

Stearns, P. N. (1990), *Be a Man! Males in Modern Society*, New York: Holmes and Meier.

Steevens, G. W. (1990), *With Kitchener to Khartoum*, London: Greenhill Books.

Stepan, N. (1982) *The Idea of Race in Science: Great Britain, 1800–1960*, London: Macmillan; Hamden: Archon Press.

Stephen, B. (1927) *Emily Davies and Girton College*, London: Constable.

Stewart, A. T. Q. (1977), *The Narrow Ground: Aspects of Ulster, 1609–1969*, London: Faber and Faber.

Stocking, Jr, G. W. (1971), 'What's in a Name? The Origins of the Royal Anthropological Institute (1837–71)', *Man*, new series, 6, 369–90.

Stocking, Jr, G. W. (1987), *Victorian Anthropology*, New York: Free Press.

Stone, H. (ed.) (1969), *The Uncollected Writings of Charles Dickens: Household Words 1850–1859*, London: Allen Lane.

Stone, J. (1972), 'James Bryce and the Comparative Sociology of Race Relations', *Race*, 13, 315–28.

Stowe, H. B. (1852), *Uncle Tom's Cabin, or Negro Life in the Slave States of America*, with 27 illustrations on wood by Cruikshank, London: John Cassell.

Strickland, S. (1831), *Negro Slavery Described by a Negro: Being the Narrative of Ashton Warner a Native of St. Vincent's. With an Appendix Containing the Testimony of Four Christian Ministers, Recently Returned from the Colonies, on the System of Slavery as it Now Exists*, London: Samuel Maunder.

Strong, R. (1978), *Recreating the Past*, London: Thames and Hudson.

Summers, A. (1979), 'A Home from Home – Women Philanthropic Work in the Nineteenth Century', in S. Burman (ed.), *Fit Work for Women*, New York and London: St Martin's Press.

Swift, R. (1987), 'The Outcast Irish in the British Victorian City: Problems and Perspectives', *Irish Historical Studies*, 25, May, 264–76.

Swift, R. (1992), 'The Historiography of the Irish in Nineteenth-Century Britain', in P. O'Sullivan (ed.), *The Irish World Wide: History, Heritage, Identity*, II: *The Irish in the New Communities*, Leicester: Leicester University Press.

Swift, R. and Gilley, S. (eds) (1985), *The Irish in the Victorian City*, London: Croom Helm.

Taussig, M. (1993), *Mimesis and Alterity*, Chicago: University of Chicago Press.

Taylor, M. (1991), 'Imperialism and Libertas? Rethinking the Racial Critique of Imperialism during the Nineteenth Century', *Journal of Imperial and Commonwealth History*, 19, 1–23.

Thompson, E. (1943), *The Making of the Indian Princes*, London: Oxford University Press.

Thornton, L. (1983), *The Orientalists: Painter Travellers, 1828–1908*, Paris: ACR.

Thornton, L. (1985), *Women as Portrayed in Orientalist Painting*, Paris: ACR.

Thurston, E. (1898a), 'Eurasians of Madras City and Malabar', *Bulletin* [Madras Government Museum], 2, (2).

Thurston, E. (1898b), 'Note on Tattooing', *Bulletin* [Madras Government Museum], 2, (2).

Trapido, S. (1980), '"The friends of the natives": Merchants, Peasants and the Political and Ideological Structure of Liberalism at the Cape,

1854–1910', in S. Marks and A. Atmore (eds), *Economy and Society in Pre-Industrial South Africa*, London: Longman, pp. 247–74.

Trevor-Roper, H. (1983), 'The Invention of Tradition: The Highland Tradition of Scotland', in E. Hobsbawm (ed.), *The Invention of Tradition*, Cambridge: Cambridge University Press.

Trollope, A. (1985), *The West Indies and the Spanish Main*, Gloucester: Alan Sutton ; New York: Hippocrene Books, Inc.

Turley, D. (1991), *The Culture of English Antislavery*, London and New York: Routledge.

Turner, F. M. (1974), *Between Science and Religion: The Reaction to Scientific Naturalism in Late Victorian England*, New Haven: Yale University Press.

Turner, S. (1823), *The History of the Anglo-Saxons: Comprising The History of England from the Earliest Period to the Norman Conquest*, 3 vols, London: Longman.

Tylor, E. B. (1865), *Researches into the Early History of Mankind and the Development of Civilisation*, London: J. Murray.

Usherwood, P. and Spencer-Smith, J. (1987), *Lady Butler: Battle Artist*, exhibition catalogue, London: National Army Museum/Alan Sutton.

van den Berghe, P. L. (1967), *Race and Racism: A Comparative Perspective*, New York: John Wiley.

Vicinus, M. (1985), *Independent Women – Work and Community for Single Women 1850–1920*, Chicago: University of Chicago Press.

Vincent, J. R. (1968), *The Formation of the Liberal Party, 1868–1874*, London: Constable.

Visram, R. (1986), *Ayahs, Lascars and Princes: Indians in Britain 1700–1947*, London: Pluto Press.

Vivan, I. (1991), 'The Treatment of Blacks in *The Story of an African Farm*', in I. Vivan (ed.), *The Flawed Diamond: Essays on Olive Schreiner*, Sydney: Dangaroo Press.

Wakeman, G. (1973), *Victorian Book Illustration: The Technical Revolution*, Newton Abbot: David and Charles.

Walker, G. (1992), 'The Orange Order in Scotland Between the Wars', *International Review of Social History*, 37, (2), 177–206.

Walker, G. (1994), 'The Irish Protestants in Scotland', in T. M. Devine (ed.), *Irish Immigrants and Scottish Society*, Edinburgh: Edinburgh University Press.

Walker, L. (1995), 'Vistas of Pleasure: Women Consumers of Urban Space in the West End of London', in C. C. Orr (ed.), *Women in the Victorian Art World*, Manchester: Manchester University Press.

Walkowitz, J. (1992), *City of Dreadful Delight: Narratives of Sexual Danger in Late-Victorian London*, Chicago: University of Chicago Press.

Wallas, G. (1948), *Roman Nature in Politics*, 4th edn, London: Constable.

Waller, H. (ed.) (1874), *The Last Journals of David Livingstone in Central Africa*, 2 vols, London: Cassell.

Walling, R. A. J. (ed.) (1971), *The Diaries of John Bright*, New York: Morrow, reprinted New York: Krauss.

Wallis, J. P. R. (1941), *Thomas Baines of King's Lynn: Explorer and Artist*, London: Jonathan Cape.

Walvin, J. (1981), 'The Public Campaign in England Against Slavery, 1787–1834', in D. Ellis and J. Walvin (eds), *The Abolition of the Atlantic Slave Trade. Origins and Effects in Europe, Africa and the Americas*, Madison: Wisconsin University Press, pp. 63–79.

Ware, V. (1992), *Beyond the Pale: White Women, Racism and History*, London: Verso.

West, S. (1990), 'Tom Taylor, William Powell Frith, and the British School of Art', *Victorian Studies*, 33, 307–26.

West, S. (1993), 'The Construction of Racial Type: Caricature, Ethnography and Jewish Physiognomy in Fin-de-Siècle Melodrama', *Nineteenth Century Theatre*, 21, (9), Summer, 5–40.

Whitford, M. (1991), *Luce Irigaray: Philosophy in the Feminine*, London and New York: Routledge.

Whitman, W. (1963), 'The Half-Breed: A Tale of the Western Frontier', in T. L. Brasher (ed.), *The Early Poems and the Fiction*, from *The Complete Works of Whitman*, New York: New York University Press.

Williamson, J. (1983), *New People: Miscegenation and Mulattoes in the United States*, New York: The Free Press.

Wood, S. (1987), *The Scottish Soldier*, Manchester: Archive Publications Ltd.

Woosnam-Savage, R. C. (n.d.), 'Gibb's *Alma*', Glasgow: Glasgow Art Gallery [record information].

Wright, T. (1861), *Essays on Archaeological Subjects*, 2 vols, London: John Russell Smith.

Yeazell, R. B. (1991), 'Do It or Dorrit', *Novel: A Forum on Fiction*, 25, 33–49.

Young, R. (1985a), 'Darwinism *Is* Social', in D. Kohn (ed.), *The Darwinian Heritage*, Princeton: Princeton University Press, pp. 609–38.

Young, R. (1985b), *Darwin's Metaphor: Nature's Place in Victorian Culture*, Cambridge: Cambridge University Press.

Young, R. (1990), *White Mythologies: Writing, History and the West*, London: Routledge.

Young, R. (1995), *Colonial Desire: Hybridity in Theory, Culture and Race*, London and New York: Routledge.

Youngs, T. (1994), *Travellers in Africa: British Travelogues, 1850–1900*, Manchester: Manchester University Press.
Zonana, J. (1993), 'The Sultan and the Slave: Feminist Orientalism and the Structure of *Jane Eyre*', *Signs*, **18**, (3).

Index